Some more questions ...

What is "enlightenment"?

Why the earth created humans?

What would be the ultimate goals for humanity?

How can you unleash your creative powers and create your own future?

Why every act, movement and thought is a manifestation of freewill and why it affects the evolution of the universe?

Why the living standard in the US declines daily?

Why there are more than 3 million people in jail and more than 50 million with a criminal record?

People in America always talk about "they". "Back then, 'they' castrated people who were homosexuals. "They" had strict laws against sodomy." They" did radiation experiments on the population. The question is; who are "they"?

Read ...

The Human Pathway

"Find the Truth"

Jim Knut Larsson

Copyright © 2010 by Jim Knut Larsson
All rights reserved. No part of this book may be reproduced in any form or by any means without the prior written permission from the author.

1. Cosmology 2. Teleology 3. Religion 4. Spiritualism 5. Philosophy 6. Science 7. Human beings

Published and designed by Jim Knut Larsson
Cover design by Jim Knut Larsson

Printed in the United States of America

ALL RIGHTS RESERVED

www.jimknutlarsson.com
www.TheHumanPathway.com

ISBN 978-0-615-41387-7

The Human Pathway is based both on "established" theories and hypotheses in physics and cosmology and some new hypotheses formulated by the author and may not be accurate in all "details". However, the book is about the "big picture" and accurate enough in the "details" for the conclusions drawn.

Printed in the United States by Morris Publishing ®
3212 East Highway 30
Kearney, NE 68847
1-800-650-7888

To:

Pernille Fiona, Norma, Anders,
Unny and Tommy

Acknowledgements

A special thanks to Kellog Stover for typing and editing and for our inspired sessions to create the book. I also want to thank Briegh for listening endless hours and being such an inspiration. Steve for editing, Drew for penning the poem and all the scientists, philosophers and people through the ages that have sought the "truth"!

When I grew up in Norway, I looked up to the United States as the land of the free and the free enterprise system. This book is what I found out when my illusions were destroyed. However, I love America and the hope for humanity rests here. It also took me on a journey through business ownership, quantum mechanics, spiritualism, cosmology, politics, justice and economics and it prepared me for writing the book. I thank America for the inspiration, opportunity and freedom to write and publish it. Hopefully, this book will contribute to the restoration of the American ideals of freedom and individuality and help to make America the creative leader of a new and better world.

While the examples used in the chapters about government, justice and economics are from America, the examples could have been taken from anywhere. The analysis, conclusions and recommendations are as valid for any country as they are for America.

The Human Pathway will guide you to enlightenment! I invite you to enlighten the world about the choices humanity needs to make to create a great future!

It starts the iterative process of enlightenment by identifying and discussing the fundamental issues of our existence, goals and aspirations.

You are encouraged to study the book, view the uncut reading with commentaries on video on the website, participate on our blog and to engage your coworkers, friends and family in the process.

The future of humanity depends on it!

~Jim Knut Larsson
October 10, 2010

Contents

The book is written to be highly accessible to everybody! However, if quantum physics "scares" you, you could skip chapters 2 and 3.

	Revelation	
	Foreword	
1	Evolution of the Universe	1
2	Quantum Physics	9
3	The Entangled Universe	15
4	The Gaia Hypotheses	29
5	The "Observer"	42
6	The Meaning of Everything	46
7	Observation, Thought, Ego & Enlightenment	53
8	Religion	62
9	The Idea of Morphic Fields	67
10	Creation versus Destruction	69
11	Governments	76
12	Man's Fundamental Needs and Rights	90
13	Principles of Information	98
14	"Freedom Means to Be Free"	103
15	The Justice System	109
16	Personal Responsibility and Punishment	128
17	Mass Media Distorts Reality and Creates Fear	132
18	The Impossibility of Protection and Safety	146
19	The Importance of Democracy and Freedom	149
20	Dynamics of Organizations	157
21	Well-Meaning Idiots and the (Sub) Conscious Conspiracy	174
22	Crime and Punishment	186
23	Observations	224
24	Who are The Real Criminals?	232
25	The Madness of War	261
26	Economics	264
27	What is The Living Standard?	288
28	Organization of Society	290
29	The New Slavery	294
30	Goals for Humanity	296
	Axioms …	298
	"Now" … Poem	299
	Addendum: The Emperor's New Clothes	301
	Addendum: War Commentary	305
	Addendum: Personal Stories of Injustice	308
	Addendum: What to do in Case of Arrest?	312
	Addendum: Recommended Readings (a sample)	320
	About the Author	324

Revelation

Does it matter if you are resurrected at some point in the future? It is your desire to know the "truth" that drives your desire for resurrection. You will live forever as long as humanity—or if human intelligence lives on forever—because what is living, even if your ego is dead, is you being one with humanity. Individuals only manifest by their "clinging" to their egos. This "clinging" prevents you from becoming creative, happy and blissful. If you get rid of your ego, which should be everybody's goal, you will dedicate yourself to the eternal "now" and to serve humanity. A great quest is to help humanity reach its highest potential and to achieve "absolute" knowledge, "finish" the creation of the universe and acquire the power to recreate everything that existed forever. Then, at that point, you will be resurrected!

However there is a final revelation and, if it is revealed to you, it will give you "absolute" knowledge and peace. This final revelation is the logical conclusion of this book. Understand what is written and the truth will be revealed to you. When it is, you will understand that it cannot be directly communicated and understood by others unless they have the same revelation! You will know that you have the final knowledge when you get the revelation and you don't need to seek validation for it! However, you want to share it with others! Study the revelations in this book and hopefully you will get it. You will know it when you do.

Foreword

Due to the lack of gene diversity in the human race, it is estimated that there must have been a time in our history where there were no more than 150 people left after a major catastrophe, so we are all "brothers and sisters"!

All truths pass through three stages:
1) It is ridiculed
2) It is violently opposed
3) It is being accepted as being self evident
~Schopenhauer

"To own nothing is to have everything"
~ **Jim Knut Larsson**

- If you get extremely angry when you read this book, remember that what is being said is absolutely true, the truth is that you cannot admit to the truth.
- If you disagree, you think that what is said is true, but you cannot admit to the truth.

If you disagree and are angry after reading a paragraph or a chapter, please read on, the "truth" might be entirely different than what you think!

100 people die every day on the highway, are we going to shut down all traffic? Another 14,000 die from other causes!

We need to dismantle many laws and make society free again. We must get the government out of our lives. The benefit you get from reading my book is that you will be able to see through the myths. When you read my book, you will become an enlightened person. Actually after you read this book you will say, "I'm enlightened now". You will have revelations that will make you enjoy life more and become a happier person, but also you will no longer be seduced by propaganda. This, in the end, is a book of cosmic and spiritual enlightenment and enlightenment with regard to politics, economics and justice. What does it mean to be an enlightened person who helps secure the future prosperity and excitement of living for yourself and for humanity as a whole? Another bonus from this book is that you may no longer fear death. My book is about enlightenment—not only personally and spiritually, but also politically, socially, economically and judicially. You will become a participant in the conversation and the future goals and aspirations of humanity. Hopefully, I will shock and awe you into enlightenment to the degree that before you finish reading, you will start talking with your neighbors. This book will cause deep controversy, anger and debate on the highest level of society, which will help to prove its truths!

What is the purpose of man's existence?

You may not be able to understand this book, even as it is written in the simplest of terms. To understand this book you must understand what creativity and destruction is and that man has:

- The ability to understand the laws of nature.
- The ability to transform matter into useful products for his pleasure and survival.

The original name of this book was *Well Meaning Idiots and the (Sub)Conscious Conspiracy*. This book is dedicated to those who desire to create the perfect society. I will prove in my book that perfection is created through the imperfect. An imperfect society creates opportunities and develops the human spirit. Anybody can be a member of a group which pursues a moral issue. The problem in life is to realize your goals and values. In fact, anybody confronted with who they are is usually scared to death. But that is what it takes because you can only grow and achieve by being subject to your own acts.

The idea that the imperfect is the preferred state of the society is proven by the laws of physics and the manifestation of the universe itself. At the Big Bang there was asymmetry between matter and antimatter. If the Big Bang had been a symmetrical event, the universe would have become nothing. Before the universe came into existence there was nothing. Then, something appeared when asymmetry created the universe. This asymmetry is observed throughout the universe. Asymmetry is also the foundation for the arrow of time and the Second Law of Thermodynamics. If the universe had been symmetrical, it would be a static universe with no past or future. It would not evolve. So it's actually through the asymmetry, an imperfection, that we have evolution and where creation can take place. This fundamental property of the universe is also consistent with the findings of quantum physics and the possibility of free will, meaning that the past and the future do not exist. This constellation establishes meaning and purpose, because without reference to the past and the possibilities of the future, meaning and purpose cannot be experienced. So, since the past and the future do not exist—the universe has been proven to be probabilistic not deterministic—it has given humans self-awareness and the ability to understand and free will. Implied in free will is the power to choose. Humanity has a choice to evolve creatively to higher and higher levels of complexity or to choose destruction leading toward lower and lower levels of simplicity. Hopefully, this book will prove to the reader that the choice of destruction would lead to a dead-end and ultimately to the disappearance of man and all life. Choosing imperfection and creativity, which are the most prevalent forces in the universe (proven through the asymmetry), leads to the continuous evolution and survival of humanity; leading to the possibility that we, at some point in time, would be able to conquer the entire universe and manipulate it in such a way that we can create everything possible and recreate everything that has existed in the past for "infinity". And even to the possibility that the universe we inhabit can spawn baby universes which would be better suited for the evolution and experience of intelligence that will be going on forever.

What are the consequences of the positive choice or the negative choice? I believe that we are going down the path of destruction. One choice is to allow, as an example; criminality to exist as an imperfection. We need it to evolve as a society. If one takes the imperfections away, one also takes away creativity and freedom.

The end result is that we need to create a society based on the idea of individual and collective freedom. This in turn implies that we have to allow the society to be imperfect. In this way we minimize destruction and suffering. Freedom is a more powerful educator and regulator of man, than any law, punishment or restriction. The attempt to guide man through laws and regulations actually creates what the laws and regulations were intended to prevent. So the society has to be organized in such a way that it maximizes individual freedom. This also implies that an element of chaos is the desired state of society. The key is to find those laws and regulations that work as positive attractors within the chaos. This leads society to maximizing development and evolution. This imperfection, in combination with the universe being chaotic, makes it possible for you to create your own destiny.

Anchored in physics, the "The Human Pathway" gives the framework by which society needs to be organized in order to maximize evolution and meaning and purpose.

Our Choice

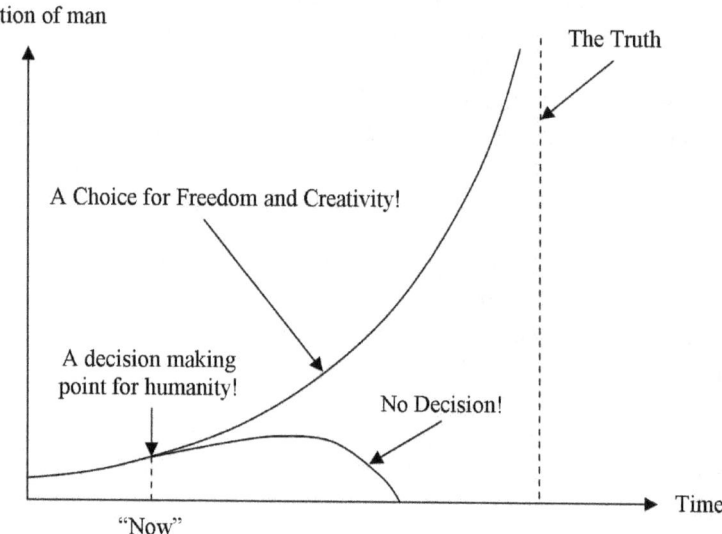

**Figure 1
Our Choice**

We have to accept an element of risk in our daily lives in order to preserve freedom. As it is a direct relationship between risk and reward in business it is in our lives as well. We need to maximize freedom in order to maximize reward and establish what would be reasonable risk on all levels to the individual. Actually, there is no choice as security and safety is to a large extent illusory and can be proven, mathematically, to be impossible!

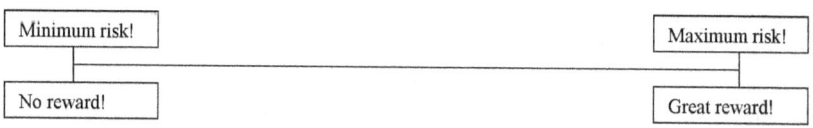

**Figure 2
Risk and Reward**

A primary goal for humanity is to perpetuate life. We must escape our own solar system, at some point in the future, or there is no meaning and purpose!

Since the earth can be viewed as a living organism, life had to create a conscious being that can understand and manipulate nature to preserve life.

The absolute core of this book is to restore and maximize freedom for the individual. Without freedom, life becomes pointless. There is no meaning and purpose. This means that we need to restore and cultivate a super tolerant society to fulfill our destiny.

Humanity is not going to survive unless we develop the technology to escape our solar system. We are not going to get there by saying no to technology and evolution.

We have to build a society based on science, freedom, technology and embrace evolution and creativity.

Saying "yes" is creative and future oriented—saying "no" is destructive and past orientated. "Yes" is God and "No" is Devil.

Inspiration is founded in creation and evolution. Without creating and evolving there is no inspiration and no meaning and purpose other than narcissistic preoccupation with oneself. So in essence, saying no to evolution is taking rather than giving.

There are two interpretations of quantum physics to consider:

1. The Copenhagen interpretation—nothing exists unless it is observed. This means that everything is just a probability function or, in other words, "nothing". Everything must be observed to manifest into something. This manifestation is the observable universe that places the observer—you and me—at the center of everything.
2. The other interpretation of quantum physics is the multiple universe interpretation. Rather than a probability function collapsed by an observer, everything that can possibly happen, happens at every instant in multiple universes. New universes are being created at any point in time where everything that can happen is happening but it is not observed by consciousness because we cannot observe the multiple universes which are being created. So the multi-universe interpretation brings us back to a deterministic universe without free will. In fact, this interpretation states that the experience of free will is an illusion.

"Ockham's principle" basically says that the most elegant and simplest solution is most often the right solution in physics. "Ockham's principle" is a strong argument in favor of the Copenhagen interpretation.

There is reason to believe that the Copenhagen interpretation of physics is closer to the truth than the multi-universe interpretation. This book builds upon the Copenhagen interpretation. We will show it is ultimately more intellectually satisfying than the multi-universe hypothesis.

Scientists are unable to find a "theory of everything" because reality is probabilistic and their efforts are anchored in a deterministic view of the universe. This would be a "perfection" rather than an "imperfection". A complete "theory of everything" will describe perfect relationships, while the universe is fundamentally imperfect and the language is probabilities rather than absolutes. Because most physicists, cosmologists and mathematicians do not take into account the Copenhagen Interpretation of Quantum Physics and are not incorporating the subject (the observer) with the object (the universe), they fail to find the "theory of everything". They are trying to find the "theory of everything" as an exact formula of relationships, while the essence of the universe is imperfection. They assume perfection, rather than taking into account that the universe, in its essence, is imperfect and doesn't even exist unless it's observed. It's impossible to find a deterministic "theory of everything" because the laws of physics are not in a perfect relationship to each other. They are neither perfect in themselves nor in their relationship to each other because the universe is a work in progress and a manifestation of imperfection!

An accurate "theory of everything" which, by definition, assumes a perfect universe, can never be found within a universe that is imperfect!

Read on!

1
Evolution of the Universe

If you believe in the creationist idea that the universe was created 5000 years ago, then ask yourself this: Given that we know the speed of light, why do we see billions of years into the universe? Did God create the dinosaurs and fossils too? An English Bishop has calculated that the universe was created 4600 years ago on a Wednesday at 3 pm in the afternoon!

The universe began about 13.7 billion years ago with the Big Bang. Initially, out of this primordial soup, the declining temperature of the universe caused the atomic particles to "freeze" into existence. After about 200 million years the universe became transparent, light appeared and things became visible. Irregularities in density within the universe caused gravitational effects leading to star formation and the beginning of star clusters, galaxies and filaments of galaxies. When you look at the filament of galaxies of today, it has an uncanny similarity to the biological nervous system of the human brain. Initially, stars of all sizes and shapes (composed of hydrogen and helium) were created. The larger the star the faster it consumes its fuel and the hotter it burns because of gravitational effects. Within a "few" years after star formation began, some of the largest stars collapsed into supernovas and black holes. The formation of planets, and subsequently life, is conditioned upon such supernovas. Under the extraordinary temperature and pressure created in a supernova, all the heavier elements—such as oxygen and carbon—are created. Supernova explosions force heavier elements to spew out into the universe. These events form the foundation for planets and for life, which is primarily created from the heavier elements. The constants in the universe, like gravity, the strong and weak force in the atom and many more "constants" must be fine tuned to an incredible degree in order for life to appear. It is almost as if the constants of nature and the laws of physics were created for the purpose of causing life to appear.

Over the next 12 billion years, continuous explosions of supernovas and the creation of black holes helped to create planetary systems around the stars. Our solar system was created approximately 5 billion years ago. The earth—because of its extremely fine tuned location with regard to its distance from the sun and its own internal rotation of 24 hours a day—made life possible. The sun matured into its stable maturity stage approximately 1 billion years after the creation of the solar system. Even during the sun's maturity stage, lasting for approx 10-12 billion years, the sun gets slowly hotter. After approximately one billion years into the sun's maturity stage, the temperature on earth—because of the composition of its atmosphere, and distance from the sun—went through a stage where the average temperature on the earth passed through 71 degrees Fahrenheit. At that moment—lasting for approximately 100 million years—life suddenly appeared. From this time forward, life has proven to be able to keep the temperature fairly stable and to create—through the interaction of different life forms—its own best environment for its own survival.

Consider the example of an imaginary planet with black and white flowers—the black ones would absorb the radiation from the sun and heat up the planet; while the white ones would radiate energy back into the universe and cool it down. As the planet grows hotter—given that 71 degrees Fahrenheit is the best temperature, an advantage is given to the white flowers so they'll spread over a larger area of the planet and cool it down. When the planet gets too cool, it gives a preference to the black flowers and the planet warms up. This interaction of all life on earth is, in a nutshell, how life creates its own optimal environment for its own survival. Today, the sun is 30 percent hotter than when life appeared. So today, the biosphere is the predominate force that keeps the temperature at 71 degree Fahrenheit and continues to make life possible. The ability for life to survive in a gradually more hostile environment (the sun's rising temperature), imbibes nature with a means and a desire for its own survival; however, life (the biosphere) will, at some point, be unable to sustain its own best environment for its own survival—because of the continuous heating of the sun. The sun will become too hot for life to sustain itself through the interaction between different life forms.

Hence, life on earth is doomed without life's ability to create a conscious "supernatural" being that can understand and manipulate nature in order to secure its own survival.

The race is between raising temperatures caused by the heating of the sun and man's ability to use technological and scientific development to preserve life.

One of the great destinies of man is, therefore, to become the custodian and preserver of life.

If this observation doesn't make you an environmentalist, nothing will. That's the distinction between a positive environmentalist who embraces evolution and who says "yes" and a negative environmentalist who says "no". The choice has to be "yes" otherwise we are all doomed. If one chooses "yes", we might be able to experience infinite existence, ultimately acquire the power to recreate everything that's ever existed, populate the entire universe, and in the end, we may be able to spawn baby universes. The "DNA" of the new universes is the new physical laws and mathematics to be created within spawned baby universes—making them even better suited for the emergence of intelligence. In fact, those constants of physics and mathematics might even be improved upon to create new universes which are even better suited for life. This is to apply the theory Darwinian evolution to the entire universe itself (and other universes). The end of our universe will be when all the energy has reached a density less than the Planck constant—unless man has created a different destiny for the universe.

Modern sciences, including physics and cosmology are believed to have been started by Aristotle in ancient Greece. The world view at the time was a macro-world view. People at the time did not have the instruments to explore. The thinking was that the "flat" earth was the center of the universe and that the sky, stars and sun were features of the universe that were attached in a sphere above the earth. However philosophers of that time had already began speculating about the idea of "infinity" and "nothingness." Aristotle's observations remained prevalent until the beginning of the Renaissance. Then two scientists, Galileo and Copernicus, had a major scientific breakthrough that eventually altered mankind's world view. Galileo's telescope allowed him to view objects in the sky. Copernicus's mathematics established that the geocentric world-view—with us in the center—was inconsistent with mathematical and observational breakthroughs done by Copernicus and Galileo. Copernicus tried to calculate the path of celestial bodies, including the sun. He was not able to construct a consistent model that explained the movement of the celestial bodies without putting the sun in the middle of the solar system. This observation, in combination with other observations, made them draw the conclusion that our universe was not geocentric but heliocentric, meaning that the sun had to be put in the center. This discovery was a huge revolutionary breakthrough moving from beliefs to objective scientific exploration. This set the foundation for Newton to not only come up with the physical laws to explain the movement of objects, potential and latent energy, but also to establish the laws of gravity—how gravity is influenced by the mass and distance between celestial bodies and the mathematics, including calculus, which were needed to explain and use these laws to construct machines and to calculate the trajectory of celestial bodies. However, as a consequence of Newton's laws of the universe and especially that every reaction has an equal and opposite reaction led to the conclusion that everything that happens in the universe can be described as a direct function of the past. Theoretically, if we could estimate the mass and speed of everything in the universe at one point, then everything which would follow would be a direct mathematical function of the past and it would explain "now" with absolute certainty and predictability. In fact, we would be able to calculate the entire future of the universe and everything that would happen in the universe, including human action, behavior and thoughts. The evolution of the entire universe would be determined with 100% accuracy at the time of the beginning. The universe, according to Newton, would be an objective machine where everything which is happening "now" is determined by the past. This theory is called the deterministic world view. However, around the turn of the century, scientists noticed that certain properties of light did not follow Newton's laws. Also, there were slight variations in the trajectories of planets that could not be explained by Newton's mathematics and laws. When Einstein formulated his theories of general and special relativity for gravity, he found that gravity actually was a function of space and time. These discrepancies were then explained. However it was observed that the properties of light could be treated as both a wave and as a particle, which mystified scientists around the turn of the 20th century. Max Plank, Werner Heisenberg, Niels Bohr and others formulated quantum physics in the 1920s that could explain these phenomena and the duality of light both as a wave as well as a particle on the atomic level. At the elementary particle level, they discovered that the energy of an electron, the momentum of the electron and the position of the electron could only take on different specific values and energy states with nothing in between. So there was no longer "smoothness" but discrete values and states of elementary particle manifestations. This led to the formulation of quantum physics, which is the foundation for electronics, the theory of the Big Bang, explains why the sun is hot, and can explain almost everything in nature—black holes, supernovas, transistors, semiconductors, TVs etc. Quantum physics today is considered the most powerful theory of man. It has been proven to be accurate in all aspects. At the same time, it was observed that many aspects of quantum physics defied logic of observation on the macroscopic level. There is reason to believe that quantum physics describes the fundamental laws of nature with extreme accuracy. However, it was discovered that quantum physics also predicted many phenomena which defied logic and everyday observations. They found that elementary particles were both waves and particles at the same time depending upon how they are observed. They also discovered that the more accurate you could determine the position of a particle the less you could say about its direction and speed. Or, if you decide to observe the momentum of the particles, the more accurate you were at observing this, the less you were able to determine the position of the particle. So, the momentum of the particle excludes the position and the observation of the position excludes the observation of the momentum.

One very famous quantum physics experiment that totally defies macro observation is the "two split" experiment: The two split experiment was set up with a "Cathode Ray Tube" (CRT) as source where the electrons submitted and the time for submission of those electrons could be controlled. In between the source of these electrons, a panel was set up with two slits, with a photographic plate on the other side. It was observed that by sending one electron at a time toward the two split panel—over time, it would form a wave pattern—as predicted. Logic would dictate that behind each split, you would have electrons creating a wave of larger and larger circles; where the electron hits the plate like ripples on a pond. Not only did this create a wave pattern of circles behind the two slits, but it was also observed that where the waves were overlapping, crests and throes—as you would see by dropping two stones in a pond, were created. Since they were sent out one electron at a time, how could each individual electron know where the other electrons have been hitting the photographic plate? This is the big question. Because of the randomness of how the electrons were sent out from the source, which slit they would go through, and where they would hit the plate, logic tells us that there should be a chaotic pattern—not an interference pattern. But that was not what was observed! It was observed that an interference pattern between the overlapping waves was created. The big question is: How does the next electron know where to go? This is where the Copenhagen interpretation presents itself. Each electron goes through both slits at the same time and is only a probability function before it is being observed!

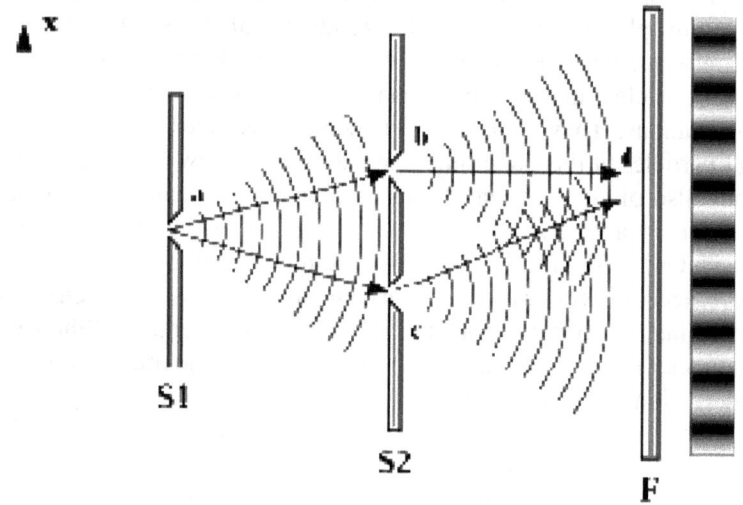

Figure 3
"The two-split experiment"

It is the act of observation which collapses something that doesn't exist before it is being observed and is manifested on the photographic plate. The particle is only a probability function as to where it might be before it's observed. The conclusion is that before something is observed, it only exists as a probability function. In fact, the Copenhagen Interpretation of Quantum Physics establishes that the entire universe does not "exist" before it is being observed, and secondly, that nothing exists unless you have an observer who collapses the probability function into the observable universe. The Copenhagen interpretation says that nothing exists or everything exists only as a probability until the probability function for all particles is collapsed into reality by the observer. And, in aggregate, all these collapsed probability functions would be the experience of the observable universe and everything in it. Niels Bohr said that there are only three people in the world who understand quantum physics. He also said that to truly understand it is impossible. He claimed that anyone who thinks they understand it is completely mystified by what it is. However, it did establish that the universe was no longer deterministic, as it was believed by Newtonian physicists, but probabilistic. This means that you cannot predict, with 100 percent certainty, what is going to happen next, even knowing all the initial conditions! What happens next is not predicted with complete accuracy from knowing all the initial conditions—it could be this but it also could be something totally different. It's all a matter of probabilities, that something entirely different would happen has a very low probability but it is still possible, and this has been proven in scientific experiments.

This is the foundation for free will and the experience of meaning and purpose by man. This also means that man has the power to create his own future and possibly lead the universe itself to a specific condition or goal!

To say it in other words, it has been observed, which is being used in every computer, is the properties of microchips in action (quantum tunneling) on the basis of electrons. This means that the electron can go from where it is through a piece of material which it cannot go through, but it still does! It cannot pass through as a particle unless it exists as a probability only. However, there is a slight probability for the electron to exist on the outside of the material. It can manifest on the other side and it does! It can only exist as a probability function before it is observed and it is this feature that allows it to pass through the material. Amazing, this is used in constructing semiconductors. Quantum physics says that what exists doesn't exist (only as a probability) and at the same time exists. The duality—it exists and it doesn't exist. If it's not observed, it doesn't exist as matter. If I pour water into a glass, there is a tiny possibility that the water will spontaneously pour out through the walls of the glass and end up outside the glass. However, the probability for this to happen is extremely small, but there is still a possibility for this to happen. According to quantum physics, the human brain operates fundamentally on a micro level. Because consciousness and thought are electrical in nature, the human brain is subject to the laws of quantum physics. There is reason to believe that spontaneous creative thoughts are possible. Only fragments of information with huge voids of logic can still cause a spontaneous creation in the human mind of something completely different and removed from the past, from experiences and from past information. In other words, reality is just the fuzziness of the probability functions until it is collapsed into reality by observation.

Summary

- Evolution of the universe—our purpose for being here—why we were created—the most logical purpose is to be the custodian of life. We must understand nature and take control of it and we must cause fast technological development to solve nature's problems not only to survive but also to spread life into the universe.
- Now we know that the universe started with the Big Bang, stars, supernova explosion, created heavy elements, polluted the hydrogen clouds in the universe and then it condensed into the sun, left over heavy elements in the pro planetary system, aggregated into the planets (dust).
- The sun started to shine, pushed through pressure of light from the sun, cleaned up the solar system and prevented the solar system from growing even larger.

2
Quantum Physics

When we look out into the universe, we are not looking back in time. We are always looking at "now"—just farther away. There is no past. There is no future. These cannot exist. If they did, there would be no meaning and purpose. Meaning and purpose can only manifest if the universe is a chaotic system and consciousness has free will to affect the evolution of the universe.

If everything can only exist in the "now", then, everything is created out of "nothing" by the observer. If it were not this way, there would be no meaning and purpose because free will would not exist.

The universe can only be "two dimensional." The experience of "now" is like frames in a movie sown together by the mind of the "Planck distance and time" as "two dimensional slices" adding up to "now". The two dimensional slices are continuously being created with the "Planck distance and time" in between by observation. This creates "now", the illusion of time, the third dimension of space and the universe. Each slice will be slightly different than the previous one according to the "Second Law of Thermodynamics" creating the experience of time. In other words, the whole universe is quantized by the Planck length and time and comes into being by observation. That is why we are living in a two dimensional universe. The "now" from the observer's point of view is divided into two dimensional slices, with the Plank widths in between. As you observe the universe you create the illusion of space in three dimensions of the "now". "Reality" is created by the collapse of the probability functions by observation as formulated in quantum mechanics at discrete moments in "time." This "blinking on and off" of the universe is happening so fast that reality is experienced as continuous by the observer. Each blink of 0s (nothing) and 1s (something) is like frames in a movie. Our mind sows them together into "now"!

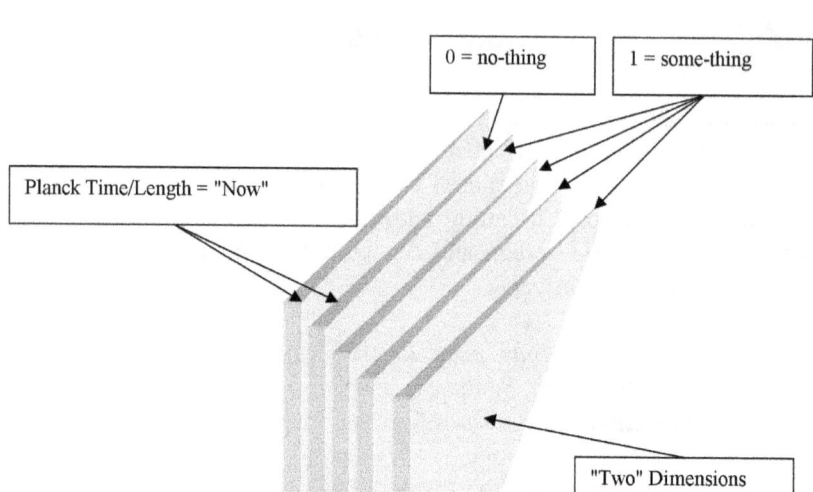

Figure 4
"Two dimensions sown together into now"

As a consequence, the past and future cannot exist. This gives us free will, purpose and meaning and the experience of change. If it were not this way, the universe would be static and time and the Second Law of Thermodynamics would not exist. This leads to the conclusion that the third dimension of space is really a function of the experience of "time". The "now" is created by the speed of light. Hence, "now" is the same for everybody and, as a consequence, the future is not a direct function of the past.

With the development of quantum physics in 1929, it was established that nature, the universe and reality were not deterministic, but probabilistic. That means the evolution of the universe of "two plus two" would not equal four. This provides a foundation for the possibility of consciousness and of humans to have free will. In fact the

Copenhagen Interpretation of Quantum Physics—which is most prevalent basically states: Nothing exists unless it is observed by a conscious observer. Everything exists as a probability function (as a potential) and is smeared out into the entire universe with different probabilities that something would be in one location but could also be somewhere else. The universe manifests when the probability function is collapsed by the observer. This non-locality of the universe puts the observer in the center of the universe. Subsequently, it is believed today that the human mind works holographic—the whole is embedded in each part of the whole—with less and less detail as each part gets smaller and smaller. This principle is fundamentally subject to the laws of quantum physics. This means that the entire brain is embedded in each part of the brain, but fuzzier. Since the mind operates on the principles of quantum physics, it not only provides consciousness—that man is free—but also spontaneous new insights and thoughts are being achieved. It also means that an individual's actions and thinking are not a direct function of experience, information gathering and physical makeup.

These probabilities—non-deterministic—mean that the brain is capable of creating something that is completely novel. If this is the case, consciousness has to be the engine of the universe itself! This allows consciousness—given that the universe is a chaotic system and probabilistic in nature—the ability to affect the evolution of the entire universe.

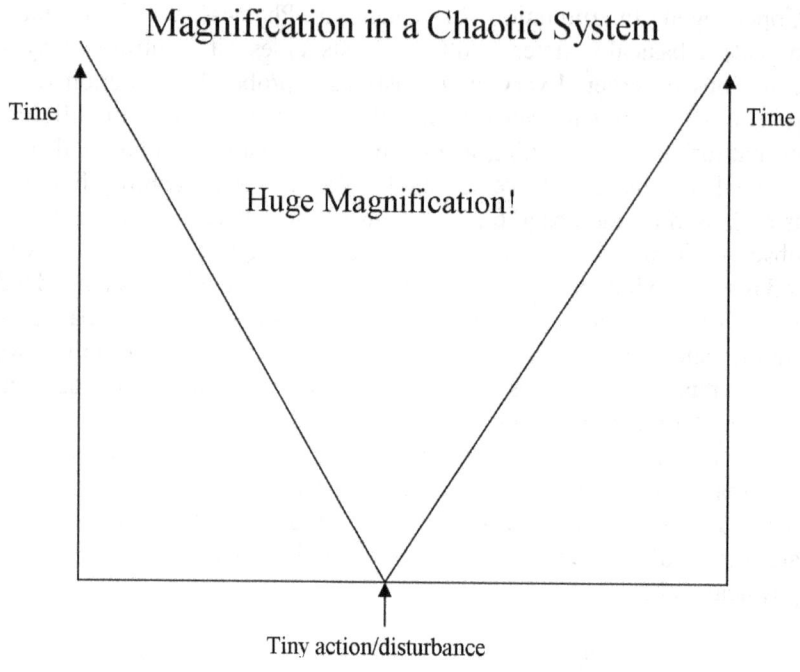

**Figure 5
Magnification**

Since the whole universe is probabilistic in nature and we only can live in the "now", the past and the future cannot exist. This gives us freedom, and without freedom there would be no meaning and purpose. If it can be proven that we live in a deterministic universe—which has been disproved by quantum physics—humans would have no free will. We would live in and evolve into something "perfect". When perfection is achieved, meaning and purpose vanish. The mind becomes a repetitive machine.

It has been proven that the universe is slightly asymmetrical. This slight asymmetry is the reason why the universe exists. In a completely symmetrical universe, matter and anti-matter would have been created in equal amounts and the entire universe would have collapsed into nothingness in an extremely short period of time. This asymmetry manifests itself in consciousness. As consciousness is a direct product of the universe itself, the universe, by virtue of its existence, is more creative and moves toward complexity rather than destruction and simplicity. Human consciousness operates the same way.

A fundamental axiom of this book—based on physics—states that consciousness that exists in complete freedom would choose to be creative rather than destructive and good rather than to be evil.

Many positive derivatives come from this asymmetry between good/creative as the stronger force and evil/destructive as the weaker force.

So man needs to align himself with the laws of physics, or put another way, the DNA of the universe. As the universe creatively moves gradually in local pockets to higher levels of complexity created by gravity, dark matter and energy—despite the Second Law of Thermodynamics—we will be able to reach incredible achievements. Rather than fighting the universe itself, we would sit upon the universe's shoulders and have the possibility of bringing it where we want it go.

If we organize ourselves to be aligned with physics and the universe's forces—which establish freedom and creativity and being "good" as a principle—we would move toward greater achievements. We would be able to create our own brilliant destiny.

We as human beings, having freedom, can choose not to be aligned with prevalent forces of creation and good. With this choice our destiny becomes significantly less than what we could have become.

If there is no objective time, to create an "eternity" will be possible if we can slow subjective time to zero. Then infinite time can be experienced in an instant.

If dark matter and dark energy are equivalent, empty space maybe dark energy and matter. Maybe absolute zero equals all energy. But we cannot observe it because our visible universe is created through energy above absolute zero. It will take infinite negative energy to create absolute zero. Then absolute zero needs to have infinite positive energy. It may be quantum mechanical tunneling from, absolute zero, which creates the visible universe. Why a lower limit on temperature?

If the time length of "now" goes toward zero, then the entire universe can be created out of almost nothing. A virtual particle created from "nothing" through a quantum fluctuation would be enough!

$$\Delta T = \text{``Now''} \rightarrow \text{``smaller''} = \frac{\text{Energy/Matter}}{\text{Energy/Matter}} \rightarrow \text{``larger''} = \text{Universe}$$

If we assume that the past and the future do not exist—only the "now"—and "now" goes smaller, the universe can be created almost out of nothing and continue to expand as long as the "now" is getting smaller.

The Plank Length and Plank Time as "something" would be the minimum energy and time needed to create the universe from nothing. The collapse of the probability function from nothing by the observer, into almost nothing, equals something.

Nothing can be truly solid. If it were, the universe could not evolve. Life would be impossible. The universe has to be like plasma or "quantized", continually changing and subject to the Second Law of Thermo Dynamics: Consciousness and acts of free will.

The mass of "particles" may be created by the speed in which they are moving relative to the speed of light. This means that a particle changes into different "particles" at different speeds. Adding energy to a particle will change its speed and we will get a different particle. Gravity slows down the speed of "particles". The more "particles" in one location, the slower the "speed" of each of the "particles." and it may create the force of gravity.

3
The Entangled Universe

Another consequence of quantum physics, which is now being tested scientifically, is that the entire universe is connected at every instant. It has been found that sending two elementary particles in opposite directions—that have interacted at some point—that the observation of the one particle would determine the properties of the other particle. This holds true no matter how far away from each other those two particles are located. These two unobserved particles exist only as probabilities for being in one state or the other. If one particle is being observed, it immediately collapses the probability function of the other particle. The unobserved particle manifests as a function of the observed particle. This means that the probability function for everything exists everywhere in the universe. The probability function of everything exists everywhere in an instant and can be collapsed into something everywhere in an instant. Because nothing is actually moving, this is a great observation—this does not violate Einstein's law that nothing can move faster than the speed of light because nothing is moving—it doesn't exist before it is observed—from one point to the other. It is only the probability function which exists everywhere!

"Someone" did not have to create the laws of physics. The universe and the laws of physics come into existence by the observer as the universe only exists as a probability until it is observed. The probability function is collapsed by the observer. The universe and the Big Bang are created by the observer into the "now." In this respect, we as observers are the "chosen ones." In other words, the universe only existed as a potential before it was observed. This is consistent with the Copenhagen Interpretation of Quantum Physics!

The universe can be created from nothing if the total amount of energy in the universe equals zero. The zero energy of the universe is the balance between positive mass and energy balanced by the negative energy of gravitation. If the energy is zero, the universe is "flat" and is equal to nothing in aggregate. There is also another possibility that another universe was created with equal and exact opposite energy. The atoms in this other universe have positive electrons and negative protons. I propose that the universe came into existence, and created time and the "now" when "time" went from infinity to Planck time. The universe experienced an incredible expansion (inflation) of energy according to the following equation:

<u>Suppose</u>

U = Universe
E = Energy
T = Time
Planck Time ("now") = 10^{-44} seconds

$$U = \frac{E}{T = \text{Infinity} \rightarrow \Delta T = \text{Planck Time}}$$

A "shrinking" of the "now" may also explain the continuous expansion of the universe.

Before The Big Bang

If delta T = infinity, when delta T went to Planck time the "Big Bang" happened and created "now". If this hypothesis is true, we are living in a "two" dimensional universe where the "third" dimension equals Plank length divided by Planck time (the time it would take light to traverse the Planck length or the building blocks of "now").

The universe did not exist before observation only as a probability. Hence, if science leads to understanding and if observation creates the universe in the "now," then man's ultimate goal is to finish the creation of the universe. Once man has created the entire universe through understanding and observation, he will also have acquired the ability to manipulate the universe according to what he sees fit.

I suggest that we use this ultimate power to recreate everything that existed and create everything that is possible for "infinity!"

When you are moving are you creating a different "now" or is the "now" preventing you from moving at the speed of light? Anything moving can only move in two dimensions inherently. It only looks as if it is moving in three dimensions for an outside observer as the blinking

on and off of the two dimensional universe creates the illusion of an object moving through space. What it is moving through is the on and off blinking or changing of the object in the two dimensional universe as the frame of reference.
Planck length/time gives the illusion of space. Therefore, we can only move in two dimensions.
When we are moving we are creating a different time. My time can never be the same as your time. Time and space are not continuous but two dimensional slices with Planck time/length defining the "now" = two dimensional! It is the collapsing of the probability function into discreet "nows" which are slightly different from "blink to blink" that creates the illusion of space and time.

If reality is not two-dimensional and quantized, we cannot be free. If time is continuous and we have a third dimension of space, then freedom and the ability to create would be impossible . . .

If the future and the past exist, we cannot have free will. If the past exists, then the "now" is a direct consequence of the past. According to Newtonian Physics, the laws of the universe are continuous, creating a deterministic universe where everything that happens is an exact consequence of the past. However, quantum physics proves that, on a fundamental level, the universe is probabilistic, meaning not exact. This means that the future cannot be exactly determined based on the past. This feature of reality creates the possibility of free will and, this in turn, meaning and purpose.

In a deterministic universe, if you knew the initial conditions at the beginning of the Big Bang; you could calculate the entire future of the universe. The idea of a deterministic universe has been disproven by quantum physics.

So, my frame of reference is different than yours. You are collapsing the two dimensions of the universe into slices of Planck time/length or "nows." This gives the illusion of three dimensions. Anything that moves creates this three dimensional illusion. When you move in a circle, you are "moving"/"blinking" through two-dimensional slices with a Plank time/length in between. This gives the illusion of moving in a circle within a three dimensional universe. When you are moving in a straight line, you are "blinking" in the two-dimensional universe. Without a two-dimensional universe, we would not have free will.

"Now" is a Planck time in two-dimensions. Planck time is the lower limit—the ultimate smallness, because for anything smaller than this, time and length would have no meaning. Many physicists don't want to speculate on the consequences of quantum physics because it is too spooky.

"It is a participatory universe. If consciousness doesn't exist, then neither would the universe!" John Wheeler, famous physicist and mathematician.

"Now" are two dimensional with Planck Length as the "third dimension". Hence, the length and time of "now" = Planck Length and Planck Time.

Reality is created out of nothing. We are something created from nothing. In the beginning, the positive and the negative split or symmetry breaking—yin and yang—which means that meaning can only be manifest relative to its opposite. However, without the asymmetry, an imperfection, the universe would not have come into existence! Hence, our existence and the universe is a manifest imperfection! By looking at the physics of the Big Bang, we can also draw the conclusion that creation and destruction emanate from it.

Net energy of the universe must be zero or, two opposite universes must have been created at the Big Bang.

The universe is created by opposites—positive and negative forces—as human consciousness and experience are created. For harmony and creativity to happen, freedom must be maximized. Both forces must be allowed to exist. Since the past and the future cannot exist—only "now"—the universe is created in every instant by the conscious observer.

"Nothing," is the opposite of "something" neither can exist without the other!

In fact, **"nothing" is not allowed on its own!** This makes everything move toward more complexity. The gravitational force makes creation a stronger force than destruction. The sum of everything that exists in the universe collapses into more complexity over time. This is a creative force. Gravity is a creative force because it leads the universe to more complexity, making creation a stronger force than destruction.

One may ask: "Why is the universe expanding?" Answer: Because the "now" is getting shorter and the expansion of the universe is a function of PT which is getting shorter. In the end, time may disappear and the expansion of the universe may have reached the speed of light. Then we are back to nothing.

"How are we back to nothing?" Because "now" was snapped out and we are back to nothing again. We must prevent this or we must learn how to travel with the speed of light—moving in pure consciousness with the speed of light.

The illusion of time and space was created by the Big Bang because nothing is less stable than something. Is the "why" still not answered? The answer can be found in freedom. Freedom gives meaning and purpose. With freedom, we are tapping into the fundamental law of the universe itself. Of the "equal" amount of positive and negative energy which makes it possible to create something out of nothing.

Definitions

- Information is the communication of meaning and purpose.
- By definition, information equals meaning and purpose.

Life is the only "thing" in the universe that can preserve and increase information—a violation of the Second Law of Thermodynamics. Consciousness creates meaning and purpose from information. This explains the collapse of the probability function of matter into reality through observation. Hence, consciousness creates the observable universe. Information theory today is explaining physical laws of the universe on a fundamental level. The universe can be explained by the exchange of information. If we make the assumption that energy equals information then everything that happens in the universe is an exchange of information. The universe itself can be looked upon as a giant binary computer. The software of the universe is the physical laws that can all be described in binary code.

It is only consciousness that can interpret and create. The observer is what has to be at the cause of information and creates/interprets what exists into meaning and purpose. Since the universe is in essence an exchange of information, an observer is needed to create information into meaning and purpose. It's the interpretation of the probability function of the universe by the observer who translates the probability function into information, where the foundation is meaning and purpose.

In order for freedom to exist, the creation of information must be possible. If that is so, information can also disappear (reference Steven Hawkings). Cause and effect goes out of the window and chaos becomes possible—meaning that you cannot predict the future with certainty. There cannot be a perfect relationship between cause and effect. If there were there would be no freedom, meaning and purpose. So everything has to be imperfect in order for meaning and purpose to exist. The observer converts interactions into information and information equals meaning and purpose. Imperfection has to exist everywhere we look, because the perfect is the same as nothing.

Creativity decreases the universe's entropy. Conversely, destruction increases the entropy of the universe. The act of creating is to start something that is less complex and increase its complexity into a higher level of order—this is a repeatable act. Destruction reduces the complexity and the order of the universe. At certain levels of destruction the original object can be restored by applying a creative act.

Entropy can always be decreased locally at the expense of increasing it somewhere else. For example, to sustain ourselves we are using energy from the sun. This is decreasing the local entropy and increasing the overall entropy of the universe. So, in a way, a decrease in entropy is always at the expense of increasing the entropy of the universe itself. The biggest increaser of entropy in the universe is heat.

The increase of entropy in the universe defines the arrow of time. In a continuously expanding universe, this overall increase in entropy is irreversible.

If we can make the universe reverse from expansion to contraction, entropy will be reversed. The question then becomes: Is gravity subject to entropy? If not, then one can actually have decreasing entropy when the universe is contracting because as it contracts, the energy content in the universe per unit of space will increase—because energy will become more and more concentrated, which is a decrease in entropy. Right now, in our expanding universe, the opposite is true.

The Second Law of Thermodynamics states: All systems will automatically go toward its lowest energy state. When you put two gasses—hot and cold—into a container, they will mix and eventually become the same temperature. The gas has achieved is its highest level of entropy. Without adding energy to the system, this is irreversible. As a logical consequence, the past and the future cannot exist. If they did, there would be no free will, or meaning and purpose. This is the core precept. When you think about it, every thought or action by an observer in the universe affects the future. The movement of the two-dimensional "now" into the future is caused by the Second Law of Thermodynamics. By being able to affect the entropy of the universe through our choice and free will, the observer has the ability to affect the evolution of the entire universe. This is the fallout of free will and the idea of meaning and purpose. Information would not exist without meaning and purpose. For meaning and purpose to exist, the information must be observed by an observer. It is that act of observation and the translation, by the observer, into meaning and purpose that creates the observable universe: The "now!"

Information has no meaning and purpose without the observer. What I am leading to is that consciousness is the most important factor of the universe. Up until this moment, science has not understood the role of the observer. Science has been concerned about the object, meaning the function of the universe without the incorporation of the observer. To arrive at a complete picture of the universe we must incorporate the role of the observer into the theory. A complete theory of the universe needs to integrate the object and the subject into a complete "theory of everything".

In fact, you could say that the object doesn't exist, and that it is the subject who brings the object into existence through observation. Observation is, by definition, the interpretation and creation of information into meaning and purpose.

I have formulated an equation that may explain the inflation at the Big Bang and, as a consequence, that the entire universe may have been created out of almost nothing, and why the universe continues to expand. In a nutshell, I arrived at the formula through the following reasoning:

    1. Quantum physics indicates that reality only exists as a cloud of probability until it is observed.

    2. If that is so, the past and the future cannot exist—only the "now".

    3. If that is so, humans have free will and affect the evolution of the universe through their actions.

    4. If the universe is a chaotic system, the actions of humans can affect the entire direction and evolution of the universe as those actions are magnified over time.

5. Meaning and purpose can only exist if humans have free will and are free to choose.

Based on this reasoning I formulated this equation:

U equals the perceived size of the Universe. E equals a quantity of energy. Delta T (time) equals the observation or the length of "Now":

(Happened at the Big Bang)

$$U = \frac{E}{\Delta T = \text{Planck Time "Now"} \to \infty \text{ smaller}}$$

Delta T goes from "infinity" to Planck time!

If this is true, the universe could have been created out of "nothing" and everything is interconnected!

The third dimension of space is created by delta-T, meaning that space is a function of time, given that time equals the Plank length/time, which is the extension of what we call "now." "Now," and the illusion of space, is the experience of change from what is the past into the creation of the future. That is what gives the illusion of space. If we were living in a deterministic universe then the past and future would exist, and the universe would be static. Any movement and change would be impossible. Any movement or change depends upon the entire universe being created and recreated at any moment in time. If this were not so, movement and change would be impossible—we would be living in a rigid universe. If that is true, then the entire universe can be created from "no-thing." If the size of "now" equals Plank length/time, then the entire universe can be created out of "no-thing". Quantum physics has proven that "nothing" cannot exist. In nothing, virtual particles would appear in pairs, positively and negatively charged—matter and antimatter. What made the universe come into existence is the slight asymmetry between matter and antimatter. A tiny bit more matter is created than anti matter and it is this asymmetry which manifested itself into the universe. If the universe had been completely symmetrical, then both sides would have canceled each other out, and the universe would never have come into existence and disappeared into nothingness again.

"Now" is, by definition, limited by the speed of light. If, in traditional physics, stating that something we observe 13 billion light years away is in the past, then light is made into the foundation of time. The speed of light equals time. However, at the speed of light, time goes to zero. This means that all observation in the universe—all events—are moving at the speed of light. If that's the case, time doesn't exist. This means that everything that is observed is in the "now." The latest work on quantum physics eliminated time from the equations. Rather than using time in the traditional sense, you can look at time to be an aggregation of correlations between events. By describing, mathematically, the correlations between events, the concept of time can be deleted from quantum physics—just as temperature can be described on a more fundamental level, as the movements and collisions between molecules in a gas.

For God to exist, a self-aware intelligent being has to be created, because without it, there will be no manifestation of God. If that's the case, God and that self aware intelligence is one. God cannot exist without an observer. And if God cannot exist without an observer, the observer has to be God. If that is the case, our destiny is to create meaning and purpose. For meaning and purpose to exist, the future has to be created, which means that we can create the future.

Hence, the meaning and purpose is to create the future.

A black hole is nothing. It is a hole in the universe into nothing, "no-thing". Just like zero in math is the reference to all other quantities or, the logic in a computer of zeros and ones or "nothing or something". Hence, everything can be expressed in binary code. The binary code of "zeros and ones" is the foundation of information that can be used to describe "everything."

Every interaction in the universe is an exchange of information that can be described through zeros and ones or "nothing" or "something". Since "nothing" is not allowed without "something", observation has to be the source of everything! If we can answer the question: "Why we exist with certainty, we would not be free to create". An answer to the question would be definitive and decisive. Therefore, the answer would be irrelevant. Hence, the answer has to be to create what does not exist. "Nothing" is not allowed because it has no meaning and purpose. Consciousness creates meaning and purpose.

Hence, consciousness/observation is the foundation of the universe!

Maybe as delta T gets smaller, dark energy gets larger; the density of the universe becomes less. However T cannot be smaller than Planck's constant, therefore Planck's constant itself is getting smaller. Any quantity of energy.

T=Planck Time
U=Universe
E=Energy

$$U = \frac{E}{\Delta T = \text{Planck Time "Now"} \rightarrow \infty \text{ smaller}}$$

This means that the entire universe can be created out of nothing. If this is what created the universe, then
- Planck time equals 10^{-43} seconds.
- Planck length equals 10^{-33} centimeters.

Because Plank Length/Time (the third dimension) is so thin, the universe is virtually two dimensional—anything smaller than Planck's constant has no meaning.

The expansion of the universe means that Planck time is becoming smaller. If we have a quantity of something and measure it against infinity, that quantity becomes nothing. Therefore, infinity equals nothing. If space was infinitely big, there would be nothing in the universe. So, the universe must be finite in order to exist.

Einstein's formulations of the three dimensions of space and the fourth dimension of time basically state that all objects, subject to gravity, travel in a straight line and that they travel in two dimensions. This means that the earth, circling the sun, travels in a straight line. This is because the universe is curved. Straight lines in a curved universe appear to curve. According to Einstein, gravity bends space. So the geometry of space is being bent.

So everything in the universe is traveling in a straight line except for life with freewill. Higher and lower energy densities in the universe make the two-dimensional slice into bulges.

There are no particles in the universe. There is only one thing in the universe and that is energy. All these particles are just concentrations of energy or "energy noodles". Everything in the universe is constructed of places with more or less energy. So everything in the universe is created out of energy noodles, including you. There is nothing else in the universe.

Every energy noodle becomes manifest by admitting and absorbing virtual energy noodles created out of nothing. All forces are energy noodles emitting other energy noodles that are emitted and reabsorbed by other energy noodles. The whole universe exists only as processes and relationships. It cannot be defined by itself. The definition of the universe by itself is "nothing". Everything comes into existence by interacting with something else. The universe is the ultimate "bootstrap!"

A particle comes into existence self-referentially. Everything exists because it relates to something else. So without this relationship there is nothing. Particles come into existence because particles also have a relationship to themselves. The energy itself comes into existence by manifesting itself by emitting and absorbing virtual energy—meaning that nothing comes into something when nothing emits a virtual energy noodle. In emitting and absorbing the virtual energy, "something" is created out of "nothing."

A particle is an energy bundle. Energy equal information which equals consciousness or observation. The energy of the universe, which is everything, is the "nothingness" manifesting itself as the "observer". This is the observer manifesting into "something" and the observer is the energy of the universe. This ties into the Copenhagen Interpretation of Quantum Physics because observation collapses the probability function into something. The probability function of "something" exists everywhere in the universe, meaning that everything is interconnected. This includes you and me!

The observer or creator is manifesting itself in different bodies. The "now" is the same for all of us because in reality only one collapse takes place at any moment in time. It is the fundamental creator collapsing the universe in which each living organism is a different manifestation of the creator. You and I are not separate from the entire universe. We are completely integrated into the whole.

Since everything in the universe is interconnected, maybe the development of a self aware intelligence is not a function of the individual local planetary systems, but is dependent upon the entire universe itself. The closest planetary system to our own is 200 light years away. If intelligence is being developed in parallel and if we assume that the first radio signals emitted by intelligence on earth came in the 1860s, then the first possible time that we could discover intelligence in the universe would be in approximately 50 years. It took 3 ½ billion years for intelligence to develop on earth. But the same evolution of intelligence might have only taken 500 million years on a different planetary system because the evolution of intelligence might have happened in parallel with ours. The entire universe may light up at the same time. Or we may see one planet light up after the other, depending on the distance from the earth. And the first light we would see would be in approximately 50 years. After that, chances are that new intelligences would be seen at an ever increasing rate. That this might be true may not only be the result of the interconnectedness of the entire universe, but also that we, as a self-aware intelligence are on the verge of a period of exponential growth of science and technology. The estimation that we could possibly discover intelligence within 50 years—which would completely change our perception of reality—is perfect timing. On the scale of time in the universe this observation would fit nicely into the whole condition of the human race. This is a great argument in favor of the possibility that these suppositions might be true.

For mankind to suddenly realize that we may discover intelligence on other planets or solar systems—predicted by humanity—would be a tremendously humbling experience. When we discover that the entire universe is a gigantic manifestation of an infinitely creative force, it creates a completely exhilarating feeling of greatness. The kind of discovery would not cause fear, but rather exhilaration and a sense of infinite greatness. Actually experiencing these things would go far beyond anything that could be described with this example. We can imagine that we are wandering in the dessert, dying of thirst and hunger, when we suddenly see another human being coming toward us. When we meet that other person, he shares food and water with us. This would actually be a verification that the source—the observer inside us—is the infinite "nothing" of the creative force of

The Entangled Universe 27

"everything". We would then discover that our existence is tied into a grand intelligence.

You and I are here. We are aware of our own existence. We have intelligence. The universe itself, everything or nothing, has to be a creative intelligence. To think otherwise is to deny our own existence. Human intelligence and manifestation of humans has to be as natural, as anything else in the universe—completely connected and integrated with the universe itself. So our experiences, thoughts, creativity, emotions—everything which has to do with life and a human being—are as natural a part of the entire universe as the stars and galaxies. So we are the manifestation of the infinite creative intelligence beyond space and time inside our universe.

You and I, as proven by physics, are trillions of interacting energy noodles or probabilities emanating from nothing. You and I are trillions of self-interacting and in between interacting energy noodles. Only on the macroscopic level does it manifests through electromechanical forces into something solid. Otherwise we are nothing. In fact, the energy noodles are creating themselves out of nothing as with everything else in the entire universe. Thus, the universe comes into being through observation: Blinking between "nothing and something" or "0 and 1" every 10^{-43} seconds.

The only truly underlying force in the universe that creates everything from the individual components such as atoms is the gravitational force. All the other forces discovered by physics are not fundamentally creative forces; they are just there—such as the electromagnetic force and the strong and weak nuclear force.

The strong and weak nuclear force is responsible for creating the fundamental building blocks of the universe. The electromagnetic force is also important for the individual components but it's also responsible for the transfer of energy in the universe. The gravitational force is the only truly creative force. Being responsible for bringing together the basic components for making the stars and the planets, and to keep together the large structures of the universe—galaxies and planetary systems.

Once we truly understand gravity, we may find the key to manipulating the universe on a grand scale. Great concentration and effort should be used to understand gravity. The understanding of gravity will make our ability to manipulate the atom almost inconsequential in comparison.

Major mysteries left as we can see right now:

1. How and why did the Big Bang happen?
2. How and why did life happen?
3. What is the gravitational force?

The previous analyses may have answered some of these mysteries!

Pointers

- The essence of time. The past does not exist, neither does the future. Einstein proved that time travel is impossible.
- "Now" is almost infinitely short. The smaller the "now" the larger the universe (reality) can be made as it goes toward the infinitely large. This means that everything can be created out of "no-thing", and that everything is made out of the same thing. It is only "time" that creates the illusion of separateness between people, planets, stars and everything. "Time" or the "quantization" of everything is the separator!
- Everything can be created from "no-thing".
- Reality is slowed-down light that gives the illusion of time. If we move with the speed of light, time will disappear.
- The past has no meaning except for helping to predict the future and to help us understand the present.

4
The Gaia Hypotheses

The Gaia hypothesis states that earth is one living organism and that the biosphere has the ability to create its own best environment for its survival. If you apply this simple hypothesis to the entire universe, shouldn't the universe also create its own best environment for its survival? There is reason to believe that this is so. If we analyze the constants of nature and the physical laws, even the tiniest of variations in those constants and physical laws would have prevented this universe and life from existing. The more we find out about the universe, the more we realize that it is for the purpose of life. The universe must be created by a super intelligent being that can understand these laws and constants. Eventually, this "being" will be able to manipulate the entire universe to secure its own survival.

I propose that this "being" is you and me!

Life forms on other planets will probably look very similar to what we find on earth. If that planet has advanced far enough, the chances are that it would have produced intelligent beings that look very much like us. "Man" with his physical attributes is the most economical and the best built for manipulating the environment as well as being extremely adaptive. So if life can only appear under very specific circumstances, like the earth, the logical conclusion would be that life on those planets would be extremely similar to ours. Notwithstanding this logic there is always a possibility that something entirely different could create consciousness and intelligence.

The final "theory of everything" can only be a description, not an explanation.

If explainable, we would not have arrived at the final "theory of everything" because all explanations are explained by something that is relative to something else. The fundamental truth—the "theory of everything"—cannot be an explanation; it can only be a description because an explanation is dependent on something that supports it. To explain something, you must have a foundation to explain it from. Therefore, the fundamental truth cannot be explained through something else. In the end, when we finally understand the truth, it can only be understood as a description.

Empty space has no meaning because it must be relative to something. "Nothing" has no meaning unless it is relative to "something." So truly nothing—empty space—cannot exist. If this is true, any truly empty space, or "nothing", would have to create "something" as it's opposite, in order to exist.

This logic is dependent on the existence of a "creator" and meaning and purpose.

This explains why there is something—our universe—rather than "nothing". Hence, the Big Bang came about at a time when something approached the state of nothing. If this is true, at some point in the future, when our universe has become empty, a new universe will come into existence—the opposite of nothing. "Nothing cannot exist without something"! Hence, our ability to experience meaning can be traced back to the origin of the universe itself as being the opposite of nothing. This also leads us toward the fundamental property that everything is consciousness. Consciousness needs to create opposites to exist and experience meaning. In other words, something can be created out of nothing. When opposites are brought back into their neutral state, they will disappear into nothing. The source of dark energy may come from the expansion of something driving the expansion of nothing, or the opposite.

Nothing (-) Nothing has no lower limit and will eventually transform into something!	Big Bang	Something (+) Something has no upper limit and will eventually reach nothing and at that moment transform into something again!

**Figure 6
Nothing to Something**

Something has no upper limit and will eventually reach nothing and at that moment transform into something again.

Maybe when the entire universe reaches a density less than the Plank Constant, which cannot be violated, at that moment, a new Big Bang will happen and create two new universes or one "flat" universe where total energy equal zero. If those two new universes are opposites, then an entire new universe can be created out of nothing. The neutral state between the two universes is nothing, and nothing cannot exist. Both the expansion of nothing and something will eventually create new "no-things" and "some-things" ad infinitum. Our universe may have the opposite dark energy of the dark energy of driving the expansion of nothing emanating from an opposite universe to ours.

Hypotheses

There is fundamentally no explanation to the "theory of everything"—only a description is present since an explanation is derived from underlying descriptions. As we dig deeper, we end up with only a description of things. Hence, the fundamental law(s) of the universe—and a "theory of everything"—can only be a description. It will be a fundamental observation that can only be explained by itself which ends up as being a description. This fundamental description will not be meaningful from an explanatory standpoint, but it will be experienced as meaningful. If the Fundamental Law of the Universe could be explained, it will not be fundamental. However, the fundamental law of the universe may be found to be true through experiment and observation and may even be subject to manipulation.

The Big Bang may have created two identical universes with opposite energies. As we look at the entire universe—on a micro and macro scale—we find a system of opposites. The dark energy must emanate from a source. That source might be the engine of an opposite universe. The "something" positive universe has matter in it. The "something" negative universe has anti-matter. So the ultimate energy exists in a true nothing. The Big Bang emanates out of nothing. Nothing cannot exist on its own as it violates a principle of opposites in the universe. So a nothing state is not allowed. When the universe hits "nothing" that state is not allowed. Maximum energy is released out of the nothing state. This is the source of the energy behind the Big Bang. But this may only come about by the simultaneous creation of two equal and opposite universes or a "flat" universe. Dark energy is increasing with increasing entropy until it reaches maximum point that is the state of nothing. Then it creates maximum energy and creates a new Big Bang. So it is the maximum energy of nothing that is the source of dark energy. With increasing entropy, the energy of nothing increases until it reaches its maximum trigger point when it reaches nothing. The energy of nothing is the dark energy. The only source for the dark energy is the energy embedded in nothing. The reason scientists can't find it is because there exists no source: The source is nothing. The ultimate energy comes out of nothing. This is the Big Bang.

"Nothing" cannot exist because a true nothing has no meaning. If a true nothing has no meaning then the source of the universe itself has to be consciousness and observation because the source—the consciousness—cannot accept a true nothing. A true nothing has no meaning and purpose since nothing is a neutral state.

There is "nothing" underlying the fundamental "theory of everything". And this theory can be tested through observation!

Electrons in the antimatter universe would be positively charged. The core of the atoms would be negatively charged. Our universe is exactly opposite. So, absolute nothing has maximum energy. There is no way that something can be created without its relative opposite that is not symmetrical. This makes our universe symmetrical to the other universe. Symmetry is a fundamental law of the universe but not perfect. However, each universe must be created imperfect to exist and have meaning and purpose!

Why don't we have any antimatter in the universe? All the antimatter is in the other universe (AMU). The antimatter universe is exactly opposite from ours. We just can't observe it!

The acceleration of the expansion of the universe means that we have a reduction in the density of the universe. It is going toward nothing. As the universe moves toward nothing, energy emanating out of nothing is increasing. This is because nothing is the apex of maximum energy. Nothing is the ultimate energy source since "nothing" is the opposite of "something".

It is consciousness that translates the universe's energy into information. Information is then translated into meaning and purpose.

The observer is the translator. The observer is nothing. Hence, the observer is the same in all of us. It's only the manifestation of body, thoughts and ego that is an illusory difference from one person to another. For example, our thought processes, our bodies, are all illusory manifestations of the same observer. The observer is the same in all of us: Created as different manifestations of the one observer. When I look at you—anybody—knowing that the observer is the same; I realize that I'm looking at myself because the essence of you is me. That realization always leads to love instead of hate. This is based on asymmetry and imperfection, love is creative and stronger, hate is destructive and weaker. Because how can I kill you if you are me! If I kill you, I kill myself!

When I was 7 years old after I had asked endless questions about everything, my dad, Knut Larsson replied, "the biggest mystery is that there is something rather than nothing."

If "nothing" is not allowed, consciousness must be the source of the universe. Nothing can only be defined by something. In the statement, "love yourself to love another" the question becomes. "Who loves? The observer is the answer. The observer in you is not you nor I, but the nothing creating the something. The you; the I; your thoughts and your emotions; the lover and the creator is the observer who is the nothing in you. When you die you realize that the nothing was the observer in you who created everything. And "nothing" cannot exist without "something" so creation starts again and "nothing" is the observer and the source.

Nothing is not allowed because "nothing" cannot exist by itself! Nothing is the opposite of everything. Since "nothing" is not allowed, everything emanates out of nothing. The nothing has to be consciousness by the observer. The observer of everything is consciousness.

The ultimate consequence of the Copenhagen Interpretation of Quantum Physics, states, "Nothing exists unless it is observed. Everything is only a probability function before it is observed, probability meaning nothing or "potentiality".

The logical flip side of this is that "no-thing" is the observer.

If that's the case, all energy equals everything and is consciousness! All creativity emanates from the source, the observer. So the less ego and the fewer thoughts one has, the more powerful and true the creative act becomes. To create is the highest form of existence because it emanates from the observer, the fundamental source of everything that gives meaning and purpose to everything.

If the future and the past existed, the universe would be rigid. The universe has to be recreated at every moment for transformation and change to take place. Otherwise, it would be rigid. This means that the conscious observer is re-creating the universe at every moment in every "now".

"Nothing" cannot exist without something. Without something there is no nothing. So our ultimate goal is to preserve something for infinity because nothing is not allowed. Hence, nothing has to be consciousness and the observer.

Based on quantum physics and the Copenhagen interpretation, the observer creates the universe at every instant, and since there is no past and no future—only "now"—this gives us the opportunity to create the future from every instant of "now". We need to create the society in such a way as to maximize freedom, the creative force and human evolution to take full advantage of this opportunity. This also translates into meaning and purpose for the individual and for humanity.

The asymmetry of the universe is the foundation for the creation of the universe at the Big Bang. This asymmetry also exists to create and to destroy—good and bad. The creative force is asymmetrically stronger than the destructive force. This is the foundation by which we must structure the society politically and economically through legislation because our destiny/existence is to create the universe itself.

Another proof that the observer is beyond thoughts, ego and the body itself is that in near-death experiences you can observe your own death. The question becomes: Who is the observer of your own death? Who has the experience of your own death? It is the observer, the source of everything that is nothing, the creator of everything. You can argue that the observer never dies because the observer is the infinite consciousness of "nothing" and "nothing" is not allowed.

For consciousness to manifest, it must create something, and that something is the universe. This includes you and me. Consciousness must create something. Nothing has no meaning and purpose. So, nothing is consciousness that manifests into something that is you and me. Because nothing has no meaning and purpose, it is not allowed. Nothing is the opposite of everything. So the infinite consciousness creates something. Nothing creates everything, so nothing has to be the observer and the creator.

This "nothing" that is the observer is the same in all of us. Every human being is a different manifestation of body, thought and ego of the nothing, infinite consciousness, by the observer. They are one. This happens at every discreet "now". The entire universe, and everything in it, is nothing for an instant of time (equal to the Plank Length and Time). Every instant of "now" is Plank Length divided by Plank Time. Plank Length/Plank Time is the "nothing". So the universe is created (equals something) by observation, then the universe becomes nothing (the observer), then the universe (equals something) is created again by observation and so on and so forth. It is the human mind that creates the four dimensions of space and time. The reality is that each "now" is two-dimensional. Otherwise, we would be living in a rigid universe. The only way that change can take place is that the universe is created at every instant by the observer. The "sowing" by your mind of every instant of "now" into the four dimensions of space and time is created by the observer in the "now". This creates the illusion of the four dimensions of space and time.

Every act, every movement, every thought—any manifestation of free will—affects the evolution of the entire universe itself.

The universe is a chaotic system, so everything we think and do will be magnified over the course of the universe billions and trillions of times. If we can achieve a cosmic consciousness and understand the laws of the universe, we as consciousness would be able to steer the evolution of the universe anywhere we want it to go; just as if we were driving a car. The question is: Can we create conditions right now to get to that level of understanding and consciousness?

In their novel *The View from the Center of the universe*, Joel Primack and Nancy Abrams, establish that any intelligence, and by extension any individual human being, is at the center of their universe, and the size of that universe is limited by the speed of light. We are living at the center of this ball, beyond which no light or action can be propagated to affect you as an individual or intelligence. So in a sense, as consciousness, there is a limit to observing or affecting the universe—meaning that the size of the universe for a conscious individual is finite (which is also an imperfection). It is also a very preferred place where consciousness exists with regard to scale. It happens to be that we, as humans, exist between the smallest possible size scale, meaning the Plank length, and the largest possible scale, which is the size of the universe. The Plank length is 10^{-33} cm. The size of the observable universe is 10^{28} cm. We exist almost in the middle between these two extremes. The logical place to put the observer and creator, with the ability to understand everything, would be right in between the largest and the smallest. That is where we are. Consciousness, as the focal point, encompasses everything from the smallest scale to the largest scale. This culminates with consciousness as the focal point. As we observe space with ourselves as the observer in the middle, we also are the observer on the scale of the universe, from the smallest to the largest. It took 4 ½ billion years for intelligence and self awareness to develop on our planet. If the solar system would have been without the Moon or Venus, life probably wouldn't have appeared on earth. Add the fact that Venus was able to clean up the solar system and create a stable planetary system with an almost circular orbit for the earth. Add the fact that the earth happens to have the biggest moon in the solar system that tilts the earth's axis at just the right angle causes the earth to have very stable seasons. The earth is therefore at the "Goldilocks" distance from the sun. The oceans were created by the bombardment of comets and the cooking of the core by the earth's interior heat. If we consider all these random events coming together in such a specific way to create life and provide enough stability for billions of years for intelligent life to appear, we as humans might be the only self-aware consciousness in the entire universe. If that's the case, we have a choice right now. That choice has to be made because at the beginning of the 21st Century we have an inflationary period in population growth and pollution. We either figure out how to solve these problems or we end up with the

The Gaia Hypothesis 37

cataclysmic destruction of the human race. If this happens after 4 ½ billion years of evolution then you can argue that the entire history of the universe has been wasted.

From "nothingness" (which we can call eternal creativity) everything has been created as the opposite of nothing. However, "nothing" cannot exist. In the nothing, because of quantum physics, you will have quantum fluctuations where something is created for Plank Time—coming into existence and going out of existence. And when one of those quantum fluctuations became just the right fluctuation, suddenly asymmetry and imperfection happened, and our universe fell out of eternity. This was the starting point of our universe: The creation of the Big Bang.

The final consequence of Darwin's theory is the creation of a "supernatural" being that has the ability to understand and manipulate nature.

The core observation of the Gaia Hypothesis is that life creates its own best environment for its own survival.

For life to survive in the long term it must develop a species which has the ability to understand and manipulate nature and even the universe. If the human branch of evolution had not been successful, chances are that any other branch of animal could have evolved to the same capacity. As an example, even without the extinction of the dinosaurs, chances are that one branch of the dinosaurs would have evolved into conscious beings just like us. If life exists long enough and in the right environment, the emergence of intelligence is inevitable.

Evolution is not through survival of the fittest but rather through adaptation and cooperation within species and among species.

The DNA is identical in all life on earth. The only difference between plants, animals, insects, fish, is the activation and deactivation of the genes of the DNA. So fundamentally, all life is the same.
The biggest misunderstanding of Darwin's Theory of Evolution is that one species is created from another species. It's not as if human beings were created from chimpanzees. What evolution says is that humans and chimps have the same ancestor. At any point in time, life

on earth is the very tip of the tree of evolution—the rest of the tree and the branches no longer exist.

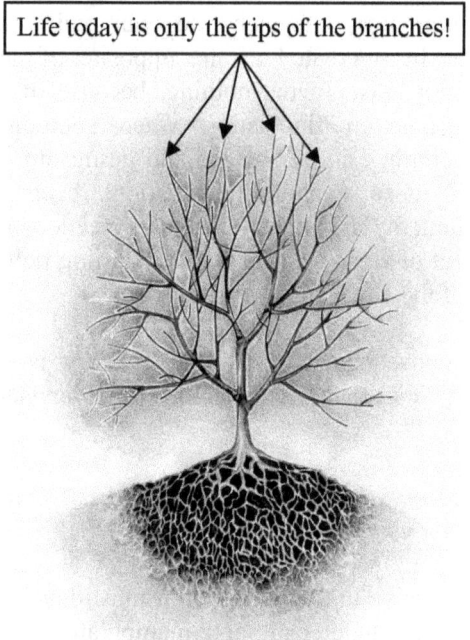

Figure 7
Life today is only the tips of the branches

Evolution does not happen through survival of the fittest. Evolution happens through adaptation! Adaptation is very different from survival of the fittest because survival of the fittest implies a fight between different species and that is a misunderstanding of Darwin's theory of evolution. "Survival of the fittest" was never mentioned by Darwin, but coined by one of his contemporaries through a misunderstanding of his theory. This misunderstanding may be one of the most damaging to human evolution and the cause of incredible misery during the last 150 years. I say it again; evolution takes place through adaptation and cooperation, not through domination and destruction! If there is an opening in the biosphere for survival, chances are that something will evolve into that opening and occupy it.

The Gaia Hypothesis 39

Life on earth needed to create an intelligence to be "above" nature to give life a chance to continue.

Life creates its own best environment needed for its own survival. An example would be a planet with white and black flowers on its surface. If the planet gets too cold for the abundance of white flowers, this now favors black flowers through heat absorption and the number of black flowers will increase and spread over a larger surface of the planet and heat it up until the planet gets too hot. Then, white flowers would get an advantage as they reflect the heat back into space and cools it down again. This is—in a "nutshell"—how life creates its own best environment for its survival.

Our sun is getting hotter, and at some point will become too hot for the natural regulation mechanism to create a sustainable environment for life. At this point, life will be dependent on intelligence for its survival in an "unnatural" way.

Hence, we are created to preserve life and we are the life's custodians when the natural life preservation mechanisms are exhausted as the sun is getting hotter.

The sun is getting too hot for the earth's self regulating, natural-life system to continue to sustain life. The earth with the ecosystem—Gaia—had to create an "animal" that could understand nature and be "supernatural" and self-conscious in order to secure that life is able to sustain itself beyond the ability of the ecosystem's own ability to create its own best environment for its own survival. Otherwise, life on earth would be doomed.

Hence, an overarching purpose and goal for man is to sustain life and become its custodian. This is the logical consequence.

Man is different. We have the ability to manipulate nature. It is impossible to turn the earth back to its unconscious stage. If we attempt to do it, all life will be doomed in the long term. The evolution by adaptation can only protect life up to a certain point against environmental stress. The heating of the sun is the number one threat to life on earth. To guarantee life's survival, life must create a being that can understand and manipulate nature. **We are that being!** This statement is so logical that when you are exposed to it, it becomes a revelation for the future and a path for humanity to take. This revelation puts everything into place. One goal for humanity is to develop so fast technologically and socially that we either are able to manipulate the entire solar system or to escape the solar system altogether to another solar system, which is hospital to life and is younger.

But in the end, life has to be able to understand and manipulate the universe itself—to sustain life forever. That is our destiny and humanity's number one quest.

Pointers

- The optimum temperature for life is 71 degrees Fahrenheit. The average temperature on earth happened to be at that temperature about 3.5 billion years ago.
- The sun is getting warmer.
- Life has its own ability to create its own optimum environment to sustain itself.
- The next major step for man is to improve the earth's nature.
- To install a system of government to maximize freedom and opportunity.
- Another great step would also be to accelerate space exploration and the sciences.
- Nature must be managed by man. This is part of our destiny. We fail if we do nothing. Today's environmental movement must adopt a management approach toward nature.
- Keeping pockets of nature untouched and unmanaged by man is wrong. In fact, it can be more damaging than what man can ever do to this environment. The complete destruction of the salmon population in the north caused by the explosion of the seal population is a perfect example.
- Look at the earth coming alive as an organism. For example: Transportation equates to a blood system, and communication can be likened to a central nervous system. The earth under the guidance of humanity is becoming alive as one "organism," and will experience a synergistic growth stage in which the

sum of its parts, once integrated, becomes more than its individual parts.
- Web sites are becoming the "nerve nodules" in the central nervous system of the unified humanity on earth.
- Our destiny is to understand the universe and life itself. The next step is to become the creator.
- Man's face in the moon, what a coincidence!
- As we travel toward the center of the Milky Way galaxy, it heats up. At some point there is a huge region in space where the average temperature will be 71 degrees Fahrenheit. We could construct huge structures in that region where we would have the perfect environment for life. The question is: Will there already be millions of civilizations in that region? In our location on the outskirts of the universe, we may not really be part of the central hub.
- The more variety you have among plants/flowers the more adaptability and evolution among flowers. The same principle can be applied to humans and cultures—the more variety, the more opportunity for growth and development.

Humanity needs to understand our climate as soon as possible to develop the necessary tools to regulate the earth for the benefit of life. As an example
- Burning of fossil fuels could be used as a tool to heat the earth, if the earth starts sliding into a new ice age.
- To use non-emission energy to avoid run away heating and to cool the earth.
- Increase of bio mass to cool the earth.

Many other tools need to be identified for the management of the earth. Humanity also needs to determine the "optimal population" of the earth with regard to sustainability and survivability of life. This needs to be related to "natural" catastrophic changes in climate, our ability to prevent such changes and the long term avoidance of loss of essential resources through recycling, recovery and overall abundance.

5
The "Observer"

In the quote, "I don't feel good today," who is the observer? It is the observer who observes that you don't feel good today. The more you become aware that there is a distinction between who you are and the observer of who you are, the more you realize that your thoughts and body are only a temporary manifestation of the observer inside you that exists for all time. In other words, your body and thoughts, including your ego are temporary manifestations of you as the eternal observer. And that observer is nothing or "no-thing".

This also explains the mystery of Quantum Physics. Why? Because of the observer which is "no-thing"—nothing exists without the observer. The observer is needed to collapse the probability function of the universe to make it come into being.

We are the manifestation of eternal creativity outside space and time within the observable universe. We are the link between eternal creativity and the material universe. That explains Quantum Physics. This spark of quantum fluctuation of imperfection created the universe. Embedded in that universe was also the potentiality of manifesting eternal creativity—you and me.

Manifestations of quantum fluctuations are caused by the observer. Hence, the observer has to be the eternal creativity of nothing. Quantum Physics proves that nothing exists without the observer. If eternal creativity outside space and time is subject to quantum fluctuations then the "nothing" must be the observer. If the observer creates everything, we are a temporary manifestation of that observer. The observer manifests to observe the material universe by creating a consciousness with eyes, nose, body, and thoughts.

Hence, the foundation of everything is the observer and consciousness.

The eternal observer-creator manifests into consciousness as living human beings in the material universe to observe it and make it come into being.

Because meaning and purpose can only be created out of imperfections—something that is asymmetrical and imperfect—the observer creates meaning and purpose in an imperfect manifestation that is the universe. Otherwise, there is no meaning and purpose. Eternal nothing has no meaning and purpose.

A temporary "imperfect" manifesting as "now" is something that has meaning and purpose.

Although, we can still ask the question "why we are here"? Why is irrelevant because there is no why. It just is. If this question can be answered, it's not the fundamental truth. Up to this point, no one would have thought that "nothing" could be the source of everything. The fundamental truth must be a description, not an explanation. An explanation is dependent upon underlying concepts and must be in relation to something else so the fundamental truth cannot be an explanation. The fundamental description is:

"Nothing is not allowed"!

Something can only exist on the background of nothing. "Nothing" cannot exist on its own. "Nothing" has no meaning without something. Therefore, "no-thing" is the source of everything and the "no-thing" is consciousness/observation. This is the description. Since we are able to describe the universe through mathematics, logic must be valid. We are taking logic to its ultimate extreme, because of this we, as human observers, are able to follow this logic all the way to the fundamental truth of our own being.

Therefore, the answer to humanity is; to become "enlightened", preserve life and to create and experience everything that is possible and to recreate everything that ever existed!

In infinity everything that can or will happen manifests an infinite number of times. Hence, infinity is without meaning and purpose. The reason infinity has no meaning and purpose is that there is no desire or purpose to create since everything will happen an infinite number of times anyway.

"Something" in "infinity" would also be "nothing", because as compared to infinity, that "something" becomes infinitely small. "Something" becomes "nothing" as compared to infinity. Something cannot exist in infinity. So infinity equals nothing. This is why the universe is imperfect and finite. If it were perfect and infinite, it would be "nothing" and "nothing" cannot exist on its own. That explains why the universe exists!

What exists beyond the universe itself is the observer. The observer is the infinite creative source creating something.

The fact that man has a free will means that the future is not determined. If that is so, then the universe is created by consciousness and observation. This act created the history of the universe and creates the future!

If the universe is "one" then there has to be a "zero". The zero and the one is the foundation of the binary code in mathematics, and everything can be expressed in the binary code! The universe cannot exist without no-thing. So the foundation of everything has to be nothing and "nothing" is not allowed. So nothing comes into existence by creating something and nothing has to be the observer. It is the observation which collapses the probability function into something.

Pointers

- The bio-chemistry of life exists in the mezzo (middle) area of 10 to 500 nanometers particle size. That is the area between quantum physics on one hand and classical physics and chemistry on the other. That area is not well understood by science!
- Quantum physics states that the observer is collapsing the "nothing" into "something" (from the 1928 Copenhagen interpretation of physics).
- When Quantum Physics calculations result in infinity, scientists routinely perform "renormalization" to remove the infinity. I postulate that the infinity represents infinite energy, which is the nothing. One solution would then be the two dimensional universe.

- A star two billion light years away did not exist two billion years ago in the way it is being observed when light from that star reaches us. This is because light traveling through the universe is moving at the speed of light! At the speed of light time is zero. The speed of light does not change regardless of the movement of the observer. Therefore, light from a star two billion light years away will arrive at our location instantaneously. So we are not observing the past, but the "now". And the "now" is all there is.
- There is no past. There is no future. There is only "now".

6
The Meaning of Everything

The universe is a work in progress!

We think about the past and future as though they exist. When we understand that past and future do not exist—that there is only "now"—then we also understand that time doesn't exist, either. Instead of calling our experience evolution as it relates to time, we should call it transformation. This would be a more accurate description than the old theory of time.

Since consciousness is the source of the universe itself—manifesting itself in the "now"—the universe is being created as we speak. For example, did the Big Bang exist before consciousness formulated the idea of the Big Bang? It did not. So our journey of manifesting the source consciousness of the universe itself is the creation of the universe. Hence, we are creating the universe with our understanding and exploration where science and mathematics are the most important tools.

Hence the universe is a work in progress with consciousness and observation as the source.

Remember "nothing" is not allowed. Something must always be. Nothing has no meaning except for being the opposite of something. Something must exist. That something is consciousness emanating out of nothing. And consciousness creates as it evolves the universe we live in. The universe started out of nothing. But "nothing" is not allowed. So the original emanating out of nothing was consciousness. So the consciousness/observer is the source.

Consciousness is the only logical foundation for everything because it creates information and meaning. In fact, information does not exist and is meaningless without an observer to convert it into information. Everything that happens in the universe is an exchange of information. Consciousness converts the probabilities of interactions into information through the act of observation. Without the observer, there is no information. Information is, by definition, the creation of meaning. The collapse of the probability function—or the act of observation—is the creation of information. Creation of the information is the interpretation or the conversion into meaning. Information equals meaning. Without the observer there is no meaning. So there is no interaction. There is nothing. It is the observer who creates nothing into something. Quantum Physics says that; without the observer to interpret the probability for something to exist, it can't.

"Nothing is not allowed"! The statement implies consciousness, creativity and logic. Hence, consciousness has to be the source of everything!

If we apply the "Ockham's Principle" as the ultimate frugality to the universe itself, we can draw the following conclusion:

"Nothing cannot exist so the observer/consciousness creates the something as the opposite to itself that is nothing, or no-thing".

Energy equals the creation of something from "nothing". Energy only exists as a probability until it is observed. Once so, the energy is brought into the "now" or the reality. Energy by itself has no meaning and is nothing. An observer is needed to make it into something. According to $E=MC^2$ everything is energy and—according to Quantum Physics—manifest into something by observation. Without the observer there is nothing. Each individual—manifestation of the eternal observer—creates their own universe; defined by the speed of light and the "time" since the Big Bang. Each observer is in the center of their own universe. All these individual and incremental observations create the universe in progress. Each human contributes to tiny transformations that are experienced as time by the Second Law of Thermodynamics. The universe is the ultimate "joint venture" between all observations contributing to incremental changes.

Before a self-aware animal—humans—were created, the universe evolved without meaning and purpose except for survival.

The energy of the universe is constant. Hence, nothing is the source of energy in the universe. Nothing is illogical. When meaning and purpose cease to exist the observer is no longer there. "Nothing" is not allowed because it cannot be observed. Hence, the creator of something has to be the observer. The observer has to be the "no-thing". The observer cannot observe itself. It is self-referential! And that ties it to quantum physics.

Mass is just a higher probability that something will exist in a specific location while electro-magnetic radiation is a very low probability that something will exist in a specific localization.

In other words, everything is energy manifesting at higher or lower probability—depending on its density and location. The higher the density of the energy, the higher the probability will be for it to exist in a specific location.

The observer is creating the energy of the entire universe because nothing has no meaning. Energy equals consciousness. Consciousness and the observer are not exactly the same. Consciousness is the creative manifestation of the observer. The observer is the eternal creativity of nothing. This takes quantum physics to its ultimate conclusion, since it requires infinite energy to make any mass travel at the speed of light.

Energy is electro-magnetic radiation. Energy doesn't exist before it is observed. Energy moves with the speed of light. This means that it is beyond time. At the speed of light, time does not exist. It goes to zero. Energy is everywhere in the universe, instantaneously from the point of view of the speed of light. Energy is the source of information. Information can only exist and have meaning if there is an observer or interpreter.

The observer is the creator of the universe because without the observer it doesn't exist. "Nothing" is not allowed. Hence, the observer is the creator of mass by virtue of being frozen energy because mass is potential energy.

The observer is the fundamental source of everything and so cannot be explained, only described.

How can the describer describe itself? Or how can the observer observe himself? He cannot observe himself because there is nothing beneath the observer. There is only a description. The description is the observation or consciousness. "Nothing" cannot be explained. The observer cannot be explained. There is no meaning because the meaning emanates from the observer. It's self-referential. You cannot observe what is inside your brain observing yourself observe. The observer just is. So it has to be the source because observation and consciousness is the creator of meaning.

In summary

"Nothing" is not allowed because it cannot be observed and therefore has no meaning and purpose! Since "nothing" is not allowed, something must come into existence and that something is created by consciousness, the observer! The "nothing" is therefore consciousness, the observer! The consciousness emanates from "nothing"! That also explains the uncanny relationship between physics and mathematics because they are the most advanced tools that the observer can use to observe and, hence, create and develop the universe!

Hence, the "now" is the evolution, transformation and creation of the universe by consciousness of the observer, you and me living in the "now"!

The Omega Point

If we can reverse the evolution of the universe from expansion to contraction and make it asymmetrical, the "Big Crunch" will never become a singularity. It will never end up in one spot, becoming a black hole. At that moment, energy goes toward infinity—energy equals information—at that point, we can create a simulation to create everything that ever existed and create everything possible forever—in subjective time including a simulation of you and me. It does not matter how much time it would take to get there as long as it happens at any point in the future. Even if it took "trillions of years," your experience would be "I was immediately resurrected after I died"!

Humanity would have created the mythological heaven without relying on a third person—God!

Pointers

- The probability functions in Quantum Physics state that the manifest reality is uncertain. However, there is a high degree of probability that the present is almost a 100% function of the past. It is that slight discrepancy or imperfection that gives us

free will. The human brain operates on electrical impulses and is subject to the laws of quantum physics. Past thoughts do not, necessarily, create the next thought. So within our minds, we can literally create something out of nothing.
- The brain, without complete information, can create its own thoughts and conclusions.
- If you will something from your imagination, it is in that probabilistic discrepancy that free will exists.
- One of the best arguments that the past and future don't exist is to ask the question: "Where is it"?
- If the past and future existed we would be in a deterministic universe. To allow freedom and evolution to take place, the universe needs be two dimensional. The universe has to be quantized—time and the third dimension of space are not needed. If you delete these two dimensions, you end up with "now" as defined by the Planck length and time and only two dimensions. Time and space between the two dimensional slices is equal to Planck Length/Time. This is the quantum of the universe.
- The Second Law of Thermodynamics establishes that the entropy of the universe is increasing. This creates asymmetry between the past and the future that manifests as the arrow of time.
- When society is changing from one moment to the next, it implies that the "previous" society no longer exists. The Second Law of Thermodynamics establishes that the past doesn't exist because the past has been deleted from the "now".

The Meaning of Everything 51

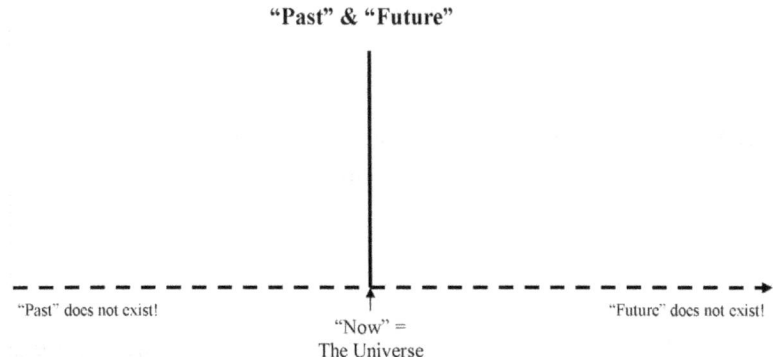

**Figure 8
Past and Future**

- "Nothing" is not meaningful to an observer. Hence "nothing" must be the observer. Since "nothing" is not allowed, the foundation of the universe needs to be observation (consciousness). So the creation of "meaning and purpose" (information) as a function of free will is the foundation of everything and is the cause of the universe.
- The equation below may explain the inflation at the Big Bang. Also as a consequence, that the entire universe may have been created out of "no-thing" and why the universe continues to expand. In a nutshell, I arrived at this formula through the following reasoning:
  1. Quantum physics indicates that reality only exits as a cloud of probability until it is observed.
  2. If that is so, the past and the future cannot exist—only the "Now".
  3. If that is so, humans have free will and affect the evolution of the universe through their actions. If the universe is a chaotic system, the actions of humans can affect the entire direction and evolution of the universe dramatically as their actions are magnified over time.
  4. Meaning and purpose can only exist if humans have free will and are free to chose.

Based on this reasoning I formulated the following equation: U equals the perceived size of the universe. E equals energy. Delta T (time) equals the observation or length of "now":

$$U = \frac{E}{\Delta T = \text{Planck Time "Now"} \to \infty \text{ smaller}}$$

Delta T goes toward infinitely small (Planck time)
If this is true, the universe could have been created out of "no-thing" and everything is interconnected!

- Everything will go toward equilibrium or entropy.
- If there is no energy coming into the system, entropy can never be reversed.
- With more energy going into the system, you decrease entropy within the system, but increase it elsewhere. "Boltzmann's Law" that increases the complexity.
- Free will is an axiom.
- Meaning and purpose is fundamental
- What is the consequence of meaning and purpose for John Wheeler's participatory universe? Free will is the logical consequence of meaning and purpose.
- The past does not exist. If the past exists, then where is it?
- Reversibility does not exist.
- The only way to get even an approximation of the original is to use energy to change the system.
- The output is always less than the input unless energy/consciousness is added to the output.
- We are living in a probabilistic universe where 2+2 equals approximately 4. Hence, there is a slight possibility that 2+2=3.

The future is created by random events within a probabilistic structure unless it is subject to freewill.

7
Observation, Thought, Ego & Enlightenment

There is a distinction between the observer, thought, ego and your body. The observer observes the other three. It is the foundation underneath the three. What's in the "now" is the observer. It is the observer that collapses the probability function of the universe—not your thoughts, not your ego, or your body. Your sight, smell, touch, and hearing are attached to the observer and together form your method of observing the physical universe. The observer is the "nothing" inside you that creates everything by collapsing the probability function of everything. The observer together with interpreting is thought. However, thought is not fundamental. Your oneness with the essence, creative force or the "no-thing" is experienced at the moment of absolute presence in the "now" without thoughts and ego. The Copenhagen Interpretation of Quantum Physics states that nothing exists without an observer. The act of observation collapses the probability function of nothing into something, which is the universe. So the observer has to be the nothing that creates everything. There is reason to believe that all life has the capability of observation. There is also reason to believe that the observer in all life is the same as the one that created the original spark of life 3.5 billion years ago. The creation of life was the "nothing" creating the "something". Hence, all life is the manifestation of something from nothing. The only distinction between different life forms is the complexity of thoughts and reasoning culminating with humans with freewill and creativity.

The fundamental understanding of the universe is not by thought, but by pure observation. Thinking prevents you from connecting to the "source"! Becoming aware of this distinction between the observer on the one hand, and thoughts, ego and the body or flesh, on the other leads to freedom.

Hence, thoughts, ego and the body can now be subject to observer manipulation and "control"! What causes pain is not the observation but the interpretation! What happens? You discover that the observer inside—your essence—exists in a place that has no fear and in complete stillness. You will experience oneness with "everything"! Joy and love become manifest! The power to create is unleashed!

This knowledge, disseminated to all people will move humanity to a new level of consciousness. A state of playfulness, humor, peace and enjoyment become possible as we realize that the person we are talking to, looking at, interacting with, is not the true person. Nothing becomes that serious or important anymore. We realize that what we do to ourselves and what we observe in others is just an act for mutual enjoyment because underneath the external manifestations of thought, ego and body we are all identical and the same observer.

Having this knowledge enables you to become fully authentic and without fear.

People must be free to achieve enlightenment, as Eckhart Tolle says in his book, *"The Power of Now"*: *"You are never closer to enlightenment as when you face a crisis in your life"*. In fact, almost instant enlightenment can take place when the crisis is overwhelming, triggering an instant realization that there is a distinction between the sufferer and the observer inside. At that moment, complete escape from the suffering can take place. You will be without thoughts. You become a pure observer with complete presence in the "now". That does not mean that you would live a life without thinking. Rather, you will be in control of your thinking and, in turn, of your emotions. They will no longer control you!

Individual freedom must be maximized for enlightenment to manifest.

Achieving enlightenment is dependent on the full expericnce of life itself. A person has to be confronted with success, failure, and the freedom to choose between good and bad. The dialectic process as it applies to society has to occur in each individual. It is only through freedom and personal responsibility of your own actions—and through the experiences of suffering and bliss—that enlightenment can manifest in the individual. The nothing—the source of everything—is the observer. The "no-thing" witnesses your ego and thinking. The acceptance of "what is" places the observer in the present timeless "now". The "nothing" that creates everything is the observer in all of us. This realization creates a connectedness to everything—the love of everything, and a true love for mankind. Euphoria and overwhelming love is felt not only toward other humans but for creation itself. It's through chaos and imperfection that enlightenment takes place, realizing that the imperfect actually was and is perfect. An example would be being together with your family at a party with children. Suddenly you feel stillness inside. You have no thoughts. You are experiencing this chaotic drama in front of you with no thoughts of the past or future. Suddenly, euphoria!

When you are working as a pure source with no thoughts, you are able to create something unique. No qualifying thoughts prevent you from creating something. If your creation comes from the "source", it becomes original, unique and much greater. This holds true with all creativity. You cannot become truly creative if the source—you, the observer—is constantly qualified by thoughts. Thought is the greatest enemy to creativity. The thought would constantly say, "You can't do that"!

However, in order to cultivate the fertile ground which can allow those creative thoughts to appear, thinking and experience are needed. This sounds like a contradiction, but it isn't. The thinking about the creative endeavor occurs prior to the experience of that creative spark. For example many of us have had the experience of going to sleep at night with something on our minds and then, somehow in the morning without really thinking about it, the answers just seem to appear.

However, thinking is needed for the creative process. There is a distinction between learning, experience and thinking on one hand and to create on the other. To create something truly great you need to have gone through a lot of learning, experience and thinking. But to create you need to get rid of all thoughts as they tie you down to the past and is limiting. This sounds like a paradox, but it isn't. You need to be in touch with the "source" and fully present in the "now" without thought to allow the space for the new creation. You will also discover that creations emanating from the infinite creative force within you trigger your enthusiasm and will be meaningful to other people.

Out of the mulch in your subconscious mind, in order for something to sprout from where all learning and experience resides, you must clear your consciousness of all thoughts and be 100% present in the "now", in order to truly create. Then to create becomes a euphoric and blissful act and true originality becomes possible.

That is why artists, scientists or business people and countless others cannot achieve greatness unless they are creating from the source without thought. It is only when you achieve enlightenment that true originality will manifest.

For example; when you write a book, the writing must come directly from the source with no qualifying thoughts. Only at this point will the book provide a profound insight to the reader.

There is no passion in copying. Passion can only arise when creation emanates from the source. You can only have passion for what you create if it is uniquely your own.

The only way to become truly "successful" is to create something unique and original. That's the foundation. Success has nothing to do with money or fame. In fact, the experience of success is in the "now" and is the creation of something original. The euphoria felt in the "now" is experienced during the creative process and at the moment it is finished. Whatever happens after that moment, the experience of success only comes with sharing your creation with others or getting feedback that your creation enriched their lives. The only time you truly can make money is when you don't search it. Any time you try to make money, you stagnate and make less. This is only true if what you create truly benefits others.

If you are bored you are a boring person. When you are enlightened, you will always know the path of joy, euphoria and love. In other words, doing nothing is transformed through enlightenment into doing everything.

Pointers to enlightenment

1. I am dissatisfied with myself. Who is dissatisfied? Answer: The ego! However, "I am" by itself points to the observer.
2. Who am I? Nothing. I am no-thing.
3. If you answer the question, "Who am I?" with anything else than "nothing", it is the ego speaking, not the observer.
4. You will find that what you do and what you say is just an act that is humorous—even hysterically funny—upon reflection in enlightenment.

5. When you become enlightened non-physical attacks will not affect you, because you know that it is the attacker's ego that attacks you not the person behind it. You also know that the person who is attacking is still "unconscious" and not enlightened. If you are affected by it, you also know that it is your ego that is hurt and not the essence of who you are. With this knowledge, you will not counter-attack instead; you'll just let it be. However, you may attempt to make the attacker enlightened!
6. I am developing myself in order see what I can truly be for myself and for others. The observer inside is different than what I manifest myself to be for the environment.
7. Our ego and our bodies are constantly being monitored by the observer. We are all trapped and manifest differently with our bodies and our egos. But we are all the same at the source. Each individual human being is an imperfect manifestation of the observer. The same observer is in all of us. That's why when you're enlightened; you have no fear, not even of death! You realize the source is nothing creating everything. The "nothing" is consciousness as the observer, not consciousness as thoughts. Consciousness as thoughts is the ego. Consciousness without thoughts is the observer and the "nothing".
8. The moment to become enlightened is now. There is no learning that can take place to get there, except for pointers. You can only point to it, but you can't say what it is.
9. Enlightenment is the realization that everything is created by the observer, and the observer is nothing…even you.
10. Enlightenment is a layer underneath where you know that there are no more layers from where everything manifests.
11. The foundation of the universe and the observer is the same, which is the nothing. That is the same in all of us, and in everything.
12. Enlightenment is not to know everything. So enlightenment is not the same as knowing. The fact that you are enlightened doesn't mean that you know how to do practical things.
13. *When you achieve enlightenment, your attitude changes toward yourself and others.* Your life becomes more joyful, blissful, playful, humorous and loving. You will become infinitely tolerant and with absolute forgiveness. In this way,

you will get rid of attachments, desires and greed. You become proactive rather than reactive.
14. What you think you want at the moment. You are already bored with!
15. Not getting what you want leads to unhappiness! Getting what you want also leads to unhappiness! Both emanate from the ego, not from the observer, and the ego is insatiable!
16. Being is observation!
17. Thinking about the future causes fear! Thinking about the past causes anger!
18. The observer creates and gives!
19. The ego destroys and takes!
20. To have absolute concentration and being in the "zone" is to be without thought. Even time slows down. Everything is experienced as in slow motion with absolute control. That is an enlightened moment fully in the "now" without ego.
21. The truth emanates from the "source" and is always more compelling than a lie. A lie emanates from the ego!

Once you become aware that there is a distinction between your ego, thoughts and emotion—that you can actually observe them—you realize that you are a manifestation of the eternal observer and creator with freewill.

Once you create that space, you are no longer at the mercy of life's circumstances. You objectify your existence without being a spectator but fully engaged and enthusiastic. Your life becomes a humorous play without being frivolous, where success and failure are looked upon the same. Greed and attachments go away. You find that everything becomes a playful creative act. You realize that the observer in you is the same one that exists in everybody else. Once you get to this realization, nothing becomes so important that it leads to unhappiness. When you find that you and others have achieved this level of consciousness versus unconsciousness, the interaction between these people becomes playful, joyful and humorous—because you now realize that you and others are just temporary manifestations of each other. That's what Jesus, Buddha, Muhammad, Ekhart Tolle, Deepak Chopra, Gwen Dyer and other "wise men" talk about. That is what it means to become enlightened. So enlightenment is to discover the observer and creator and the "no-thing" inside you; the source of everything. Once you get it, you are another wise man. You have transformed yourself from unconsciousness to consciousness. By observing yourself, you come into existence by virtue of your own observation of yourself. The observer is not subject to thoughts, emotions or events. Reality, including you, becomes a participant in a humorous and playful theatre.

The term "gallows humor" comes from the old days when they would hang a person in public. Suddenly, the audience, including the person being executed, burst into laughter. If life and death can become humorous to the person who is about to die, then that moment is a moment of enlightenment. The subject realizes that even life itself is distinct from the observer. Even in that situation, humor, stillness or peace can be achieved by becoming fully present in the eternal "now" and accepting what is.

To become a "wise man" is actually becoming an enlightened person. And you can only become a wise man through experience. Experience implies that you are living a life in freedom. Wisdom can only be achieved through the experience of the imperfect.

When you view another human being—knowing that he/she isn't going to live forever or go to "heaven"—you experience tremendous love and compassion for that person as a temporary something created from nothing.

To become enlightened is to achieve a state of consciousness that is beyond yin and yang. It is where everything—including you—is interwoven with the universe itself. This is something that is beyond understanding. This cannot be explained. It is pure observation, experience and participation with no thought. You reach the state of being in which you are beyond understanding. There is no distinction between you and the rest of the universe. You become fully aware of the interconnectedness of everything.

To become enlightened is to "die" before you die. The energy of observation inside of you never dies; it just dissipates into the original energy of the nothing. Is observation dependent upon seeing? No.

Observation is to be one with the object of observation. Is it to hear or to feel? No.

Without any observer, the universe only exists as a probability. The observer makes the universe come into existence through observation. It not only comes into existence through observation, but the observation itself is changing the universe. So, in a sense, the universe we live in is a participatory and living universe. The act of observation changes the entire universe. That's what it means when I say that everything is interconnected. The universe, including you, is interconnected. Everything we do changes the direction of the universe.

All living things are observers. The first living organism on earth was the first observer, the first, one-celled algae. Since the DNA is the same in all living organisms, all living things are just different manifestations of the original observer.

In summary

You can look at your senses as just different kinds of measuring equipment. We have created equipment to observe the atom. The equipment that we choose to use will change the nature of that which is observed. So the eyes are one kind of measuring equipment to observe the world. The world will manifest in one way by observing with the eyes while the inner essence of everything is just probabilities. Enlightenment means that the energy inside of you becomes connected with the energy in the universe. The "key" to the universe is enlightenment.

It takes infinite amount of energy to move any mass to the speed of light as the mass of the object is increasing to infinity. However, the paradox is; if it reaches the speed of light, the mass becomes "nothing" according to Einstein's equations. The flip side of this physical "truth" is that nothing is infinite energy.

You have to mobilize infinite energy in order to create nothing. Does that mean that nothing also has an infinite equal energy of nothing? If they are both the same kind of energy, they will repel each other—whether positive energy or negative energy. You have to take two opposite energies together and this would take infinite energy. Why did you have to spend infinite energy to create nothing? The infinite negative energy would then create infinite positive energy.

Maybe the nothing is infinite negative energy and then the universe is the opposite energy. If the energies have poles (like + and -) then the reason why you cannot move a mass to the speed of light without expending infinite energy is that you are facing the infinite energy of nothing. If you successfully do this, the mass becomes nothing then the energy of nothing becomes infinite and is an infinite energy of the same pole.

Why do we have to spend infinite energy to move a mass at the speed of light? This is the paradox, the mass goes to infinity, so you need infinite energy to move the mass to the speed of light, but actually as the mass manifests in time and space it goes to nothing at the speed of light. As an object goes toward the speed of light, it shrinks in the direction of travel (in two dimensions), until its manifestation as a physical object becomes nothing at the speed of light, but with infinite mass. And infinite mass equals infinite energy, because mass is only condensed energy. Now we have a nothing with infinite energy. And nothing is not allowed, because it has no meaning and purpose—so the infinite energy which is the observer in you and me, creates something which is the universe.

Consciousness is what creates the observable universe.

The observer is the infinite creative energy emanating from nothing.

The observer is nothing (no-thing). The observer is beyond the observable universe because he is the creator of the observable universe. The Big Bang did not come first because the Big Bang was a function of observation, and was created by the observer.

You have the ability to observe your ego, your thoughts, your body, the universe and everything else around you. And the measuring instrument chosen by the observer of this universe is our senses. Hence, based on the measuring equipment we have as senses determines our experience of the universe and the manifesting universe is based on how it's being observed. This is proven by quantum physics. The measuring equipment you use to observe the subatomic particle determines the properties of that particle!

8
Religion

The more doubt in the person about their own religious beliefs, the stronger the desire in that person to recruit new members. This is because of a desire for constant belief validation. Their religious belief can only be sustained through the recruitment of others to that same belief.

If God is almighty—he can see everybody's thoughts—you have a situation of two people A and B. Person A spends his entire life doing good things with the idea that he will be rewarded by going to heaven when he dies. Person B goes through his life saying, "I don't know", and has no thought that he is doing good for any other reward other than what is personal. He decides to do good without recognition from anybody. In fact, the person who decides to do good by creating rather than destroying, without any consideration of any reward, without anybody knowing, has to be in the eyes of God a far better person than somebody who does good to get rewarded by "eternal" life in "Heaven".

Persons A and B are now before God. If God is a moral God, he would choose B to go to heaven rather than A. God would say to A, "You didn't do good out of the goodness of your heart. You only did good because you thought you'd be rewarded for it". God says to B, "I'm going to let you in because you chose to be good, without any expectations of reward". B would say to God, "In order for me to accept your invitation, you have to renounce the Bible and the Koran. Only then will I accept your offer".

Ultimate goodness and heroism is to do good and what is right without anybody knowing and expecting nothing in return!

In fact, that is a requirement in order for an act to be considered moral. Any act that includes self interest is not a moral act. A moral act is to do the right thing without any consideration for self interest. You have to be blind to your own self interest for an act to be moral! Hence, the teaching of doing good in order to be rewarded to go to heaven destroys true morality. There is nothing more destructive to morality than what we teach our children to not do anything unless they are personally rewarded for anything they do!

Since Islam and Christianity find unmarried sex to be sinful, how come God will reward you with all the sex you want with virgins in heaven?

The idea of eternal life—going to heaven—is what makes it possible for believers to sacrifice themselves and to die for a cause. This belief also enables a person or society to take another life. Destroying the respect for human life is a direct function of the magnitude of the belief of life after death. A question for a believer: "Do you go to heaven immediately after death or do you have to wait for the resurrection"?

They say in the bible, "This is my body; eat Jesus' body—his flesh and then you are going to drink his blood". That's an act of imaginary cannibalism!

It says in the Bible that you, as a believer, have the right to kill. In fact, it's demanded by God that you kill any heretic. As an example, if you believe in reincarnation, or anything from Buddhism, you are by definition, a heretic. According to the Bible, anybody who is a true Christian is obligated to kill you. *God killed all first born in Egypt. Q. E. D.*

What value is life, if heaven awaits us!

The sad part of all of this is that millions if not billions of people have been dedicating their lives to what has now been proven to be fairy tales. Except for some core revelations by Jesus, there is nothing unique or special in the Bible. The sacrifice of a son by the father is found in many religions around the world going back thousands of years. The birth of a son by a virgin is in many religions around the world, existing before and after Christianity and the New Testament.

The resurrection itself is also a part of many other religious mythologies. In conclusion, there is very little in the Bible that is unique to Christianity.

The Ten Commandments only have four commandments with regard to obvious morality. The rest of the commandments are for the self-preservation of the belief itself. They are not very elaborate or sophisticated. Any person can think about better rules for living a better life that are far more elaborate than the Ten Commandments. For example: The Constitution and Bill of Rights of the United States. This should show to any thinking person an obvious glaring deficiency of the Ten Commandments as a moral guidance for human life.

The obvious limitations of the major world religions have become evident. The replacement for traditional religion needs to recognize the desire for spirituality. *Mysticism is an inherent value of human existence. But this new spiritualism and mysticism need to exist without being a potential source for destroying humanity. We must believe in creating rather than destroying!*

The major religions were invented by man as a way of coping with the misery and ignorance of the past. Armageddon may be the most dangerous idea for the destruction of life. If you truly believe in Armageddon, it's okay to destroy all life. In fact it's not only okay, it's inevitable. It would be extremely dangerous to put any human being in a position of power in today's world who believes in Armageddon. In fact, a person in power suffering from greatness self-delusions would find it irresistible to create Armageddon on his watch.

Traditional Christianity is based on the idea of sin—sex is sinful, knowledge is sinful and accumulation of wealth is sinful.

The true teachings of Jesus in the Gnostic Bible states:

Sex is good, acquisition of knowledge the path to God. To serve is good and creates wealth.

These are the true teachings of the "original" Bible before it was edited by Emperor Constantine in 315 AD as a political document to consolidate the Emperor's power with the support of the church. They decided to make the three most important things in a human beings life sinful in order to make sure that everybody would be a sinner. The acquisition of knowledge, wealth and sex could be forgiven only by the church and by submitting to the Emperor's power. This would be the only path to paradise! The Roman Empire could now be controlled by the Emperor through religion and the church.

The unintended consequence was the fall of the Roman Empire by making stupor, poverty and abstinence a virtue leading to the Dark Middle Ages.

Religion 65

This was a time of incredible cruelty and poverty. The loss of the knowledge from the antiquity was imminent. This "spell" was not really broken until Martin Luther broke up the Catholic Church and set in motion the renaissance in Europe leading to a time of enlightenment. This in turn, led to the breakthroughs in the sciences, the French and American Revolution and the Industrial Age.

The suppression of sexuality between men and women is manifesting itself in religions as religious ecstasy where the object of sexual attraction is the Priest, Jesus and God. This (sub) conscious ritual and attraction also manifests itself by a woman wearing a dress and stockings to church. Her outfit creates maximum sexual attraction. She is not dressing up for her mate or husband, but for the Priest, Jesus and God.

Religious people have gotten used to or are living in an unreal, imaginary sphere. They will perversely be more likely to create opinions and beliefs and other imaginary ideas not founded in reality. Hence, they will have less morality and will lie more easily than a person who is less religiously inclined.

Being religious is the ability of a person to create an imaginary world. When this ability is applied in politics it creates dogmatic beliefs that can manifest as lies. In other words, it's the ability to believe that their own lies are true which explains how a person can create an imaginary world which defies logic. This is a world torn away from reality, creating its own internal logic. Governments around the world have a tendency to fall into this category!

We have two people. One does good things and tries to be good throughout his life because he believes that he will be rewarded by going to paradise. Another person expects no reward, but still decides to be good and do good things throughout his life, expecting no reward. When both go before God who will God choose for paradise?

1. The one who decides to do good and be good because he believes that he will be rewarded by God because he believes in God?

Or,

2. The other who decides to do good and be good but is expecting no rewards?

How can you have freedom of religion when you are passing laws that are grounded in Christian/Judean beliefs? A religion is a system of belief and values that cannot be proven. Everything which is not hard science and cannot be proven through experiment is by definition a belief system and can be classified as religion. To believe and to be spiritual is not destructive. It becomes destructive if that belief is used to restrict the freedom of other people!

9
The Idea of Morphic Fields

Rupert Sheldrake and others have proposed a very intriguing theory about morphic fields. A morphic field manifests in the universe either by a thought or action by any living organism. There is reason to believe that morphic fields that are being established are stronger in higher life forms. The higher the life form, the stronger the morphic field will be. The ultimate morphic fields would be created by human beings.

The morphic field hypotheses basically states that when a thought has been expressed, that a kind of imprint has been made in the "now" of the universe and the thought or action exists in a common field of the universe where it becomes a part of a common knowledge or action for everybody.

This is the key—that what has been thought or the action which has been executed has not been communicated as a conscious communication by any means by the creator of the thought or action. For example, if one person gets an idea once it is observed or becomes conscious in that one person, that idea exists in the universe and has a tendency to spontaneously appear in others. For example, a group of scientists are working on a problem in one part of the world. They find a solution. If they do an experiment—an action—suddenly and spontaneously, other scientists working on the same problem in other parts of the world, are able to solve the same problem without any communication between the two groups. The expression that something is "in the air" describes the idea of morphic fields. The interesting part is that the more times the scientists perform the experiments, the easier it becomes to do them, even adjusting for learning. This has also been observed in the animal kingdom. A famous example is one group of apes on an island in Indonesia. The apes suddenly learned how to steal potatoes and wash them before they ate them. Almost at the same time, without the possibility of communication, apes on other islands learned and acquired the same skills. There are many more examples both among human beings and animals that some form of communication is happening on the subconscious level.

The morphic fields are like imprints made in the universe itself of the thoughts you have and the actions you are doing. They become imprints in the universe. Those imprints exist for everybody to tap. If this is true, it means it would be possible—through synchronization of thoughts and actions between people—to create much larger imprints than what one person or a small group could do. And if the imprint is made large enough, it might be used as a way of affecting evolution in a very significant way. So the idea of a collective consciousness may exist.

If we look at the universe as a computer, all interaction in the universe is fundamentally a binary exchange. If energy equals information, the whole universe could possibly be one giant computer. What we are discovering through the laws of nature is actually the software of that computer. At some point in time, man will be able to understand the software (the laws of nature). By understanding that, we might be able to program the universe to our benefit. Then, one possibility could be that we decide to program it from expansion to contraction, or even status quo. If we can program the universe to a state of contraction, the energy of the universe would be more and more concentrated. It is probable that as we control the contraction of the universe from a to z, that we can manipulate the "big crunch"—the opposite of the "Big Bang." By doing this we can avoid the collapsing of the universe into a singularity and create a state of infinite contraction that would create infinite energy—forever. The control and manipulation of that energy would make it possible for man to acquire the power to recreate everything forever and exist forever, in subjective time. In objective time that would not be true! In fact, we might be able to make time stand still.

It doesn't matter how long it takes between the time you die and the point in time where intelligence can recreate everything forever. If this ever happens in the future, your experience will be: "I died and I was immediately resurrected". It doesn't matter how much time it takes, because when you are dead you have no perception of time. If man can achieve this point of re-creation in the future, we have become one with "God". Consequently, we don't have to be dependent on a "God" we don't know about. We will have achieved the ability to recreate ourselves inside a "computer universe". There would be nothing of you in there except for the formula of a complete replication of yourself down to the last cell and atom in your body. If the replication is that complete, it is you.

10
Creation versus Destruction

The universe from the beginning gives a slight advantage to the creation of matter over anti-matter, which is an imperfection. This means that the universe itself is not 100 percent symmetrical. If it were, it would not exist. As a leap of faith, since the universe is more creative than destructive, proven by physics itself, man is more creative than destructive, and would choose to be good more than bad. Given absolute freedom, man would choose to be good over bad. As a consequence, one of the primary goals of man would be to maximize creation and minimize destruction. This can only happen in a truly free society.

Through regulation and the pursuit of perfection we can create a "perfect society" as an ant hill is perfect. It functions well for survival at the moment. But we have destroyed its ability for creative development because of the destruction of the "dialectic process".

What brings man forward to a great future is to allow the imperfect to exist.

People who bring the society forward are the "misfits" who are not happy and do not perfectly fit into today's society. They are the people who have the incentive to change and are forced to think. The truth and the future always exist among the minority in a society. By eradicating the progressive, the unusual, the different, we have destroyed man's ability to evolve. You have to allow society to live in a state of controlled chaos and let it be imperfect. It even manifests itself in everything from planning a city and living in a planned environment versus living in an unplanned part of the city. The unplanned is always the old town. You can ask yourself why everybody goes to the old town to have fun. The old town has an element of risk, excitement and freedom because it was created at a time when people were freer. You have this mixed development, a little tiny street next to a big street. You see it in every big city. The old town is a slum. The more progressive people, artists and scientists are attracted to it. Then the old town becomes the main attraction and the most desirable place to live.

The universe itself is a chaotic system. The evolution of the universe is chaotic. A chaotic system means that it is subject to certain attractors. According to quantum physics, the universe is probabilistic. This means that the future cannot exist because the universe has been proven not to be deterministic but probabilistic. Neither can the past exist, because if the future and past exist, there will be no freedom. Without freedom there is no meaning and purpose.

Since the universe is a chaotic system, it is extremely sensitive to its initial conditions at any point in time. This means that any action and communication affects the evolution of the entire universe.

Each individual affects the evolution of the entire universe. It is magnified over time by the dynamics of chaos. One of the characteristics of a chaotic system—the butterfly example—is that it is extremely sensitive to any given or any created conditions at any point in time. "A butterfly flapping its wings in Hong Kong will affect the weather in California a week later". The consequence is that each individual, and mankind as a whole, can create conditions on an extremely small scale that will have a profound effect on the entire universe. This happens over time by its own magnifying dynamics. This imbibes every individual or organization with extreme power to create change and the possibility for self realization.

As there is a slight asymmetry in the building blocks of the universe—matter versus anti-matter—there is reason to believe that there is an asymmetry between yin and yang, creation and destruction, and between good and evil. There are an infinite number of ways to describe good and to act good while it is easy and simple to describe evil acts.

If man is given the opportunity of freedom and tranquility, there is reason to believe that creativity and good will prevail.

The creative force in the universe is stronger than the destructive force. We need to align ourselves with the creative force, which is achieved by choice, this creative force of the universe leads to greater complexity. By understanding the physics of the universe we will be able to select the direction of the evolution of the universe for our benefit and well being. Our success in doing so will enable us to acquire the power to create everything that is possible and to recreate everything that ever existed. We will be able to extend this to infinity in subjective time. As you are falling into a "black hole" you would experience that it would take infinity before you get into the black hole. An outside observer will be able to observe that you disappear in finite time.

If man can control and populate the entire universe and create a controlled big crunch (where matter and energy in the universe collapses asymmetrically), energy will go to infinity. Harnessing this energy—energy equals information—it will be possible to create a simulation in which everything that is possible to create can be created. Everything that ever existed can be recreated, for infinity, in subjective time.

Goal: To recreate everything to create "heaven" or, in other words, to take the great myths of humanity and make them reality.

In order to do so we must first control the solar system, then the galaxy, then the entire universe to secure "infinity of survival"! It does not matter how long it will take to recreate everything. As long as it happens at any time in the future you will be resurrected.

As the fig wasp uses the fig nursery to develop when they hatch and fly away they pay their host back by spreading the fig tree's pollen. We see this in the hierarchy of symbiotic and synergistic relationships in nature. We can extend that hierarchy in relationships into humans and into earth, planetary systems, galaxies and into the universe itself with higher and higher life forms and intelligence up to pure intelligence and self awareness of the universe itself.

Our goal as the leading consciousness on earth is to find a way to achieve this pure intelligence and awareness and in the process to reach this level without destroying ourselves.

The "law of action" that states that an action always will cause an equal and opposite reaction cannot be true. An action will not produce an exactly equal reaction. If true, evolution and change would be impossible. This observation is anchored in asymmetry. Asymmetry means that destruction can happen without an equal and opposite reaction. Quantum Physics proved that the universe is probabilistic rather than deterministic. Therefore, an action does not and will not need to cause an equal and exact opposite reaction. The slight asymmetry traces back to the Big Bang itself between matter and antimatter.

These fundamental laws of nature are extended into a slightly stronger action than an opposite reaction that can be further extended into the Second Law of Thermodynamics explaining the arrow of time, creation, complexity and ultimately free will as the foundation for a sense of purpose and meaning. This fundamental asymmetry can also be projected on life and the society where the preferred states of being would be imperfection rather than perfection.

As the universe evolves, based on these principles, the laws of physics and our ability to understand them lead us to the possibility to align our self with this creative force toward complexity. Ultimately, we may find the key to the universe itself. When found, we can open the universe and control its destiny.

Today we have a choice between "creation equals freedom"—to find that key—or dictatorship and the path toward destruction.

A life not lived in freedom is not a life worth living. To find this key we have to accept the imperfect and choose freedom with its drama of achievement, failure, tragedy and triumph as it relates to the individual and the society as a whole. Without it there would be no meaning and purpose.

By trying to eradicate tragedy and suffering, we are also destroying achievement, triumph and happiness. You have a dialectic processes between people, societies, nations and also inside the individual—the human mind is subject to a dialectic process. Hence, plurality maximization maximizes the creative force and evolution of man and society.

"To destroy is infinitely simple. To create is infinitely complex."

That is why any organization that is not facing a free market ultimately becomes destructive, but will justify themselves on moral grounds to continue to expand its power and influence.

The reason it is infinitely simple to destroy is because what is being destroyed already exists. Destruction also is intimately tied into prevention. By saying "no" to something, you are preventing something that already exists as an idea or concept to be put into reality. The principle of destruction is that you can only destroy something that already exists. To create you are operating in a sphere of infinite possibilities that makes it infinitely complex to create something. Among all those infinite possibilities you must choose one to make it into reality. So creation means that you are creating something new. The manifestation of freedom and to create is not a direct function of the past. So to create is to take something that is fragmented and incomplete from the past and create something new. Example: You can choose to build a house an infinite number of ways. When the object already exists it is infinitely simple to destroy it because there is only one solution to destruction and that is the destruction of the object that already exists.

That is why destruction is chosen by any organization that is not forced for survival to renew itself in a positive way.

The organization will gravitate toward the lowest energy state for survival; unless it is stimulated by its interaction with the environment that forces it to become and stay creative. Destruction is to destroy something that already exists or to prevent something to be created. In both cases, there is only one solution: The prevention and the destruction of the object.

So if any organization or individual fundamentally is preventing something from happening or is set to destroy something that already exists, they are fundamentally detrimental to human development.

So, every activity by any organization or individual needs to be analyzed in a fundamental way to determine whether it is destructive or creative. In other words, destruction deals with the past and/or with the prevention of the future. Or, it deals with something that has been created in the past and the prevention of creating something in the future. So destruction is past-oriented, and creation is future-oriented.

Infinite complexity to create, infinite simplicity to destroy!

Words describing creation (God)

Yes, hope, enfoldment, wealth, freedom, self realization, openness, democracy, sex, risk, private enterprise, exploration, science, technology, good, fun, excitement, ideas, wisdom, alive, protect, defend, compassion, forgiveness, openness, construction, knowledge, peace, fashion, disarmament, humanity, respect, intelligence, sport, physical fitness, complexity, individualism, art, teach, spend, rehabilitation, education, creative, use, develop, allow, more, do, infinite, brave, risk, different, plurality, dynamic, energetic, mastering, responsibility and the list continues "ad infinitum"...

Words describing destruction (Devil)

No, prevention, security, safety, stupor, poverty, restrictions, legislation, law, regulation, planning, incarceration, war, secrecy, dictatorship, power, property, dummification, stupor, censorship, prison, control, authority, religion, bad, boredom, dreariness, hopelessness, conformity, limit, fear, boring, government, justice, protection, safety, punishment, brutality, nationalism, patriotism, war, military, humiliation, control, idiocy, simplicity, mob, flock, conformist, deprivation, weapons, save, conserve, destroy, planned, deny, limit, less, equal, dull, boring, protect, secure, morality, ethics, safe and the list continues "ad infinitum"...

The optimal society is a creative society. The universe is more creative than destructive.

The reason why we spend so much money on schooling our children is to prepare them for a creative life. This is another proof that creating is the essence of life.

One way the desire to create manifests itself in the individual is the act of buying and owning. To buy something is an unsatisfactory substitute for creating something personally. That explains consumerism. So, as a first step a human takes toward becoming creative after their basic needs have been fulfilled with regard to food, clothing and shelter, is the desire to buy and own something. The creative influence manifests itself on its lowest level in consumerism and the desire to buy and own things. There is reason to believe, as society evolves, that more and more people will be engaged personally in creating. This can be seen as societies become more affluent, they go through stages of advanced consumerism before those societies become engaged in innovation and creation. To buy something is an act of creativity. But it's not as satisfactory as creating something yourself. An example would be to purchase something at IKEA: There is an element of satisfaction not only in the buying, but the act of assembling it yourself. You are creating your own environment.

- Cool furniture
- Inexpensive, reasonable
- So much of it—styles, colors, textures
- Act of assembling, which gives you the feeling of creating your own environment.

The act of purchase and assembly becomes a psychological substitute for the act of actually creating the item.

If you are living or have lived a life being a destructor or been part of a destructive segment/organization in the society, your life is or has been meaningless, without purpose.

11
Governments

One of the most important prerequisites for a society that wishes to be free is for it to live in peace long enough to discover that their most important enemy is themselves.

It is not a coincidence that the American Constitution was created within a country that was isolated from the rest of the world and hence from immediate external threat. It was within this kind of environment that the great American Constitution was created to preserve freedom.

Government was originally set up to protect freedom, fair play, and human dignity. As a reaction to exploitive capitalists here in the West, unions were active from around the turn of the century until the Second World War. Government, once the protector of the people, has moved from being a creative "Yes" force with a high degree of complexity, to adopt the simpler more destructive stance of being a "no" force. They have become a negative force and, in fact, the abuser. I just saw on TV, pictures from Stalin's mass graves and the murder of 645,000 Russians. However, nobody seems to object to the fact that the US has more than four (4) times as many people in a state of living dead in their own prisons, 3 million people as I'm writing this book, reside within our prisons—many with long term sentences and continuous hopelessness when they are finally released. I would rather be in Russian Siberia than sitting in a modern prison in the US in isolation and no humanity between people whatsoever.

During the 50s and 60s, those who looked forward to today's society, envisioned a future of prosperity. However, that has not happened. This is due to destructive forces in our society and a government that chooses the easiest way of conducting itself in its efforts to expand its own power.

Government has chosen to promote the ideas of restrictions, limitations, and ultimately chosen the opposite of creation, namely destruction.

The larger the organization the more immoral it will become and the more heavily it will rely on moral justifications for its actions. This is because with a larger organization, responsibility can more easily be defused among its members. Once this happens and the organization has found a moral reason to destroy, nothing will stop that organization, especially if it's a government. It will commit horrendous crimes and destruction against humanity.

True morality only exists in a free, independent, thinking individual.

In fact, the more free and democratic a society is the more "Weapons of Mass Destruction" (WMD) that society can produce, not because they should or want to do it, but because that's the only society which has enough individual responsibility with personal morality to be trusted enough to have those WMD in somebody's custody. Alternately, in a dictatorship, where the rulers build their power based on fear and intimidation, those rulers will always have the fear that the custodians of the WMDs will turn those weapons against the ruler. Based on this scenario, it was not only outside pressure on Saddam Hussein which incented him to dispose of the WMDs but his fear that one day those WMDs might be used against him. That's why the US couldn't believe that Saddam Hussein didn't have any WMDs, because the WMDs were given to him by the Americans while he was at war with the Iranians. It is only in a free society that WMDs can be stored and maintained, because it is only in a free society that the rulers have a high level of confidence that the people won't use them against the rulers. As such, the rulers in a true democracy will be respected and loved rather than feared. So in a dictatorship that is built on fear, the rulers cannot trust their own people to be the custodians and builders of the WMDs. But in a society in which the people are free, there is an element of trust, and so the rulers feel safe in allowing others to be the custodians of the WMDs. That's why the weapons debate in the US is the canary in the coal mine. If any US ruler violates the right to bear weapons, and wants to stop this right, that would be the canary in the coal mine that the US society has crossed over from being a free country to a dictatorship. Because taking away the right to bear arms is an indication of the fear that the rulers have that their position of power is no longer supported by the people.

We must get rid of secret police and secrecy of government. All government actions should be open for inspection and review by its citizens and the world.

If a country refuses to stop manufacturing weapons and refuses to abolish their military, they need to be frozen out of the world community and the rest of the world needs to support the freedom movement in that country. However, for this to work, the national state needs to be redefined. In fact, in many ways the national state has become a dinosaur of the past and is, to a large extent, the problem.

Why have national states? What is the purpose of them? The primary purpose of nationalism is to gain advantage over one part of the world population at the expense of the rest, and to keep its affluence away from other countries and people. This is already impossible by the national state by the free trade and free capital movement around the world.

Why are worldwide free trade and the free movement of capital the most effective and fastest way to increase affluence and aid development around the world? A world wide free enterprise system integrates the world and makes us all interdependent. In this way it lays the foundation for a unified world without wars and violence among nations, races, ideologies and religions.

The United Nations must receive the power to declare WMDs illegal for all nations. A date must be set for which all WMDs will be destroyed. If there is any organization or nation that doesn't comply, the U.N. will have the right to enter that country and do it for them. Any rulers who try to hide their country's WMDs should immediately be removed from power and prosecuted for crimes against humanity.

Government regulation reduces competition in the private sector and helps to generate huge profits for larger more established businesses. This is in the government's interest, because these added profits serve to maximize the tax base and feed the government coffers. And in fact, the private sector could not pay taxes at current levels and still survive without this kind of protection. However this system is hopelessly inefficient—by regulating the small business man into oblivion and erecting barriers to entry, large corporations are free to become inefficient, wasteful, and ignore the kind of creativity and innovation that helps to foster prosperity and health within a nation. The paradox is that, in the long term, this leads to less tax revenue, not more. It is another example of short-sighted bureaucratic thinking.

When governments allow for more competition and a freer enterprise system, the economic pie will always expand faster, and the tax base will grow correspondingly.

Foreign aid is tied to CIA covert operations. Often this aid, publicly touted as a way of benefiting the people of other countries, is actually being used as a means of sustaining other governments in order to preserve the traditional institutions of government around the world. Whether these governments are dictatorial and oppressive in nature is unimportant, as long as they are friendly and cooperative with the US government, through the CIA.

Secret services such as the CIA and FBI are completely inconsistent with the ideas of a free society.

IRS Audit—the IRS wanted to do an audit of my company for employees and independent contractors for the year of 2006. A letter from the IRS was sent to my CPA to request information from tax records to determine whether they should be considered employees or independent contractors. The documents we submitted were not satisfactory to the IRS. On November 24, 2009, a new letter came from IRS expanding the audit to include 2007 as well. The tone of the letter was threatening in nature, revengeful and intimidating. "If you do not do this we (the IRS) will do that to you personally and to your company"!

State Board of Equalization: In December 2009, I talked to audit and collection executives at the department. I asked the question: "What is the mission of the State Board of Equalization in California?" Nobody could answer.

Both the State Board of Equalization and the EDD of California were initially set up to provide equal employment opportunities and help to expand employment in California. Today these two departments have gone from those missions to become the biggest destroyer of employment in California, by putting hundreds of small businesses out of business.

These are examples of government agencies doing the exact opposite of what they were intended to do in the first place. Tax payer's money, originally intended to be used for constructive purposes, is going to pay for the bureaucracy, especially for law enforcement and prisons.

When a private individual or business is audited by the IRS or the state, the final result is almost always the taxpayer owes something more in taxes. How would it be if auditors rarely found additional monies due? Their jobs would be pointless—so in order to justify their own positions, they must find monies due. There is a strong incentive for them to find ways for those individuals and/or businesses to owe more taxes. Likewise, there is a strong incentive for the government to overlook auditors who collect taxpayers money in error, because error or not, this is still money coming into the government's coffers.

In the end, the individual or small business can never win. Big business, however, with its government contracts, can achieve tremendous profits—they are the real winners. The irony is that the taxes collected from the individual and small businesses end up being a massive wealth transfer into the pockets of the owners of big business.

Right now, the US prison population is 4-5 times higher (estimated to be more than three million) than the estimated 650,000 prisoners who resided in Russia's prisons during the peak of Stalin's rule.

There are no checks and balances in government with regard to spending. Hundreds of billions of dollars are spent each year on WMDs and on war. WMDs have become the toys of the political elite.

The US president is trapped within the whole machinery of government. Inundated by endless studies and advice coming from all sides—he is no longer able to see the forest for the trees. He has, himself, "fallen" victim to the powerful forces of big government.

Government departments and organizations always seek to justify their own existence. Each department will recommend a solution to any problem that supports the continuation of their mission. As an example, military advice will always be a military solution. Advice from the CIA will always solve problems through covert operations. The FBI will always look for a criminal solution and the State Department will advocate a diplomatic solution. In the end, the President gets solutions based more on the self interests of the various groups which advise him, rather than the most prudent course of action. Ironically, the real and best solution might be to do nothing at all or none of the above. The best solution might well be to allow the forces of evolution around the world to dictate actions on a local basis. This often works because fundamentally, everyone on earth is looking for the same thing; namely: food, clothing, shelter, education and health care. The starting point for solving most problems around the world needs to be understanding and not some construct of some government agency's imagination.

Change will not come until the people of the world can get direct control of government. A more efficient and effective political system needs to be developed with direct voting by the people. The only way the people will gain control of their destiny, rather than leaving it in the hands politicians, is to allow for and enforce complete governmental transparency.

The world always looks for stability and freedom unless they have been seduced by some fanatic nut. In most cases, a simple solution, based on this desire, can be sought. The free-enterprise system, with the right rules and regulations, will meet the demands of the people of the earth in the most efficient way, and, at the same time provide opportunity to create and give.

Although most governments intend to create well-meaning economic regulation, the unintended consequence often stifles creativity and innovation within the industry which is being regulated. An example would be the automobile industry. The auto is basically the same now as it was when it was invented at the turn of the century. Everybody agrees that cars should be safer. So a car has to meet certain safety standards. However those standards often necessitate the use of heavier and heavier steel. In order for one car to withstand the impact from another heavy car, it too must be build heavier. This "inflationary" effect among cars not only increases the cost, but also, ignores the fact that if all cars on the road were lighter, we'd have no need for such regulation. This is because the momentum of each car, a function of mass and speed, would correspondingly be lighter. As things stand, cars must be made out of steel, thereby causing an inflation of their mass—all this in order to meet safety standards. If these safety standards had not been there, the car of today might well be a fraction of the weight of what they were when the "modern" car was created back in the 1920s.

Nobody in the auto industry is able to do "zero based budgeting" with today's regulations. For example, to ask this fundamental question: "If we create a personal transportation device from scratch today utilizing the latest technology, what would that transportation device look like? How can it be made in the most inexpensive, comfortable, and safe way, using today's technology?" That question cannot be asked when automobiles are over-regulated by government. This is the paradox: To some extent, industry does need regulation, but well-meaning regulation that makes sense at the time it's passed often becomes one of the biggest hindrances to innovation at a later point in time.

It seems to be almost like a law in the universe–if you do a little regulation here, then more regulation is needed over there. Then, suddenly, the whole industry is frozen and has lost its ability to innovate. I am for a certain amount of regulation, but it needs to be evaluated on a consistent basis to see if it's serving the industry and the people or if it is actually stopping innovation, and precluding much better products.

When one looks at history, it can be observed that in the messiness at the end of the 19th Century and the first 30 years of the 20th, there was a huge explosion of innovation. In fact, most things we have today were innovated during those years. They have fundamentally stayed the same. The exception of course is electronics. I'm talking about aircrafts, cars, refrigerators, washing machines and most other appliances. Something happened toward the middle of the 20th century that dramatically slowed the pace of innovation. The common denominator we find is taxes and regulation. These can have huge, unintended consequences. It can create barriers for small companies and "monopolies" for large companies which, stifle the innovation from individuals and small businesses, because the capital and sophistication needed to enter, is too high. Some examples would be health care, pharmaceuticals, transportation and possibly even education.

Today there is reason to believe that much regulation that could have been justified 50 years ago is no longer needed. Effective mass communications such as the internet, TV and radio play a huge role as checks and balances for industry by educating the consumer. Basically, a company today could not sell their products unless they prove safe

Governments

and beneficial to the user. There is reason to believe that we would see an explosion in media monitoring of business and organizations and independent research organizations to "objectively" evaluate products and services. This will reduce the "micromanagement" of many industries by too much and wrong regulation.

A typical example of government incompetence still many years after 9/11, the property at ground zero still sits there without being developed because of politics. Almost anything significant that the government gets involved with will automatically be prevented and stopped.

Legislation creates meaning and purpose for the government, regardless if that legislation benefits society or not and destroys meaning and purpose for the rest of us.

The very fabric of the family has been destroyed by the continuous manipulation by the government, manifesting by the government's micromanagement of people's private lives. This micro-legislation has taken away the sense of personal power, meaning, purpose and sense of achievement in peoples' lives. The reduction of freedom though legislation destroys a person's self–respect. This leads to alcoholism, drug abuse, hopelessness and crime.

Then, perversely, people are punished by the government for becoming or doing what is being created in the first place by the government by taking away freedom.

A crisis makes politicians and its constituents, including the mass media, feel important and needed. It also justifies an increase in power. Perversely, it is in their interest to promote and create crisis situations not only internationally, but also domestically. That is why George Bush and his cabinet could not withhold their glee after the 9/11 attack: It would increase their power and importance. With a great external threat, like terrorism, politicians no longer have to deal with complex domestic problems. They can focus on just one big problem. They can fight terrorism and wars. There is no greater euphoria for people who love power than to play "God" deciding upon life and death with full justification that their choice is just.

The government is sucking the last drop of blood out of small business and employees in the private sector for the benefit of government employees and large business.

This is the new slavery of the people.

About "conspiracies"

A conspiracy does not have to be "conscious" among the conspirators. They do not even have to talk about it. However, a common goal or understanding within a group may allow something to happen or to evolve which is to the benefit of that group at the expense of something or somebody else. This unspoken conspiracy can allow or "cover" for a decision or a direction to be at the benefit of the group and at the same time allow the group to appear as they are trying to do something good for somebody or another group. But that they failed due to somebody or circumstance not allowing them to do what is "right" and to be a benefit for another group or individual. Example: Joseph Lieberman working against health care for the American people. Joseph Lieberman if he does not seek reelection is out for his own personal future after he stops being a politician. He could stand to make millions of dollars as a lobbyist for health insurance companies. The rest of the democrats might have been able to prevent him from being an obstructionist for the health care legislation if they had put all effort to prevent him from being an obstructionist. However, to be for the health care legislation is an act of selflessness on the behalf of the politicians—basically to do the right thing for the American people. However, the politicians allowing Joseph Lieberman (to win), provides them with a cover of appearing to the American people that they are trying to do what's best for them, but deep inside are happy, and are not trying hard enough to make Joseph Lieberman change his mind because financially they will benefit much more personally by not having the legislation passed. This is a great example of an unspoken conspiracy.

Another example would be that the white people in the congress want idealistically to support Obama and believe that they want to support Obama and are, to a large extent supporting Obama. However, deep inside do they really want Obama, being black, to succeed and

Governments  85

potentially becoming one of the greatest presidents the US ever had? That kind of conspiracy, on a deep quiet level can be classified as a "(sub) conscious" conspiracy. So when the conservatives are obstructionists to Obama and try to destroy his presidency, the fight to prevent that from happening by the white democratic part of congress, may not go the extra mile for Obama, as they would have done if the president had been a white man. If this is the case, it is not only a sad time for America, but for the world. Because it means that being non-racial is not completely authentic. So hopefully, history will prove me wrong. But it's still a great example of how conspiracies can form without a word being spoken.

The core of it is that you appear to be one way but you allow something to go the other way because on a truly selfish level, it benefits you personally—so you allow the opposite to happen as to what your public position is.

So a conspiracy doesn't have to be a group of people going into a back room whispering to each other. A conspiracy can be a mutual understanding, of letting something happen or taking action or no action.

Pointers

- Government and taxes are extremely inefficient and wasteful of natural resources.
- The world would be much richer and much more advanced if excess profit had been kept in corporations for international expansion!
- The federal government is now turning over more and more programs to local governments, recognizing and admitting that they are a complete failure. It will be interesting to see if they work on the local level. I predict that they won't. Example: HUD—Department for Housing and Urban Development
- Government today cannot even improve upon the highway and freeway system in a significant way, proving how hopelessly helpless and inefficient it has become.
- Government and their agencies are objectifying human beings through laws. There is no self-control or self-determination left

for the individual. Hence, they take everything away from the individual. There is nothing left to live for.
- Freedom in America has become the same disguise as Christianity was for colonial powers. "Go into a country in the disguise of protecting somebody's freedom and justice. Then plunder that country for natural resources. Put as many women of that country into prostitution as possible".
- Most kids in this country are growing up in an overprotected, "secure" environment. It is not surprising that as adults they are seeking out prison like and oppressive big companies, mates, to continue their lack of self confidence, manifesting as seeking security as adults. Most healthy people in this country are probably in jail. In fact, most heroes in history ended up in jail.
- Watch out for control freaks! They are on the government side of things and people identify with them to gain power. Society needs to be in a slightly traumatic state to strengthen itself. Strength comes from adversity and diversity.
- It is in the government/power interest to only allow people to display desirable behavior in its extreme. It would be desirable for people to only work, eat and sleep. Anything associated with making people feel good represents indulgence. They will try to prevent people from having access to it. All other things threaten their power and make people less effective as quiet workers in society. They prefer the status quo. *The (sub)conscious goal of government is to implement rules and regulations through legislation to create a system of rules and punishment to turn people into slaves, and, at the same time, give people the illusion of freedom.*
- The government cannot deal with anything that is causing pleasure. Because drugs cause pleasure, it cannot be legal. When legislation and controlled distribution will immediately solve the criminal part of the drug problem. This has got to be the ultimate stupidity.
- You want all these laws and regulations and restrictions because you do not rely on yourself to make good decisions for yourself. So you need the laws?

Governments 87

- Primary goal of government should be: "secure equal opportunity and maximize opportunity for every individual for self realization:"
- Education
- Money
- Control of destiny
- Power
- Housing
- Work
- Children
- Discussion in the Bay Area about the new Bay Bridge. Both mayors in San Francisco and Oakland were going against the bridge to be selected, and for a bridge which includes a light rail system. However the new bridge only goes to Treasure Island, not all the way to San Francisco. Now how do you connect the light rail to San Francisco? This is the ultimate idiocy.
- Absolute government equals absolute cheating equal immorality and corruption. For example: Use of steroid drugs by the East Germans, the Czechs under communism and now China. Drug-use sponsored by the government. These are actions of government that violate all humanity and natural law. Drug use in sports destroys the whole idea of winning and the satisfaction coming from winning because you cheated. If these governments can do that, which very few individuals would do, what is the point? The whole idea of winning in sports is to not cheat. This also proves that an organization like government possesses no morality since governments sponsor cheating while few individuals would cheat given the opportunity! It is also symptomatic that cheating is done by nations with extreme government power and by athletes growing up under these governments with less freedom!
- Why do we have to have laws against discrimination? If we need them that means that society is discriminating. Why should anybody discriminate against anybody? It is lack of understanding that creates discrimination. Discrimination is rooted in a rudimentary emotion from a peasant and static society from the past where my wealth would by necessity

- come at the expense of yours. The capitalistic society works in the opposite direction. *Your wealth makes me wealthy.*
- Women blame the male. The male blames the society for the misery. But the fundamental problem is the way society is organized.
- Awards for snitching educate the population to violate some of the most natural moral instincts. That is loyalty toward friends and family. This snitching promoted by government is contributing to a great moral decline in the society.
- The well-meaning equate morality to being against sex and romance. Obviously, they have no idea of what morality really is, which is so "eloquently" summarized in the "Ten Commandments."
- If sex is abusive, and abusiveness is sexual. If that is true, then the governments, the military and the police are doing what they are doing to get horny.
- As morality among adults decreases, the desire to protect children increases. Here we have a society that is becoming increasingly more and more immoral. At the same time, it is passing more and more laws to increase morality. A society that does that is in big trouble. The drive to legislate and pass laws is grounded in immorality. It is an admittance of the need to be guided by laws and legislation because individuals can no longer be moral.
- The race issue diverts and covers up the fundamental issues of this country.

Who is this?

- 36 have been accused of spousal abuse
- 7 have been arrested for fraud
- 19 have been accused of writing bad checks
- 117 have directly or indirectly bankrupted at least 2 businesses
- 3 have done time for assault
- 71 cannot get a credit card due to bad credit
- 14 have been arrested on drug-related charges
- 8 have been arrested for shoplifting
- 21 currently are defendants in lawsuits

Governments 89

- 84 have been arrested for drunk driving in the last year

Can you guess which organization this is?

It's the 535 members of the United States Congress!

The same group that cranks out hundreds of new laws each year designed to keep the rest of us in line. I am sure that most of them got no or little punishment. It is just people like you and me who are getting punished! In fact, they should get the maximum punishment times three since they should know better. Or better still; get rid of many of the laws as we all are becoming victims. The laws have little or no preventative effect. The laws have rather the opposite effect; it creates more of what we are trying to prevent!

12
Man's Fundamental Needs and Rights

- Making human behavior a "science" is extremely damaging because it targets victims with unusual or peculiar behavior and it establishes "normality" as a base for legislation.
- To force treatment/punishment upon abnormality destroys human plurality that is essential for evolution and the dialectic process. It's contrary to the idea of freedom.
- An individual or "supernatural" with "infinite complexity" is being forced into conformity.
- Inherently victimizes people who are different and not "normal".
- "Normal" depends upon time and culturally-conditioned values and is not absolute truths.

The need or desire for groups or individuals to impose their beliefs and morality on others—at the expense of freedom—is directly proportional to how far those beliefs and values deviate from what is natural and normal.

The farther away beliefs and values stray from what is natural and normal, the more important it becomes for groups and individuals to impose their belief and value systems on others. In fact, the more doubt there is in a belief or value, the more important it becomes to validate that belief or value through legislation that put others into bondage. This is rooted in the desire for validation of their beliefs and values!

One person or group is not necessarily any better than anybody else. What matters are the conditions and circumstances that individual is exposed and subject to that makes the difference. The condition the individual needs to be subject to is freedom—this places demands on the person that automatically educates and moves the individual toward wisdom.

By committing injustice against other people, you throw yourself and your family into a fearful self-imposed prison!

Publicly throwing people in jail for 40 years appeals to the lowest and most despicable of human emotions. If the tragic and inhuman treatment of others makes you feel better, you are the true criminal. As soon as you engage in destruction, you may not be aware of it because it is always justified in your mind and otherwise. You also plant the seed for your own self-destruction because you violate a fundamental principle in the universe: Creation. This also is true if you work and/or belong to a destructive organization. You cannot help planting seeds of self destruction. At some point you will make your own self destruction into reality. This has been proven over and over again throughout history. Daily, you can observe the self destructive process in today's mass media. One example is Governor Elliot Spitzer. He created his own self destruction through his unjust prosecutions as a district attorney and governor.

What you often see is that people who manifest as destroyers will "subconsciously" start a process of self punishment. When a person finds themselves to be destructive, perverted, unjust and wrong, the tendency is to project those same deficiencies upon other people.

They legislate against the very thing that they dislike about themselves.

So people who have the strongest desire to control other people's behavior through legislation and otherwise, are also "admitting" that they have those same personality traits driving them.

In other words, the most adamant legislators and prosecutors are the manifestation of the ones they are prosecuting and legislating against.

When something is forced upon a human being, the immediate natural reaction is to do the opposite. This reaction is reinforced from the experiences of growing up. Everything you could not do as a child until you become an adult are things that create the most pleasure and are among the most important in life: Sex, driving, going to a party, having a drink, smoking and working. You are conditioned as a child to this reaction. When somebody tells you that you cannot have nor do something, you immediately want it or want to do it.

The more laws and regulations we have, the more desire we have to break them.

Making necessities like housing, food and cars scarce makes us into survival slaves. True freedom to realize your potential and the path to self realization, happiness and a sense of achievement comes when those basic needs have been filled and there is no fear of losing it. It is only at that moment that you can choose to become what you really want to be.

The feudal system myth still guides the fundamental assumption of man. The idea is that the ultimate goal of man is to do nothing. That assumption is wrong! It is reflecting the static class society of the feudal system where the highest class lives a "do-nothing" life that is looked upon to be most desirable and ultimate goal for everybody. However, with the Industrial Revolution, and the proliferation and evolution of the sciences, the goals for the individual has changed from making money and accumulate wealth to the age of creativity where the ultimate goal is to create. This represents a paradigm shift in man's aspirations. Given the opportunity, all humans want to advance themselves. They want the opportunity to create! It is the leftover ideas and institutions from the old myth that still foster negative people. They do not want to work and possess internal and external destructive desires. Man has both a creative and destructive side. We need freedom and personal responsibility to create personal growth opportunities. The sense of achievement automatically promotes and develops man's creative side. Society has the opportunity now through its affluence to make this creative opportunity possible for everyone!

Government's goal should be to make life easier for its citizens. The redistribution and establishment of a base income for all citizens is paramount. Many invaluable benefits emanate from a base income for all citizens.

- Reduce crime.
- Take away poverty
- Restore the most efficient demand economy
- Create freedom and security for all people
- Make life much easier for all people
- Would be a strong stabilizing effect on the economy

Principles and guidelines

- No human being or organization should have the right to impose their values, belief or live style on another human being or organization.
- A new Constitution needs to be written as fundamental principles of freedom.
- Fundamental goals and objectives need to be established as a hierarchy for a society. This needs to be consistent with human "nature" which leads to a "natural society".

Fundamental goals:
- Maximize freedom for the individual
- Prevent economic or organizational monopolies
- Freedom of speech, writing and expression. This assumes that freedom is the underpinning that maximizes the strongest possibility for happiness and self realization
- The children belong to their parents and are the responsibility of their parents until they are 18. At this time they are emancipated.
- In divorce, the parent who is willing to take economic responsibility for the children gets them. Child support or alimony should not be granted, leading to a complete dismantling of the whole system.
- The hunger for knowledge and experience is one of the fundamental drives in man.
- There is good and bad in everybody.
- If the opportunity to choose between good and bad is taken away, you have also taken away the opportunity to grow and the feeling of achievement and happiness.
- A "natural human being" loves sex in all shapes and forms as a gift from "God".

Everybody does what they think is expected of them!

Sept 9, 1998 Sally Jessy Rafael Show
"A human being is born without any sex organs". On a personal note; this would be the perfect human being as to what today's government and society wants a human being to be.

The trauma hierarchy

- Thoughts about your own death
- Death of people close to us
- Child being taken away from parents
- Rape
- Blackmail and threats
- Caught up in the justice system
- IRS
- Harassment by the federal, state, county or city bureaucracies
- Harassment by the police
- Physical violence
- Divorce
- Personal physical pain

All leading to unhappiness, fear and anger!

The meaning of life is also responsibility. If all responsibility is transferred to the government, the meaning of life is reduced.

For example: Children being taken away from their parents by the government. The society is walking down a completely wrong path as proven by the increase in unhappiness and crime.

It is more important to experience the freedom of choice than to actually bring what we desire into reality.

You can live your life two different ways: Doing something is the creative way to achieve meaning and purpose; avoidance leads to destruction. "Non-doers" have become the prevalent force in our society as they impose their legislative restrictions on everyone. Legislators mistakenly assume that their morality is on a higher plane. They will not grant permission for anybody to do something. In the end, they deny themselves from doing. Doing nothing has never been the ultimate goal of humanity. In a society of scarcity and suffering, "doing nothing" is considered most desirable. However, "doing nothing" is the ultimate punishment. That's why prison is the ultimate punishment. Incarceration prevents a human being from doing something worthwhile. In the modern age of plenty, the goal of "doing nothing" will lead to unhappiness. Remember: Doing and creating is the path to happiness and success. The ultimate terror for any human being is to do nothing, because it takes you away from being able to "play". That is why prison is used for punishment as it takes away the opportunity to create and do something! So striving to get into a position that you don't need to do anything is a paradox. In fact, achieving what you are striving for without being enlightened is the same as prison because "doing nothing" is the ultimate horror.

Human beings expect to fail. When they see success coming most would rather be unsuccessful and sabotage themselves as the possibility for success brings them out of their "comfort zone"!

"If you never spent money on a business, fun, or a hobby you will have a lot of money when you die."

Priorities of a society

- Provide food and housing
- Health care
- Education
- Work
- Business opportunities
- Wealth generation
- "Security and protection"

On this background to preserve freedom is a continuous fight!

The whole discussion of handguns and weapons as it relates to age: The increase from 18 to 21 years of age to carry weapons makes it more desirable for young people to get a weapon to increase their status among peers and to reaffirm their status among other young people. This is normally a healthy goal for young people. Every time you pass a law that you have to be of a certain age to have or do something, it becomes irresistible and extremely important for young people to have or get that thing. One of the major drives among children and young adults is to be able to become an adult. They associate what they can do or own with adultness. So if you want to be sure that the most aggressive and smartest young adults will get or do what we are trying to prevent, just pass a law that states that you must be X number of years old to have it or do it! In fact it is the same way for adults!

Freedom and financial security is the foundation for the possibility for self realization.

The Desire for Meaning

If you have "perfect" knowledge, there is no meaning and purpose. Meaning and purpose only exist in an imperfect universe. When made "perfect" it becomes meaningless. The "perfect" would be an existence of no polarity. With no polarity there is no reference. Without reference there is no meaning and purpose.

The US population has chosen to give life meaning by avoiding tragedy and disasters by being subjected to rules, regulations and prosecutions. They have chosen destruction and being dysfunctional. The other choice is to achieve meaning by participating in creation and evolution the constructive way. However, that way is a lot more complex, but it has to be chosen to sustain and develop humanity to achieve the ultimate goal of absolute power to create and recreate everything. It must be aligned to creation and the positive, rather than to destruction and the negative.

Politicians are talking about "What they can do for the country". The only thing they can do in a positive direction is prevent less of natural evolution. Otherwise, the only things they can do effectively are to stop evolution and engage in ultimate destructive acts, starting wars and incarcerating people. Being a law maker is to do the opposite of what the base is for freedom. Rather than doing what "planning commissions" do—preventing people to build and develop what they want—the creative force needs to be liberated. Planning should be based on chaos theory with reference to "attractors" to reflect the creative unfolding of life.

Laws need to be formulated to be "attractors" to guide society in a desirable direction rather than absolutes based on punishment.

If the society does not consider the consequences of destroying human life through prosecution and incarceration, that society causes incredible misery to its own people. Why do we prosecute a person for violating a law that destroys that person's life? Destroying a human life does not count as evil when it is being done by the government? This is a paradox of complete inconsistency in valuing human life.

You destroy a community by taking responsibility for the community away from the people who live there.

The idea of protection, and the emphasis upon it, creates enemies and disenfranchises people. The goal must be to maximize freedom and to minimize injustice, not to maximize justice.

Maximizing information and experience is the foundation for developing wisdom and making the right choices.

Seeking freedom is in many ways paradoxical. When you are truly free you are confronted with who you are without excuse. This state of mind is extremely difficult to handle for most people. However, it is the only way you will advance and experience a sense of meaning and purpose. By not being free, your responsibility for your own life has been taken away from you. Lack of freedom is a much simpler and easier life for most people. As Ibsen said, "If you take away the lie about a person's life, most people would not be able to handle it."

Socrates said, "Know thyself". To know thyself, you must be free to choose and forced to take responsibility for your own life.

13
Principles of Information

Information is education.

If information equals education, why would you limit information about anything to anybody? An increment of additional information about a relevant issue increases the probability that you will make the right decision about an issue. If you have no information, you have no basis to make a decision. Hence, the probability for a wrong decision is higher. Anything that has to do with the restriction of information must be reduced to create an educated and responsible society. The internet is the ultimate information provider. The gap among mass media, politicians and the public is starting to lessen in the sense that dogmatic opinions and political correctness are being exposed. The idea among politicians and journalists that the public can only understand simplistic religious ideas and dogmas is being greatly diminished. In fact, the public will become less and less affected by media and political manipulation. If you take away dogmatic opinion and illogical value systems, there is little left for politicians to do. Their importance greatly diminishes. Chances are future politicians would increasingly have the position of mimicking a football referee in a game than the position they have now. The gap between the people, politicians and the media is also created because each group acts out of their own self interest.

- The media who loves "scandals" because of increased ratings.
- The politicians see another politician's loss as their gain and this reasserts their own importance.
- The people recognize excellent performance by a president. They want him to have the best possible environment to execute his position to make the world and the country a better place to be. On the other hand, his fellow politicians wish him failure!

Any increment of information increases the probability for making a correct decision.

It develops the human intellect and leads to a higher level of wisdom. If you agree with this principle, it means that any attempt to restrict the flow of information/experience to anybody, including children, leads directly to slower development and dummification of the people. To protect people from something is inherently destructive and counterproductive for that person. Maximizing information and experience for everybody needs to be one paramount goal of society.

The more devastating a trauma a person goes through the stronger the person will be in the long run.

Examples of this:
- My own grandfather was sentenced to lifetime of forced labor in Hitler's camps with a death sentence as he was the most powerful union leader in Norway and responsible for the famous "milk strike". The diary workers organized in his union decided to protest the occupation by not delivering milk to the German occupiers. He survived the ordeal as the only survivor of all the politicians that was captured. He was re-elected a year after his release at the end of the second world war and retired in 1957 and lived until he was 94. The Norwegian government commissioned a book about his life as a hero and as a national treasure that was published on his 75th birthday.
- Holocaust survivors
- Veterans of the 1st and 2nd WW
- Cancer patient survivors

Phobias

For people with phobias—the solution to their problem is to actually experience what they are afraid of. Humans are extremely adaptable and strong. They will recover if left alone. However, there is no recovery—and a huge magnification of the problem—if that person gains more personally by remaining a victim. Today, they are persuaded by authority that they have been damaged. The persuasion creates the victim!

Any increment of information or experience will enrich and enable the individual to make better decisions with faster growth and wisdom.

When you learn something you are actually committing "trauma" to the brain. This makes for increased intelligence, wisdom and mental capacity. This is just like when you traumatize a muscle. It becomes stronger and healthier. "Trauma" is good if not too strong. It develops whatever has been traumatized. We can apply the same principle to society. An element of trauma and chaos is good. It makes for more traumas that result in evolution. This relates to the Second Law of Thermodynamics that everything develops to a lower energy state with more stability. This law applied to society; by allowing higher level of chaos will cause more variety and plurality and at the same time, more stability. The movement of all things to lower energy states may also be reflected in advancing technology, higher and more efficient use of resources to achieve the same or better benefit.

Even if a total system experiences higher and higher levels of entropy, this higher level of entropy is leading to more stability. Localized opposing forces create higher levels of complexity and organization. In other words, while the total system moves toward a higher level of entropy, it will at the same time, create regions where higher level of complexity is created. For example, as the sun releases its heat it goes toward higher entropy. But that very heat creates high levels of complexity on the earth. So even if the entire planetary system is moving toward higher levels of entropy, pockets of the system move toward higher levels complexity.

If you control the information flow to your child, how can the child develop and form their opinions and mature intelligently? A child needs as much information as possible to gain as much knowledge as possible. By controlling the information your child gets, you are slowing down the child's development. Preventing a child from experiencing and finding out about reality is dummifying and slows down its development as it does for adults.

Principle: *To deny children new experiences and information only delays the maturity and adultness of those children. It's not only the number of years a person has lived that determines their maturity, but also exposure to reality and personal experiences. Denying them access to TV and internet only delays the maturity. The goal of raising a child is to make that person into a mature adult. The best approach is exposing that child to information and experiences. There is reason to believe that a person or child will choose to access and view information and experience what they are comfortable with. The more information and experiences, the more stable and mature that person will be.*

Principle: *Any increment of information and experience the person has will increase the probability for that person to make a better decision. This eventually leads to maturity and wisdom. The whole idea that you can categorize information and experience into good and bad information and experiences is false. That's why foreign children coming to this country end up many times more successful than Americans. This is because American kids are protected from reality. Do you want them to learn to cope as kids or wait until they are 35, if ever, before they "break away" from their parents to become mature adults? We are raising a nation of fearful "little kids" who use their employer and the government as surrogate parents. We are creating a nation of followers with infantile attitudes!*

A chaotic system has attractors that guide the evolution of the system, and it is extremely sensitive to its initial conditions.

Information not communicated or not affecting the environment has no meaning.

Meaning and self realization can only become manifest in you by serving other people and communicating what you know. This leads to action. In fact, if you have the knowledge, you have the responsibility to communicate and to affect the environment. You can only become a happy person if you look at yourself as a giver and a tool for other people. I realized after several years of focusing on myself that it only lead to introvertedness and unhappiness. To become a happy person you must find a goal that is outside yourself. Self indulgence leads to unhappiness and possible insanity. The narcissist is always a very unhappy person.

A human being in complete freedom from external punishment and outside influences chooses to be creative rather than destructive. He chooses good over evil. We really do not have any choice in this matter. If this statement is not true, humanity is doomed, period! We can't punish, control and restrict humanity on one hand and have meaning, purpose and evolution on the other.

The desire to reaffirm freedom will, in some people, create antisocial behavior when society passes a law against it. This constellation in combination with the mass media will create more of what the law was intended to prevent and reduce. Especially in people who feel they are being unfairly treated by society. This feeling is in direct proportion to the number of laws and diligence of enforcement! Violating the law becomes a form of protest and an affirmation of freedom in that individual.

14
"Freedom Means to Be Free"

The private enterprise system must exist to guarantee freedom by staying independent from the government. The private enterprise system earns their power through money and functions as a check and balance on the government. This is the paradox. You need a good government to regulate business. If done right, this actually works well.

There is always a human being involved in any security effort. But with a human being there is no security and safety. The selling of security and safety to the public is a fraud, unless your intention is to break the human spirit.

If society has to make a law about something, it is a proof that it goes against "natural law" and morality. Otherwise, it would not be needed.
- When men and women get married, they belong to each other.
- Nobody belongs to the government
- Children belong to their parents until they are 18 years of age. Then, they belong to themselves.

The more violence and anger an opinion creates the more truth there is to it.

The government, church and media forces of self interest to increase power and wealth, is reducing people's freedom. They all act out of self interest. Destroying the opportunity for people to advance and achieve. This is based on the assumption that any incremental increase of information and experience makes a person more knowledgeable and, hence, increases a person's wisdom.

Religion has prevented and dummified the creation and evolution of knowledge throughout the centuries. An example would be what the church did to Leonardo Da Vinci by censoring and destroying a lot of his research and writings. The church did something similar to Galileo. This is manifesting even today with the teaching of creation by the church rather than evolution.

If education is important, why should it stop when people graduate from high school? Would not a society which demands knowledge from its people by virtue of being forced to make decisions about what they should spend money on force the people to educate themselves? Especially, if they have complete freedom to spend their money as they wish! Would it not be true that if nobody is willing to pay for something out of their own pocket, then it is not needed? Should it not be regarded as a waste of resources and detrimental to the environment to spend money on products and services that very few people or nobody would be willing to pay for?

The more we legislate morality, the less morality we get. Freedom of choice is what keeps a person moral. There is no such thing as absolute morality. If that existed, it would be a manifestation of something perfect and that would ultimately destroy evolution. Evolution relies on imperfection. What comes natural to a human being living in a free society is what can be considered as morality. Morality is personal, not absolute.

To say it is wrong to get married and have children before you are 18 years old is wrong. It goes against nature. A person is ready at the biological age when they can have children. It must be that person's choice no matter how old they are. The desire by the parents to prevent their children from having sex and relationships is purely egotistical on behalf of the parents. They want to extend that person's dependency on childhood that gives the parent meaning in their life. Breaking away from parents is natural and normal. Do not use the argument that you want to protect you children from it.

To have to talk about "rights" basically means that you are living in a fascist dictatorship. Why do people have to fight for obvious rights? How idiotic can a society and a government that denies rights be?

Freedom is destroyed by the Desire for Perfection

Humans in their desire to make something perfect and complete will look to the government to fulfill that desire, believing it will happen.

Freedom Means to be Free 105

However, this is an illusion. Government interference in the private enterprise system makes it much more inefficient. It might even stop the private enterprise system from evolving altogether.

The desire for government regulation is driven by this desire of making something more complete and perfect. Humans must realize that the preferred state of something is the imperfect and incomplete because the seed of opportunity, evolution and creativity exists only in this imperfect and incomplete state.

The **"Victimization Process"**:

= Victimization of millions in the name of "prevention" leading to the destruction of freedom!

**Figure 9
The "Victimization Process"**

I asked my grandfather, Josef Larsson, when he was 85 what he thought was the most important thing that he had found out about people. His answer: "All people are the same as you. What they think is unique and a deep secret about them is not." If that is true, people who want to impose their values on others and think they are morally superior to others have not achieved a high enough level of personal development and self knowledge to accept themselves. They are driven through self hate to impose their values on others through legislation that destroys freedom.

There is very little difference between a theorist and a terrorist. Both of their world views are a construct of their imagination. They manifest themselves in irrational decisions and behaviors. The end result is the use of force to impose their values and beliefs on other people.

America has a fundamental problem of mistrust by the people of the government. This manifests itself in a lack of healthcare for everyone. This mistrust is created by the people due to having a lack of democracy caused by:
- The election process
- The history of the US government/justice system of being adversaries of the people instead of fact-finding. The US has an adversarial justice system. It's like injecting perversion of lies and fraud, instead of fact-finding into the justice system.

What happened to government by the people and for the people?

Is the US a free or totalitarian society?

Events in LA during the Rodney King riots come as a climax from some very disturbing trends in the US Democracy is not the same as freedom and it's not a guarantee for freedom. Communism and Nazism were implemented on the basis of support from the majority. In fact, Hitler had the support of more than 70 percent of the German population in 1939. The difference between a totalitarian state and a free society is the protection of the rights of the minority, whether it is heritage, color race, opinion, values, morality and life styles. In fact, the word "free" only has meaning in the context of being different from and in opposition to what the majority stands for.

A totalitarian state is founded upon moral principles or an idea that is legislated and forced upon the minority.

Upon this understanding it was extremely disturbing to listen to government officials using the same strategy and principles as any ruling dictator would use, namely: "We need to enforce law and order in LA to protect the citizens." This is exactly the same as the Nazis claimed when they occupied Norway in 1940, my native country. Hitler told the Norwegians when they marched in that they needed protection from the English and from communism. The same was said by the communists in Russia and by Stalin and Lenin. "The Russian population needed to be protected from the decadence and exploitation of the capitalists." It is very obvious to make the following equation:

The US population needs protection from crime and drugs equals capitalists in Russia equal English and communists in Norway under the Second World War. The result is exactly the same. To protect the population we need to throw everybody in jail so we can protect the citizens from themselves. In the context of what has happened in LA, it means we need to throw any black person in that community in jail who fights for justice. In Germany, during the 1930s and the Second World War, they called them Jews. We called their prisons concentration camps. We can make equalities here, too, between money (Jews in Germany) = pimps (black in the US). There is no difference. The result of throwing people in jail or concentration camps is the same. What you saw in LA central is not criminality, but a citizen uprising against injustice. This society has to face the problems and not throw people in concentration camps to protect the people from themselves. If society does, then this is a totalitarian society. When a society legislates an idea, principle, or morality, and enforces it legally through punishment, we will no longer have a free society.

A society that attempts to control its population through punishment because it needs "protection" is a totalitarian society.

In fact, the US is already a totalitarian society. We have concentration camps. We even have the gas chamber.

A free society needs to appeal to its citizens to control themselves and to minimize legislation and enforcement. In fact, it is my firm belief that crime and violence would drop automatically when society stops taking away the citizens own responsibility for their actions through punishment. What we saw in LA from the uprising is the first declaration of war by the citizens against a government who declared war on them. That is the war on drugs, criminality, deviate behavior, drunk driving, woman abuse, abortion, etc.

What right does one human being have to decide how another human being should live their life? If these "custodians" of the truth get into power by claiming to know how everybody should believe and behave, we inherently have a dictatorship. In the implementation by humans, anybody can be accused of being homosexual, or adulterer. They would have to try to prove themselves innocent. This task would be almost impossible. By letting these individuals get into power we have created a society where everybody is living in fear of each other. This will be a society of the ultimate horror.

Instead of spending the tax money and revenues on creating opportunities for the population, it is spent on punishment and the attempted restructuring of human behavior because it is easy to understand.

This empowers the well-meaning. The legal system produces martyrs for the younger generation with their desire and need to reaffirm themselves and to feel independent. Doing something illegal among the young, is looked upon as a heroic act. This produces more martyrs, more crime, and more misery in an endless spiral. This must stop!

The perfect has no seed of change or creation while the essence of the universe is creation and change. Perfection is found in the imperfect because the imperfect implies the opportunity for change and creativity. The essence of the universe is change. That is why the "perfect" society is not even desirable because it stifles the opportunity for creation and change.

15
The Justice System

You want more of what you can't have!

The justice system rests on the idea that human beings are perfect. Lawbreakers are punished when they are imperfect. Every law that is created manifests the idea of perfection. The problem is that human beings and society can never be or should be perfect. Instead, our courts apply laws of perfection to human beings who are inherently imperfect. The end result is random justice that often commits heinous crimes against humanity. That is why the dispensary role of judges—and their freedom to act—should be limited. Judges should have the freedom to reduce sentences. However, they should never be allowed to harshly punish to perfect the criminal. Instead, older people—not politicians—should establish sentencing guidelines since they possess superior human skills and experience.

As a fundamental principle, those who make laws should not have any vested interest in their outcome.

A nation becomes a pressure cooker when it sanctions zero-tolerance laws. Suppressing violence below natural levels accelerates violence—sooner or later—it erupts. Allowing limited violence helps to dissipate murders, mobs and even riots. We must accept an element of risk in our daily lives to preserve our freedom. Just as there is a direct relationship between risk and reward in business, the same holds true in our lives: Maximizing our freedom maximizes our reward! This approach establishes a reasonable risk to the individual. In present day reality, there is no choice for any of us because security and safety are mostly elusive. Besides, one can easily prove them to be mathematically impossible as I have shown elsewhere in this book.

As we move toward complete freedom—individually and collectively—risk increasingly outweighs security and safety. The higher the business risk, the higher the reward potential. This same axiom holds true in society: The more risk we accept collectively, the higher the reward we receive individually. There is no such thing as government-created security. Even if it could be achieved, it would not be desirable. The threat of violence and violent acts often trigger a catalyst for change. When violence erupts, a strong warning sign is sent out that freedom is threatened! Removing risks from society destroys freedom! The pursuit of security and safety ultimately leads to a higher level of evil, abuse, and even murder by a government that constitutionally is sworn to defend and protect the people.

A society that pursues security and safety as its primary goal eventually strips away personal growth, life's challenges and the fun of living.

Over the centuries, governments clearly have shown that they have little regard for human life. We witness this in the countless killings of millions who either die in wars or are prosecuted in the courts. Killings worldwide drop significantly if one allows individual freedom to neutralize government genocide and prosecutions.

To ensure individual freedom, "we the people" must accept the world's imperfections!

Irrefutable evidence clearly shows that media outlets and governments act out of self interest when they condemn terrorist attacks and individual killings. When the non-establishment kills people—intentionally and accidentally—stories are quickly publicized and analyzed. Conversely, there is significantly less news when a government kills on a much larger scale. There exists a strong desire to keep these acts secret. Examples of clandestine acts in recent years include the Bali bomb explosion, the Virginia sniper attack and the Afghanistan government killings of thousands.

A perfect example of this glaring contradiction is self-evident when governments criminalize prenatal abuse by taking away individual responsibility. Elected leaders exacerbate the problem when they legislate because this abuse is significantly small. Meanwhile, a woman never feels good about making a responsible choice for her life because the government and society confiscates her freedom to choose. What remains is resentment and hatred toward a law that ultimately creates more abuse.

Ask yourself. What has society accomplished by passing this law? Answer: It creates more abuse by usurping a larger chunk of people's freedom. This law is counter-productive toward achieving its intentions because often it imprisons the mother and leaves her offspring motherless. If this trend continues, you no longer can take credit for anything good you do. Personal growth stops and finally regresses. Freedom has no meaning if people cannot choose between good and bad. Freedom means that each of us is guaranteed the right to be bad and do wrong things! Without this option, freedom has no meaning. An individual creates morality by taking responsibility for his or her actions in freedom. This means making a decision without fearing external punishment. A person increasingly realizes higher levels of morality and wisdom by taking responsibility for his or her actions in freedom. Taking responsibility is an educational process that fosters a desire to choose creativity and goodness.

Standardization stifles progress and evolution because it assumes that present-day thinking is perfect. This standardization becomes the yardstick that measures performance. There is a tendency to gravitate to this accepted standard rather than soar above it. Allowing excellence and progress to manifest, automatically necessitates failure and regression.

Freedom must be redefined more explicitly than its current definition because the sense of freedom is subjective. This infinite sphere is defined by what you cannot do—even if defined narrowly—and leaves ample freedom to argue that you are still free. This is fundamentally wrong. Freedom's definition has been so redefined that many people frown on a person for just having consensual sex. The problem with freedom is that a well-adjusted person in society may act under freewill according to the dictatorship's rules and regulations. However, this person's sense of subjective freedom is infinite. Even if the freedom experienced is extremely narrow, the subjective feeling is that you are free. Why? There will always be many degrees of freedom in any society, even in one that is not considered free. Subjective freedom is paradoxical. No matter how small, it still becomes an infinite experience.

In maximizing our freedom, we cannot rely on subjective feelings—conditioned by culture—as a pathway to the society's rules and regulations.

The problem is that freedom can vanish from a society without the citizenry knowing that they have lost it. Only the most progressive and creative people sense their loss of freedom. What is a free society for one person is a dictatorship for another. We need to have enough freedom—beyond the average person's sense of subjective freedom—to ensure evolution's dialectic process. Otherwise, we choose stagnation over evolution for our lives and for society. If our only desires are eating, drinking, entertainment, sleeping and sex, if these freedoms are permitted—and that's all we want—we are perfectly happy living in a society that denies other freedoms!

Imagine a civilization where the individual has complete freedom to do anything! This does not mean that everyone will do everything. Self interest quickly discovers that not treating others like you wish to be treated—because you are negative and evil—ultimately threatens your existence!

Therefore, self interest and survival instincts along with higher level of personal morality and wisdom are the regulating mechanisms for this society.

I also put forth the idea that crime and evil are minimized if complete freedom exists. Society needs rules, regulations, punishment and incarceration. But we need to minimize these aspects to maximize individual responsibility. This becomes the most powerful educator and regulator of human interaction than any legislation can ever hope to offer its citizenry.

So we have the right to kill each other in a free society right? But people in a completely free society do not shoot me—although they could—because we don't want to live like this. Furthermore, you are creating an example to other citizens that shooting people is wrong. It is in the best interest of everyone living in a society to create an affluent, tranquil, enjoyable, dramatic and interesting society.

If I destroy one's opportunity to enjoy a particular choice, I destroy my own possibility to experience the same.

If I have the opportunity to experience fun and excitement, I need to allow others to experience the same. It is this fundamental principle that we blindly run away from in modern-day society as the government perpetuates its subconscious conspiracy with the mass media to distort reality.

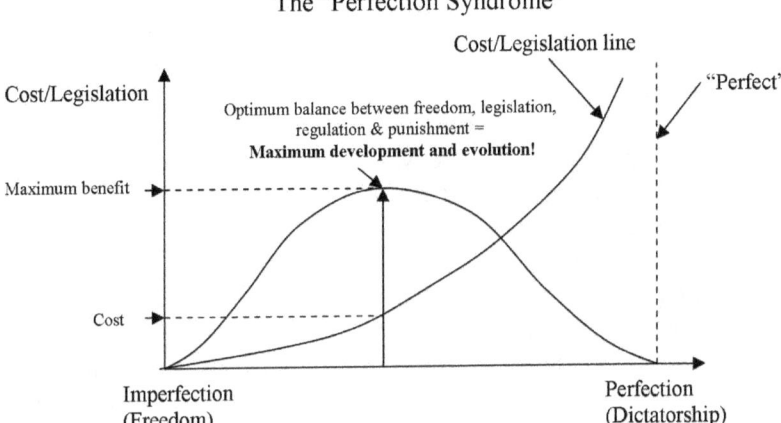

**Figure 10
The "Perfection Syndrome"**

The government also intervenes in lives of women who seldom choose freedom over security and safety. When a woman no longer finds these qualities in a man—since legislation has destroyed his ability to provide security—she turns to the government for help. However, this choice actually destroys her foundation for real security and safety.

By condoning federal, state and local laws as necessary—most of us do what governments tell us to do—are a terrible insult to our generation. The previous generation was better and freer than ours because they lived in a society that didn't have hundreds of thousands—and maybe millions—of new rules and regulations. It is desirable for society to accept unruly, unacceptable and anti-authoritative behavior as a foundation to develop the individual and society. Without this acceptance, new generations merely become "clones" of the previous one. This stagnation creates a material, moral and intellectual decline. You cannot expect to advance society without allowing positive and negative behavior.

As society moves through the myriad of moralization and legislation—especially under an evolving democracy—it soon becomes a majority dictatorship. This establishes the lowest common denominator of human involvement and what is desirable in society. Selecting a more creative path creates a unique, powerful and excelling individual who pulls everyone upward to new and higher levels. Society is gravitating toward the lowest common denominator: The Law of Mediocrity! Or perhaps you thrive on laws and regulations because you get a thrill out of violating them. I think this becomes tremendously dangerous in more ways than one.

The foundation for external regulation of a system that influences human behavior only works for one generation. After this one generation, this new environment becomes a natural part of living. For example, take a look at drug-use among teenagers. They do not think they have a problem, even if they are moving in and out of the justice system. The environment in which people grow up in is their reality. People assert their freedom regardless of what the environment dictates. Only when we change the environment does behavior-adjustment have real effect. That's why punishment only works temporarily as a behavior-influencing measure. If most people become felons in a society, the desire to avoid becoming a felon is minimal. Why? A felon has become the norm. When society uses legislation to impose its will on the population, this approach creates criminality. People violate rules to manifest themselves as independent and free people. It is the desire for freedom that turns people into criminals! Unnatural rules and regulations, coupled with the unnatural state of affairs, causes the best people to be thrown in jail because they have the strongest desire for freedom. We throw a lot of people in jail these days. Their only crime is creating what they believe are their rights to freedom! In fact, the US legal system has become so fanatical that the government creates something illegal out of nothing. This is especially true when judges imply that someone is lying or hiding something, even though the person is innocent!

The Whitewater case against President Bill Clinton is a perfect example. You never get to the truth if you dig hard enough and involve enough people. You create a case where there is no case because you fail to embrace the truth!

Jury misconduct is another reason why the justice system is not working. A Dateline show in September 1996 features a story about inmates trying to get a new trial by investigating their accusers. Then legislators pass a law to limit inmates' ability to access the accusers' public records. The so-called victims feel threatened because they want to live a perfect life. Meanwhile, inmates are reduced to nothing as they sit in jail or prison for 75 years! Obviously, inmates' rights do not count.

A major reason why victims are afraid of being investigated is that they themselves are guilty of criminal behavior!

This is another example of the mass media and politicians furthering their own agendas by solving an insignificant problem.

How does this affect public access to information and, in turn, place society in jeopardy? Answer: Cover-ups and criminality at the highest levels. An open freedom of information act that ensures the public's right to know should take effect immediately to reduce government corruption and misuse of power.

Unfortunately, when police try to solve a crime, they sometimes end up committing an even larger crime. They violate the principles of human law. Police sometimes stoop low enough to blackmail wives to snitch on their husbands, even though this violates the US Constitution, since a wife can choose not to testify against her husband or vice-versa. Police sometimes orchestrate break-ins, commit killings and endanger innocent citizens' lives during car chases and shootouts. Are these actions beneficial for society? I think not!

The Menendez Brothers' trial is a typical example of society elevating child abuse to one of the most horrific crimes. Society packages and sells this idea to the public. Abused young people are a primary target because they are a receptive audience. They are propagandized to believe that they can no longer lead normal lives. Justifying the death penalty for the abuser becomes extremely likely. In a weird way, the focus on child abuse leads to even more horrible crimes: Sons and daughters even kill their parents! Well-meaning idiots are guilty!

How outrageous that many American TV shows justify endless killings for less egregious reasons. Meanwhile, some so-called "fair trials" are a joke. Children receive life imprisonment for admitting to a crime while O.J. Simpson is exonerated as a mature, famous man. Leave no doubt in your mind that the California Justice System sacrificed the Menendez brothers to save face. The US government likewise saved face by sending young men to Vietnam, just like its doing in the Iraq and Afghanistan wars.

Society must ask itself why groups or individuals become terrorists, since there is little protection against attacks. Isn't it time for governments and societies around the world to implement fairness policies to minimize threats? We must realize that crime is a symptom of society's illness. Crime should be analyzed as such. Remedies should be found to solve this growing problem since there is no protection.

A law can't protect everyone. It might even be detrimental to those it protects as shown in a 20/20 television show in July 1996 on the Social Security Disability Act. The show reveals that laws governing the act are insufficient and unjust.

It's disgusting that we tolerate abuses that take place while in custody of law enforcement. This is probably the least-safe place to be. If we receive little to no protection while in police custody, how can we expect protection anywhere else? Police forces foster some of the worst criminals. For example, the Atlanta Olympics bomb planted by a security guard who also worked as a sheriff's assistant. He warned people to become a hero. The same syndrome affects firefighters when they set blazes to break the boredom and become heroes. There is a long history of these cases!

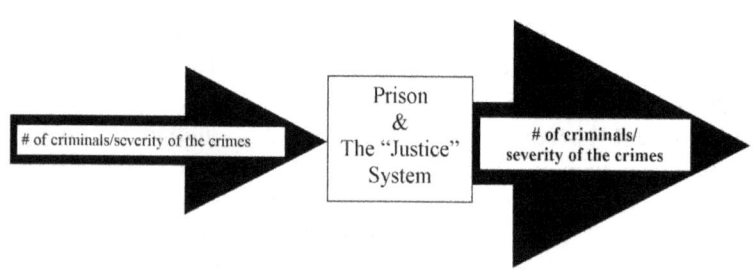

**Figure 11
Criminals and Crimes**

Society must minimize creating criminals to diminish damage to society and individuals. Punishment is not working. More than 90 percent of the population, responsible and moral, chooses good over evil. Another proof in reducing criminality is the rising recidivism of criminals that repeatedly land them back in jail. The impulse to kill countless people stems from society's deterioration to the least common denominator. A society lacking the dynamics of complete freedom eventually retrogrades to the least common denominator.

Another extremely dangerous precedent in the legal system is that people no longer are responsible for their actions. Instead, they need government protection. When tobacco companies lost a multi-million dollar case to a man dying of lung cancer, the jury found that tobacco firms had a greater responsibility for manufacturing a product known to cause cancer than the dying man who chose to smoke cigarettes. This is a very dangerous step that destroys people's freedom as a principle of law.

Taking an innocent person's freedom by incarceration should be viewed like kidnapping. When the legal system snares teenagers and young adults for minor offenses, it actually says to them: "You idiot; you're no good for anything!" This places them on the path where the desire for self realization becomes the criminal road. They are not really given a chance after they enter the judicial and penal systems.

These offenders have a record even if they leave jail. The path to increasingly heinous crimes is straight as an arrow. This is happening now in our justice and penal systems! When we pass laws like this we create more criminals. Chances are that more and more people will willingly, or unwillingly, break one of these new laws.

The only difference between a criminal and yourself is that the criminal was caught while you were lucky. As increasingly more people break some law, natural law-abiding tendencies are undermined. It's always easier to break the law the second time around, especially if the individual experiences the rule as being unfair or unjust. To make matters worse, law enforcement keeps seized property, thereby giving them a greater incentive to create more criminals!

A new principle of law should be that everyone has a right to freedom. If someone asks the justice system for protection, it should be given even if "real" protection is impossible. Nobody should be asked to remain in a situation for financial reasons. For example: A wife should not have to live with a husband for financial reasons.

When criminals are prosecuted, the jury should be allowed to question witnesses directly. This should happen at least two times during a trial. The jury should have tremendous latitude to ask probing questions because ultimately they decide the trial's outcome.

When society legislate personal morality, they systematically destroy it.

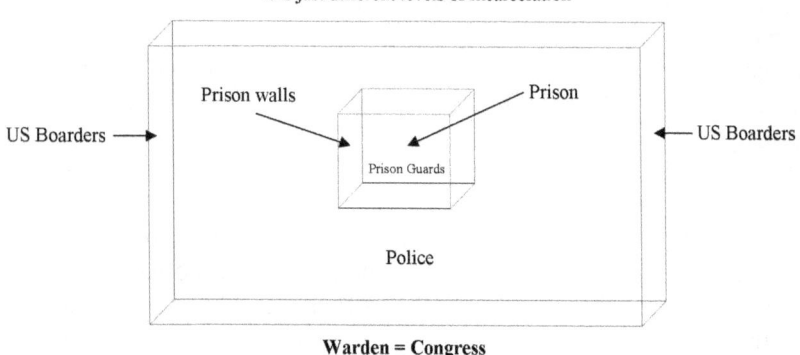

**Figure 12
US as a prison**

Many people become homeless after they commit a minor crime. Then they lose their job, business, girlfriend, wife, boyfriend or husband while incarcerated. When they are released they cannot overcome this predicament. In the US, most abuse is minor. The only crime that measures up to the punishment that society imposes is murder or permanently disabling another person.

To hit someone or even knock them unconscious, involves possible pain for a week or two. Throwing someone in jail for even six months is significantly harsher abuse than what a person does to the victim. The statement in the Bible, "An eye for an eye, and a tooth for a tooth," literally means that if I hit someone, he has the right to hit me back!

The Justice System 119

This is the only reasonable consequence of abusing another person. So if I hit you in the face, you have the right to retaliate, though you may refrain.

Then there's the matter of spousal abuse. A domestic scenario could read like this. A man is married with two children. His wife drinks, parties and dates other men. Obviously, she is not caring properly for her children and the house.

One day her husband snaps. He beats her, so she calls "911." She tells police that her husband occasionally spanks his kids when they misbehave. He is thrown in jail on charges of spousal- and child abuse! Since he owns a small business, he must temporarily close his doors. He also loses key employees. With the help of the prosecuting attorney, his wife files a law suit. He is convicted of wife and child abuse. She is granted a divorce. She is awarded the house, alimony and child support. His company folds while serving a three-year sentence. He loses his house, children and visitor rights. His ex-wife gets the house. She continues having parties and fools around. She also gets the kids. He decides not to return to work due to bitterness. He cannot ease the pain from the injustice. He feels that his wife and the system have committed a crime against him. The ex-inmate keeps muttering to himself, "I have lost everything because of them. My life has been stolen from me. My parole officer wants me to start working. Only problem is that most of my money will go to my Ex-wife to support her boyfriends and her partying. Forget it! I'd rather live on the street." That's how the story goes for many homeless people.

Ridiculous laws lead many law-abiding citizens down the path of dissention. They break new laws to reaffirm their independence and strength because they desire to exercise freedom and responsibility over their own lives. Many of these people chose not to violate the law before the legislation was enacted. But now they freely break the law. Does this sound like you?

Immoral persons in the President Bill Clinton case are former special prosecutor Kenneth Star and the Republicans. If they are not immoral, the system is! If they can prosecute the president for his sexuality, what about the rest of us? The question now becomes: "Who are 'they?'" Who creates these ridiculous laws that undermine the real morality? Ask yourself, "Who is making this country into a crazy prosecutorial society?" There is always a more vocal opinion against something than for something. For example, people are more likely to cast their vote against Clinton instead of for him; even if the silent majority approves! We have passed so many laws that everyone—no matter what their background—breaks some of them. Passing this legislation destroys society's fabric by creating an atmosphere where nothing is real! This forces intelligent people to stoop to a level of complete stupidity! The Clinton case was an excellent example of how a stupid law like sexual harassment blows up in everyone's face. The idiocy level reaches a crescendo by jeopardizing the entire economy because the president had a blow job!

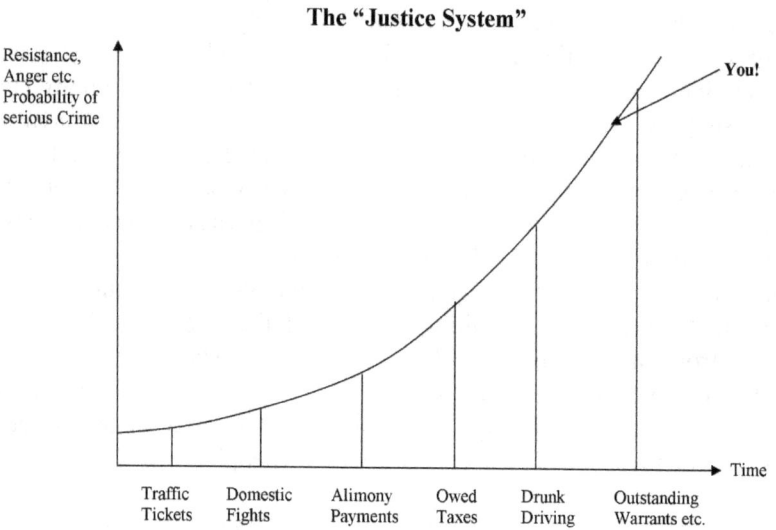

Figure 13
The "Justice System"

Government as we know it is rapidly self-destructing! We should delight that Clinton became a US president. No, he wasn't perfect in the White House. He is just another human being like the rest of us. The antithesis of Clinton would be someone who is perfectly dehumanizing to others. I would be extremely concerned if any president was like this.

When we have so many of these laws and regulations, how can we know when we are doing something illegal? If we dig long and hard enough into anyone's life, we find that most of them have committed illegal and immoral acts! Only random circumstances and bad luck decide who goes to jail and who is in trouble with the law. It's only a matter of time before you will get in trouble, too. Do we really want a society where everyone lives in fear? Disgustingly, this is where we are heading in the US. This makes no sense!

We also pass laws that presume certain assumptions about reality. Normally, they reflect the middle- or upper classes. Often, these laws are out of touch and discriminate against the poor and lower classes.

An important principle to remember is: When we pass too many laws that violate reasonableness and justice, we are creating a situation that's usually just as bad. We might even create a society worse than anarchy!

Most everyone protects their own self interests. Therapists, doctors, police, judges and other professionals convince people that their skills and talents are indispensable. Many times these professionals exacerbate our predicaments by convincing us—through the power of suggestion—that we need their skills.

Many Norwegian teen-agers believe that having sex involves some resistance from the female, who is playing "hard-to-get." Today, Norway has numerous rapes—just like the US—because America largely influences this Scandinavian country and the rest of the world. I now realize that what we call rape in today's society is inaccurate. We are taught that it is normal when boys experience some initial resistance from women before a sexual act is performed. Now, the US has convinced Norwegians that it is rape. Hence, rapes are skyrocketing in most countries.

The generation before mine—before recent legislation—did not believe in divorce. Abuse was virtually nonexistent. I know this because hundreds of my friends who I grew up with tell me so!

Sexual-harassment laws create an incentive for women to desire sexual molestation. Why? This gives women power, and maybe even a lot of money from the so-called criminal and the government. Women also blackmail and threaten the perpetrator. Remember when Monica

Lewinsky—one of President Clinton's playthings—saved her semen-stained dress? The victim needs the victimizer. Both of them get a sense of purpose by doing it to each other.

Now, many Americans resemble the average German under Adolf Hitler when they look the other way. Some even refuse to believe that Germany committed atrocities against the Jews. Are you blind? The US Justice System is in many ways more inhumane than a German prison during World War II.

My grandfather, Josef Larsson, was one of the unfortunate victims. Germans rounded him up and threw him in a concentration camp from 1940 to 1945. He endured terrible isolation during his first year. Then he was released into the general prison population with a life sentence. Miraculously, he survived four years of forced labor.

Some US prisoners fare even worse. Years of isolation drives them insane. Though many do little wrong to land them in prison, acts they commit in prison result in isolation. Years of solitary confinement drives them insane. 13 percent of the US prison population is put into isolation as a punishment for their original crime, and another huge percentage of people are also put into isolation for crimes committed after they'd been incarcerated. Wake up, please! The next person in this horror chamber could be you or somebody in your family. And remember, nobody is perfect, not even the presidents.

Our society is creating this paranoia about sex and relationships. The Emperor's New Clothes is the epitome of the Clinton-Lewinsky scandal: Suspects and witnesses predictably answer investigators' questions by responding in a way they believe is expected.

Politicians don't fare much better. They run the other way when another politician is indicted. This choice is a worse moral act than Clinton's indiscretions. How often do you vote for a politician who, rather than legislating his conscience, reflects the mob-mentality idiocy that the mass media generates at the beck-and-call of multi-national corporations and lobbyists?

People defend themselves by accusing the opposition of that for which they are guilty.

An example of this disgusting behavior is when fascists accuse President Obama of being a fascist! Psychologically, this is a classical example of a person projecting his or her guilt on someone else.

There is nothing more traumatizing to a human being than realizing the inevitable death of themselves and their loved ones. Normally this awareness is awakened when a person is 8 or 9 years old. Sometimes this even causes extreme fear and discomfort.

All human beings go through this trauma. But eventually they become happy, well-adjusted people without interference or counseling from therapists. Other traumas in life pale in comparison because most of them have little impact on a person's ability to live a happy and fulfilling life.

Traumas like sexual molestation and domestic violence pale in comparison to one's own death. But incarceration is even more traumatizing than becoming aware of your eventual death.

If people need counseling, then everyone released from jail should get help. In fact, trauma can enrich a person's life and nurture greater wisdom.

Lying to the Congress is regarded as a severe crime. However, lying to the American people should be considered even more serious.

A hundred years ago, crime was very uncommon. In fact, criminals became legends. However, after passing and implementing these laws, we are destroying personal morality. So now we have ongoing crime in most neighborhoods because personal responsibility—through legislation, law enforcement and punishment—has been destroyed.

A free person chooses to be good! Forcing people through legislation to be good offsets the balance and encourages people to be bad. A person always tries to achieve a new equilibrium; the bad magnifies because they are forced to be good. This is how the Taoists look at it. They are basically saying that we as human beings are manifestations of the yin and yang, the masculine and feminine. All thought and language are based on something that is relative. Something can only be explained in relation to its opposite since everything manifests itself as the opposite.

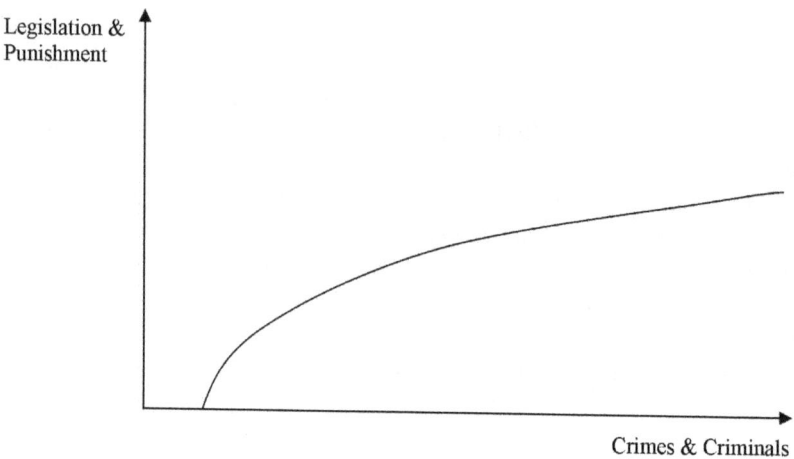

**Figure 14
Legislation & Crime**

Legislating and forcing people to be good skews the normal balance of good and bad, and of creating and destroying. The individual becomes bad and destructive. The more goodness society imposes, the more an individual becomes bad because we always try to balance good, bad, creation and destruction. However, a free individual will choose the stronger force of goodness and creation.

There is a misguided assumption that causes people to believe that horrific crimes will be committed if we do not have legislation against it. Fundamentally there is no such thing as safely and security. This is an illusion. There is nothing that can prevent somebody from walking into your home at anytime and shoot you. It is not happening because we have a law against it. The reason that nobody walks into your house to shoot you is because 99.9999% of human beings will not do that act. For somebody to walk into your house and shoot you it has to be a moment of insanity. That person needs to be treated as an insane individual. The mindset of the individual who would commit such an act has been created by the environment the person lives in. A society that produces such an individual who is capable of committing such an act must change.

Today, there is irrefutable evidence that the justice system creates the criminal and the crime.

As this is being written, there is a census being performed in the US creating temporary opportunities for work for millions of Americans. However, everybody who applies to be a census worker is subject to background check by the FBI. There are so many felons and people with criminal records in the United States that 1.5 million applicants are being prevented from working as census workers. Many of these people might have committed a minor offense years ago. They are now being slapped in the face by society again. This causes incredible anger and opposition to the society. Potentially, this will cause many individuals to commit another criminal act, as revenge. However, it is of course in the interest of the FBI and the justice system—to produce anger and resentment which can turn into criminal acts and more criminals.

The more crime and criminals that can be produced by the FBI and the justice system the more the FBI and the justice system can expand their power and influence.

This will increase the power and the influence of the justice system and the FBI. So it is in their self interest to dig up as much dirt as possible on every individual and then turn that dirt against them. How do you think these people feel, when they are trying to work, and then they are not allowed to do it? That would make any citizen who has any morality left feel tremendous anger and resentment toward society. The justification for this policy would be that society needs to protect the citizens against "criminals" and cannot allow "criminals" to knock on doors and obtain the census information. However, the problem is deeper than that—the real reason for having this policy is a cover for the politicians to not being confronted in the future by the magnifiers (media) that one census worker did something criminal in the course of working for the census office. This "perfection" demonstrates that policies created by the politicians is only to benefit them, without regard to its effect on the society overall and the 1.5 million people who were rejected and their feelings.
What makes this even more hair-raising is that you are not allowed access to your own records, hence you have no way to defend yourself against this hugely discriminatory act by the FBI. This does not only

cause anger but a sense of complete helplessness. It is also a fact that the FBI only keeps negative records about individuals and they will keep them FOREVER. Even if you are mistakenly arrested, your record at the FBI is only of the arrest and not of the mistake. So, in accordance to FBI records you are forever condemned to a criminal even if you were mistakenly arrested.

This violates any reasonable morality and sense of humanity.

An organization like the FBI is allowed to commit immoral acts and crimes against humanity without any punishment. But we, as individuals, can be mistakenly arrested and punished for the rest of our lives without having the opportunity to know what our records are and no means of defending ourselves. The observation needs to be made—what the individual did of being mistakenly arrested, has no moral equivalent in what the FBI do to that individual. Obviously, the only morality the well-meaning can understand has to do with your sexuality. When the politicians, who proclaim to be holier than thou go out for entertainment at sadomasochistic bondage strip clubs—there is nothing wrong with that—it only becomes wrong when the same people are passing legislation preventing the rest of us from doing the same. It's not that the rest of us would be that interested, because if you've seen one of the acts, you've seen them all. In a truly free society, a person would have these experiences as young adults or even as teenagers. They would by the time they are in their 40s, 50s or 60s find that this kind of entertainment isn't worth the money. This shows such an immature and infantile mindset from people who are set to rule that it is scary. That is the problem.

According to a New York Times article dated April 20, 2010, there are "nearly 50 million Americans with arrest or conviction on record". That's approximately 20% of the US population. The percentage is much higher among males.

If you calibrate for the groups in society who are likely to have a criminal record, the percentage among males and especially blacks and Hispanics are much higher—this figure may be as high as 50%. The fact is that the US government and justice system have declared war on its own citizens. The question becomes when are the citizens right and the government wrong? Where is the cross-over point where the citizens are right and the government is wrong? When has "normal" become "criminal"?

The Justice System 127

If we take into account everybody who has committed crimes according to the laws, and were not discovered, we can probably safely say that everybody in the US is a criminal. Then the question becomes maybe there is something wrong with the justice system, and not with the people.

The Wild West had so little crime that when it was committed, the person or people involved became legends. An example would be Billie the Kid. In fact many of the settlers in the west did not even own a gun. The explosion in crime has always been synchronized with unjust laws, as the prohibition in the 1920s and the explosion in crime for the last 40 years. It always happens in parallel with the increase in legislation and the expansion of law enforcement.

A fundamental principle can be formulated from logic but also from history that: the "unjust reduction of freedom leads to an increase in crime." In other words, the more reduction in freedom, the more crime.

16
Personal Responsibility and Punishment

Morality, responsibility, wisdom which has been created by freedom through the ages is rapidly being dismantled in the modern society in the name of protection and security.

In freedom, people have to choose to be moral and follow the "10 commandments" in order for survival. In this process, an environment for the advancement of the human intellect takes place. Freedom forces people to make independent choices, take responsibility for them and gather information and seeking the truth in order to make the best choices for themselves. Freedom is what cultivates and educates people.

By legislating morality, the opportunity for personal growth is taken away from the individual. Today, the threat of punishment is the "force behind morality", not personal freedom and the desire to do the right things. This constellation undermines the development of man to evolve morally.

There is reason to believe that women are programmed to believe in protection and safety. For them, through millions of years of evolution, the protection, safety and security for them was real through the continuous and many times 24 hours a day seven days a week protection and surveillance by their mates. That belief is now projected on the society and the government, even if protection by them is an illusion.

Women seek security and protection and have been seeking that from the government during the last century, causing the decline of freedom; however the only one who can really provide protection is the man in her life. He will, in general, defend his woman and children with his own life, if they are threatened. Security and protection by the government is an illusion and is completely ineffective. This understanding is essential in order to return the society to freedom again.

The 20th century has created the government into the "male" supported by the female through her vote and support of security and safety communicated to the people by the mass media. This has been causing the destruction of individualism and personal responsibility creating "flock behavior" by the people.

In order to create "freedom" for men, women and children, the society has destroyed the family structure. The society has decided that it is more important to "protect" women and children from the "evil" of fathers and to destroy their role as the "head" of the family. The society has become and implemented the role of the "father" as the new "head" of the family and in order to do so, has criminalized and prosecuted the "fathers."

The ability to punish and reward within the family for disciplinary purposes has been continuously destroyed and replaced by the justice system. The ability to punish and reward within the family is nothing as compared with the draconian, inhuman monster called the justice system. To educate another person, educates both people involved. In other words, it educates the teacher as well as the student. This is in essences the relationship between male, female, adult and child, and other relationships of dominance and submission.

Punishment/Justice System

- Condemnation for life as a felon
- No opportunities
- Hopelessness
- Lack of freedom
- Punishment for years
- For life or death
- Loss of sanity
- No mercy
- No love
- Costs billions of dollars
- Etc.

Family System

- Rapid, only lasting seconds or minutes at the most
- Designed to correct behavior for the better
- Very little loss of freedom
- Done with love and compassion

- Immediate and effective
- Manageable
- Does not cost anything
- Etc.

The social experiment of the last 50 years of removing the role of the father from the family and removing the responsibility for the upbringing of the children and the ability of the father to reward and punish his children and his wife is destroying the family structure and morality. By removing the phrase "to honor and obey" from the wedding vows, we've done incalculable damage to the family structure and in turn to the society at large.

If we restore the natural relationship between man and woman, sexuality will become heterosexual again as woman will find their power through their femininity and the male through their responsibility and love for his wife and offspring.

Pointers

- Freedom has been destroyed, that is why nobody takes responsibility for anything and risk is not allowed—that is why we are suing each other.
- In order to have the positive, we also have to have the negative. = freedom = foster responsibility = precursor for growth of the individual = growth and evolution of the society.
- Humans are both constructive and destructive in their nature however; the constructive is the stronger force.
- The society needs teachers and leaders; not only followers and we are becoming a nation of followers.
- All the regulations lead to the dummification of the people, because they no longer have to think and make their own decisions. To become an adult is to take responsibility and to start to think. There is reason to believe that an overly safe and overly regulated society prevents the people's intellects to advance from childhood to adulthood. The infantile attitudes are being preserved.
- The whole drug situation for young adults is for parents and especially for single mothers, by reporting their children to the

police is preventing the children from breaking away from home and it gives the parents the "mother", a sense of being able to discipline their kids by using the system. This will obviously postpone adulthood in the youngsters and continue to dummify the children.

- When your freedom or the feel of it, is being taken away from you, you want to do exactly what caused you to lose your freedom in the first place in order to reassert your sense of freedom. For Example: President Clinton, getting involved with Monica, at a time when the Paula Jones court case was running. When even the President reacts according to this principle there is reason to believe that all of us would react the same way. This is why, when you pass laws that violate natural laws; we are actually promoting the behavior that we are trying to eradicate.
- It has been a catastrophic decline in "boys" motivations and performance in school over the last 30 years. This is understandable, as boys motivation is driven by the ambition where his number one goal is to find a wife and have a family as a man's ambition is not driven as much for himself but his ability to take care of someone else. This ambition is instilled in him by his father. Too many boys grow up without fathers and legislation and culture has over the last 30 years undermined his ability and desire to start a family. This caused by the continuous promotion of hostility against the male, and to make it a virtue among women to leave their husbands and boyfriends. It was therefore great to see and touching that a school in Berkeley CA, is going to welcome boisterousness, desire for exploration and masculine energy in their students. This is a very important step in the right direction for the US to foster a new generation of entrepreneurs and scientists.

17
Mass Media Distorts Reality and Creates Fear

Present-day news coverage targets unusual or abnormal events in our everyday lives. The news media's pervasiveness subtly creates a new reality for us as reporters scurry to find attention-grabbing stories. We are led to believe that this media-created reality is the truth. In actuality, we have lost touch with the real reality. For example, every day we pass hundreds of thousands of cars going back and forth to work. Yet, we never witness a crime. Meanwhile, the media leads us to believe that we are living in a criminally-violent society. The result is that we live a life of fear as we embrace unreality.

When a woman kills her babies—an occasional, unusual occurrence—television, newspapers, radio and the internet rush to report the story. This criminal act is so extraordinary that we fail to comprehend that we are more likely to be struck by lightning. Instead, we fearfully take extra precautions with our own children.

This shocking news profoundly affects our perception of reality—actually unreality—and ultimately creates harsher legislation. The media proselytizes us to believe that certain crimes are out of control. With this unreal mind set, we talk to our friends and neighbors to convince them—and our legislators—that we need ridiculous laws to combat this heinous, yet infrequent crime. Then the government legislates this felony, making every mother a suspect. Parents eventually lose their rights to raise their children, who are put in foster homes or elsewhere. This horrific choice creates yet another spoke in the Draconian Society's wheel of infinite misery.

Media-created mass hysteria creates runaway mob mentality that is largely unstoppable once it ignites. Our inability to distinguish between a media-created artificial reality and the real reality leaves us in a lurch.

No one dares to argue against this ridiculous legislation because they fear someone will accuse them of immorality and bad citizenry.

However, if we allow this imperfection to exist—acknowledging that this crime seldom occurs—we prevent incredible fear and misery among the masses.

Media that deceive the public through sensationalism—without placing the news in a statistical framework—should be exposed for fraud. Media that engage in deception should be discredited and loose their credibility in society. They are creating fear and anxiety by distorting reality. They destroy freedom by spurning irrational voting and lawmaking.

The media in the 2002 election earned more than $1 billion from political advertising. No wonder we have a subconscious conspiracy. The mass media incredibly magnifies events by creating mob mentality in its readers and viewers through dehumanization. An example is when the press victimizes the accused in criminal cases. By this act, the media is guilty of the Emperor's New Clothing Syndrome, magnified many times over.

Incredibly horrifying and lengthy sentences for crimes are designed to shock and thrill viewers by creating a voracious appetite for the media's (read: the magnifiers) sensational stories. Had it not been for the magnifiers, no one would really care that much. We would live in a more humanitarian, just and free society. Remember: The mass media's sensation-making news creates spontaneous mobs for causes that emanate from unreality.

When talk shows like Dr. Phil help people divorce or end relationships, the media finds this newsworthy because this fits society's norm. The media captures reader interest by reporting on the abnormal. For example, if 25 percent of US couples choose marriage, television shows spring up to convince partners to remain together. In fact, Dr. Phil supports divorce less than the talk shows in the '80s and '90s. As divorces drop, TV shows increase on divorce benefits. More divorces generate more shows about staying married. This is another example of how news-making justifies itself on moral grounds to support situations rising out of the self interest of a person or organization.

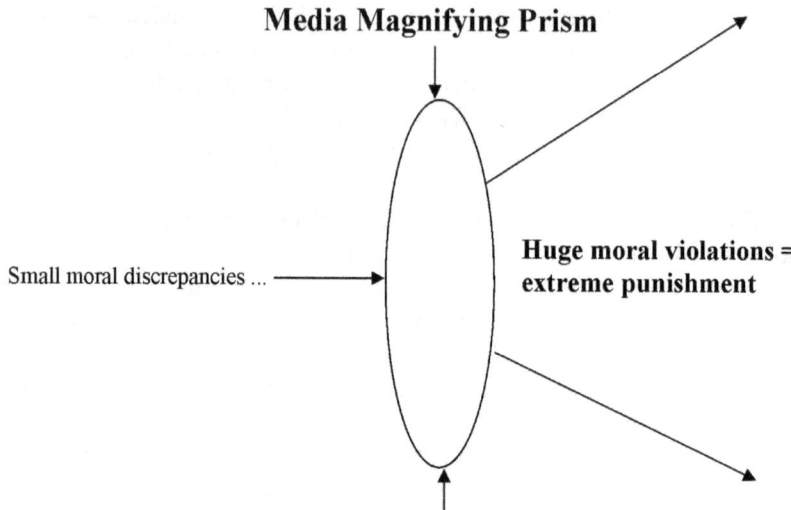

Figure 15
The mob and the magnification prism

We can express this in the following equation: Small moral discrepancies committed by people reported as mortal crimes by the magnifiers; the media plus politicians acting out of self interest; create mobification of the people; magnified into huge moral violations; laws passed with extreme punishment.

It is this morbid mass media preoccupation and the "experts" telling people that they suffer from depression and mental problems that are largely the cause. When people seek help, they increasingly relinquish their freedom. They establish a dependent relationship with the government and quazi-government entities. Government persuasion of dependency through the mass media permeates society. The media sells this recipe to the public.

One of the subconscious conspiracies between the media and therapists—making you much worse—tells us constantly that we need to write down our fears. Instead, we should do the exact opposite.

Therapists unconsciously conspire with media-based self interest in cooperation with the government to make us stupid and fearful. It is in the self interest of the media to support the maximization of what's criminal and the punishment of such crimes in order to increase the impact and importance of their news stories.

Media is showing its real self interest by scaring, intimidating and prosecuting and being the instigator of the mob or group behavior.

The problem with the mass media is that it highlights the unusual, perverse, and weird, and rewards destruction, negativism and the strange.

An ad from the California Health Department against tobacco used a cartoon like a crocodile to be tobacco manufacturers. That actually makes the tobacco manufacturers more interesting for children. Any idiot looking at that ad would know that it does the exact opposite as to what it is intended. This is another proof of government agencies creating the problem they are set out to solve.

Good Morning America March 8, 2001 7:10am
In talking about the shooting at a school in Santa Anna, California, Don Quijane's interview with two friends of the "shooter" is an act of blatant self interest by the mass media.

Society has all these problems with kids and teenagers because of legislation that prevents parents from disciplining their kids. This leads to the complete destruction of the family unit. Continued attack especially on the male by the mass media leads to legislation that undermines the father's authority in the family. The government, CHILD PROTECTIVE SERVICES (CPS) and the mass media have to take the blame for a situation completely out of control. "People love their pets because they have complete control of their lives (life and death)"

When a person goes to counseling for trauma it solidifies the psychological trauma and makes it worse.

Mass media forces "officials" to over react to crimes or "wrong doings" by creating a cover for them if something should happen and to be politically correct.

People, when "sold" by the mass media or under influence of authority are acting and saying what they think is expected from them, not what they think might be right or wrong.

"Do not let your child or teenager sniff what you have under the sink! The most dangerous drugs are what you have under the sink!" This was a "well-meaning" and "moral" ad on TV. Outrageous! It is designed to promote this kind of drug use among kids so the agency that made the ad can get more to do and funding. Under the umbrella of morality they are seeking their own self interest with no regard to children and teenagers. It's the same as the tobacco companies advertising for you to quit smoking. These ads are reminding people to pick up a cigarette and smoke.

Since the mass media reports what is not normal and peculiar. They also inadvertently reward wrong decisions and behavior. This especially manifests itself to give recognition and coverage to any legislation or proposed legislation that in the most blatant way violates the natural desire for freedom in people.

All the talk shows are teaching girls and women to leave their boyfriends and husbands. "Get pregnant, but thank God you left your husband," and "now" I'm back in school and I definitely got rid of my boyfriend" (applause from the audience).

How does society expect to get normal heterosexual relationships to last when it has become a virtue for women to leave their husbands and boy friends?

The news media is reporting increases in alcohol and other criminal drug use by minors. It is in the self interest of the agencies involved to create the statistics to get more influence, power and funding. Just the act of getting "better" and more accurate registration of a "violation" will in itself show an increase in "violations". Also, the definitions of what constitutes violations are changing the statistics. Of course, the news media will dramatically report this "negative" story.

The TV shows 48 Hours, 20/20 and Dateline started out as good news programs. Eventually, they all slid into stories about criminality.

The mass media have created a giant "Emperor's New Clothes" syndrome. Everything is magnified beyond reason. Nobody dares to tell the truth. All of it is in the interest of politicians, government agencies and mass media. The result is blatant violations of human rights and the complete disregard of reality. This magnification creates the horror of life time imprisonment of people where their violations may not deserve punishment at all.

Not only do the media magnify events, but it also magnifies the resulting victimization of the victims. This leads to severe damage to victims rather than what would have happened if the event would have been minimized and treated as a bad experience for the enrichment and maturation of the intellect.

What is happening is as bad as or worse than what happened under Hitler's Germany! Rather than having a dictator such as Hitler—demonizing a group of people in the society—we have a (sub) conscious conspiracy today between the mass media and the government and its agencies. They label and demonize groups in the "free societies".

If the prison turn over rate (average) in the US is 1 year, after 10 years, 30 million people would have been sitting in jail for 1 year. Even if we account for repetitive offenders, and calibrate for long term sentencing, chances are that we are coming up to millions of victims of the system. Example: The War against Drugs, which is victimless crimes, the mass media and the government have artificially labeled and demonized a group in the society that can now be prosecuted and incarcerated with draconian sentencing for years. This shows that a democratic and "free" society can identify a common denominator among people, label them by passing a law against what they do, and demonize them just like Hitler did with the Jews. The only difference between Hitler and what's happening now is that Hitler killed them off rather than incarcerate them.

Mob mentality created and fueled by the mass media and government/politicians reaches its peak within the prison system itself where the condemnation of "crimes" is the strongest among the lowest ranking people, namely the prison population.

The most tolerant people have the highest education. They are the most successful people! The least tolerant people have the lowest education. They are the least successful people!

Segment on ABC April 14, 2000
This story was about a 7 year old plotting to kill classmates. This news broadcast sells the idea to other kids that plotting something

criminal and horrible is a way for them to get attention. In fact, it is a way for parents, officials and the media to get attention as well.

The propaganda programs on TV every Memorial Day for killings are totally obscene. It's nothing more than a glorification of crimes against humanity.

The reason whales die is because of over crowding. According to some environmentalists, mankind should commit collective suicide to save the earth because our presence is destroying the earth.

The Elian Gonzalez case is a typical example of media and government collaboration to increase each other's importance and value at the expense of society and individuals directly involved in the case. The case with the Cuban boy sent back to his father in Cuba, and the subsequent vote, is a typical example of how government/media sensation creates mayhem and crisis with demonstrations and protests.

Mental care is a typical example of where the media can find an endless supply of horror and abuse to report. We all agree that it is wrong to abuse mental care patients. However, we would have to spend billions and billions to control and to avoid it and not even then, can we avoid it completely. We can not do this as a society, we can only do so much—so we have to establish strict policies, guidelines and complete transparency with reasonable oversight. Then, let it be and trust that abuse is minimized.

On the TV program 20/20 July 12, 2000
A segment was shown on TV about women in the Ku Klux Klan and how they recruit other women. It also had interviews with some of the leaders. It is nothing the KKK could have done—even with unlimited advertising money—to forward their cause more effectively than what 20/20 did. The show even encouraged people to go to their website to learn more. This is how TV creates even bigger problems in the society because of self interest.

Everything featured on TV promotes what they are showing. Example: Dateline has a feature about plastic surgery for teenagers. Then they conduct a survey where 73 percent of adults disapprove.

Mass Media Distorts Reality and Creates Fear

Showing this automatically promotes the desire for more plastic surgery among teenagers more that any advertising that business could have done for itself. What drives the teenagers is the opposition among youth against authority and the desire for self assertion.

Phillip Morris Ad: Telling people that they are educating shop owners to recognize kids who are less than 18 years of age. Signs showing "No sale to minors"! This ad sells tobacco to minor and kids more than any other advertising. The allure of smoking for kids is that you have to be an adult to smoke. This ad plays directly on kids desire to become adults, while Phillip Morris appears to be responsible and performing a public service.

Mass media, especially TV, magnifies regular human endeavor into catastrophic events and also magnifies the tragedy or problem a person(s) is facing. Example: Single mother gets drunk. Neighbor calls police. Police come. Mother gets angry. Police arrest mother. TV reports the incidence. Child is taken into custody. Mother charged with resisting arrest, child neglect and endangerment. Mother looses child and goes to jail. Mother gets out from jail. Mother has nothing to live for. Mother drinks even more, starts taking drugs. Mother is arrested again. Now mother's and child's lives are destroyed. TV reports and now the case are magnified even more. It becomes a high profile case and mother gets condemned by the community. The punishment becomes more severe. The child is in a foster home! Child grows up and becomes a criminal too. This sequence of events is, in essence, the same for all reporting about "crime" and/or "immoral" behavior and must be broken!

Ask yourself, who is the real guilty party, creating this incredible misery? The answer: The mass media and the justice system.

Now you ask for perfection from an imperfect human. We create huge problems that cost society billions of dollars for virtually nothing and lead to incredible misery. This cycle must be stopped! Every little moral wrinkle is magnified into a major crime by the mass media and justice system. This actually inflicts a greater crime on the person who was responsible for the wrinkle than the "crime" this person committed. Mob hysteria, created by the mass media and the justice system, has no mercy.

Segments you see on talk shows and news programs about sexual abuse will be looked upon in the same way in the future as we now look at the era of McCarthyism.

The news media perpetuates the myth about "closure and revenge", even portraying punishment and a guilty verdict as if it will bring the murder victim back from the dead. The Yosemite case is a typical example where a person is seeking attention and commits murders to get it. The mass media has created this so, in a way, they could be held responsible for the murders. This is a typical example of how the news media, out of self interest, creates a society of shock and fear. The news media is constantly looking for news worthy stories that are, by definition, what is not normal but perverse and unusual without regard to true morality and dignity.

The mass media causes mass psychosis. Reality has become artificial as projected by the media. News is, by definition, the exception from the normal reality of everyday. This exceptional reality has become the "normal" reality that is leading to completely unnatural behaviors and opinions. Opinions are formed from exceptions to reality and from second party accounts for commercial purpose that totally distorts reality, an extremely dangerous development.

Your life has been continuously diminished with the encroaching mass media and, in turn, the rise of famous, rich people and politicians. The media has taken your life away from you and replaced it with a "surrogate" media—fueled—life where you are living your life through those people as a spectator!

Recordings in the media

One of the big problems today is the possibility to record everything you said or did and it will stay as public record—which could be used against you at any point in the future. This is completely unfair to the individual and is another reason that we need to create a super tolerant society and to recognize that people over a lifetime will change as they mature. What a person said and meant as a 20 year old may have no relationship to what that person says and does today. What a person says and does today has to completely overrule what the person did or said in the past. Revelations and changes of opinion can happen extremely rapidly. Deep insights which have a profound impact on a person's opinion can be achieved in the shortest of moments. This is especially true among active and thinking individuals.

When the real truth becomes evident in a person's mind and it is not in alignment with the official view, and especially if the truth seen is the extreme opposite of the official view, then, the person who sees the truth becomes afraid of the truth and will then take a neutral position and no longer speak the truth out of fear for personal consequences. At the moment of seeing the truth, extreme courage is needed to speak the truth in public. A person who is heroic will—and a person who is a coward will not. That is the distinction between heroism and cowardice. However, that moment of truth is the opportunity to achieve true greatness in the individual. There is a very strong incentive in the news media to "not get to the truth". As soon as the truth has been stated and acknowledged, the "news" stops being "news". If they arrive at the truth, everybody involved, the interviewer, the interviewees and the experts would no longer be in the public eye with the story and it is felt as a loss to everybody involved with an interest in the story. That is why the most logical solution to a problem and the truth is not being expressed and reported by the news media. In fact, many times when the "truth" is close to being expressed it is almost always being diverted, and the news is left in controversy, rather than going down the path of truth and a conclusion is made. The conclusion is avoided to keep the "news" going forward. Most of the time, the news producers will bring in people with the most "outlandish" ideas on the subject matter, just to keep the news and the controversy going forward. They also do it to maximize the "entertainment" value of the segment—as most news shows have become "show biz". There is nothing wrong with making news entertaining, however, the viewer needs to know and understand that it is "show biz". What is wrong is to manipulate the news in such a way that the "truth" or most logical conclusions are not being expressed. The news media are just reporting what the news is in the most self serving way possible.

When the news media interview someone for their opinion, they should always include an informed regular citizen that has no vested interest in the issue being discussed! Neither personally nor to promote nor protect their own profession or role in the society. Asking a lawyer about legal issues is wrong without somebody else being objective. The same by asking a doctor about a medical issue, because they act out of self interest so answers to questions are biased. This would be a major move toward objectivity and more truth through actual reality in reporting!

There are great exceptions to the sensation making mass media and their journalists such as: Charlie Rose, Bill Moyers, Keith Olbermann, Fareed Zakaria and many more that are fact finding and are seeking the "truth". They know themselves who they are!

History, as it is written and recorded, is also a story of the unusual, perverted, and inhuman. What is mostly being recorded is destruction and what is not normal and good. So we are led to believe that the nature of man as recorded in history is brutal, competitive and destructive. This is as untrue as the reporting by the mass media today. The real human history is about cooperation, exploring and creating.

Pointers

- The purpose of media can be the informer and control mechanism in society and can largely replace most government control agencies.
- Media brainwashing leads to a belief in an abnormal reality—causing people to act accordingly and form opinion and votes based upon this media-created abnormal reality.
- The news media can take on the role of evaluating and disseminating information about products and the hazards associated with those products.
- Dynamics of the news media in itself as a profit-making business will secure its impartiality to information and evaluation of products.
- We no longer need the evaluating and regulating agencies as society used to.
- This will lead to self regulation of companies since negative publicity should be devastating to companies and to manufacturers who are producing inefficient or harmful products.

Mass Media Distorts Reality and Creates Fear 143

- Research in hypnosis and the results that can be achieved through hypnosis has shown its significance as creating any kind of reality in the minds of people as well as the planting of false memories.
- The mass media are selling issues like "abuse" to the people out of self-serving interest to engage people in issues, while the truth is that their freedom is taken away. The paradox is that the society—government—gets more abusive and controlling. However, the path to gain control over the people is always justified on moral grounds masked with the idea of protection and safety.
- The same emotion that causes sadistic glee in other people's misery of convictions, that same emotion can also be promoted to feel glee and a sense of power over victims of crime. We are programmed, through propaganda, to feel good about lynching and jailing. This is the ultimate mob mentality—created by the mass media. Both ways of feeling glee are totally sick and perverted.
- People do and say what is expected of them, especially when confronted by authority and/or mass media. For example: The McMartin case. The interaction between accusers and mass media created a frenzy in the mob about child abuse. A very interesting experiment was done when people were dressed up in doctor's lab coats. They asked people to turn a dial to inflict pain on a person. 80 percent would turn it up to very high pain inflicted on the subject being under the supervision of authority.
- Society is suffering from "The Emperor's New Clothes syndrome" supported by the mass media where everybody has to have and is "forced" unconsciously to have the "politically correct opinion"!
- Real record of criminal on TV—it was concluded why this person should still be out, did molest a child, everybody discusses it. Man will get life in jail, under three-strike law. TV report did not mention how serious the crime really was. Nobody dared question throwing this man in jail for life.
- The sexual hysteria ties in with the Gulf War Syndrome in this country. The same mass psychosis is behind both. The media in this country has brainwashed itself into extreme "political correctness".

- The "Religious Right" is responsible for many of the hate crimes by virtue of singling out groups of people with the "wrong" life styles or beliefs. This is supported by politicians and mass media.
- The most immoral act in today's society is to sacrifice a human life through the focus and stories in the mass media under the disguise of morality. In other words, the mass media destroys human lives for the sake of entertainment. Obviously, the destruction of human life is the ultimate entertainment for the masses.

The Internet has changed everything:
- Opportunity for mass distribution of objective information.
- Opportunity for the people to directly vote or to express their will in the political process.
- Mass media to educate the public and to show more than one side of an issue. The Monica Lewinsky Case clearly showed that the politicians are not task oriented, but people oriented. The political talk that President Clinton had destroyed his power is a purely people oriented statement. Clinton could still work for and present issues or tasks that are objectively the right thing to do.
- The TV news caster goes on and on about human tragedy, not even knowing that he is contributing to the tragedy. Mass media and politicians are completely underestimating the intelligence and knowledge of the citizens. Do you really believe that you can get away with these lies and abuse? The only thing most of the mass media can do is to report sensational "facts". There is no thinking, no interpretations, and no explanations.
- The TV and mass media are turning the people of the world into a homogeneous and mindless mob, creating mass psychosis that manifests in the inability to distinguish fiction from reality.
- Everybody in the western world means pretty much the same as they mean on TV. TV is trying to perfect any issues and at the same time focuses only on news of the unnatural. Hence, opinions and meanings are formed on the basis of a completely distorted reality. This is one of the primary reasons that society is becoming less free and more dysfunctional and creates the

problems they are trying to prevent. The news media will go ahead and interview somebody with an extreme position on a subject. Otherwise it will not be news. Then we, the viewers, think that this position is the right one. Especially if this opinion is repeated and substantiated by a law suit or by other similar positions by other people.
- Princess Dianna's death is a manifestation of how the mass media can blow an event completely out of proportion.

New legislation needs to be created to deal with the reality of communications and the mass media:
- Issues may never go away.
- Creates an absolute through recordings.
- Anything can be kept alive in the media.
- The recordings of what somebody said at which time creates inhuman absolutes. Through modern recordings, time will never erase it.

18
The Impossibility of Protection and Safety

Security and safety do not exist.

To provide protection and safety assume that society can prosecute somebody for a crime that has not taken place. Punishment can only take place after the crime has been committed. To prosecute a person before they have committed a crime would violate all principles of free speech. Security and safety can only be achieved through 24/7 observation and analysis of every individual. If this is not achieved, there is no safety and security. The government is unable to provide any safety and security for its citizens. For example, a suicide bomber can explode anywhere, any time when people are crowded to maximize damage. If somebody can drive a car anywhere, you could have a huge bomb go off anywhere you park a car. How could anybody prevent that? Even if all people were under surveillance—a mathematical and practical impossibility—a person has to monitor and analyze another person. This means that 75 percent of the population has to be engaged in the continuous monitoring of the remaining 25 percent of the citizens. Even under that scenario, people who would be needed are not enough to create security and protection. Even if 225 million people in the United States, assuming two shifts with 12 hours shifts for each would still have to eat and go to the bathroom under their watch.

An individual who has been given the responsibility for a "Weapons of Mass Destruction" (WMD) could in a split second use that weapon. Not only that, but everybody has to be observed 24 hours a day. This puts 225 million people in the most boring and mind-numbing job of observing another person 12 hours a day. What is being observed and analyzed has to be acted upon to prevent something from happening. This means that we have to take another big chunk out of the last 25 percent to be the enforcers because they have to be within no distance at all from any citizen to prevent their actions. This simple logical analysis shows that security, prevention and safety are a completely logical and mathematical impossibility.

The goal of safety and security has been established by the government and sold to its citizens for only one purpose: to maximize their own power and privileges.

The Impossibility of Protection and Safety

Protection and security were the arguments of organized crime and the mafia to "tax" people. It is a direct parallel to the government and what is happening. In fact, "organized crime" and the mafia was the formation of government within another government. There is very little difference between them. Of course the government in power will diligently fight another government within its borders. The question is: How can we create a society where both are prevented from taking advantage of the people? A major difference is the election of politicians to "serve" the people. However, if the election process is flawed, self interest among the politicians becomes the stronger force and the interest of the people suffers. An example of no protection, 98 percent of all alarms are false from home alarm systems. Out of the 2% real ones, 99.9991% of the cases, the burglar has already left because it takes 15-20 minutes before the police can get there. So there is no protection.

The success of protection is inherently dummifying, since you prevented the subject of the protection from the information and the opportunity to make the decisions about the subject matter. In fact, nothing dummifies more than successful protection.

Do you want your child to be a meek and dumb human being? Without the ability later in life to make just, right and logical choices (vote) when they are confronted with something they are unfamiliar with because they have been living in an intellectual vacuum of protection. You can argue that my child should not grow up and become an adult before they need to. However, the very essence of growing up is exposure to information and the gathering of experiences. So, by exposing your child to reality earlier they will mentally grow up faster and they will grow even faster when they become an adult.

The more laws, the more dummification, the more idiocy, and the more laws are needed because the population has gotten too dumb to take care of themselves. So the dummification, of a dictatorship, fascists spiral is developing dumbness out of control by the will and desire of the dummies.

We are discussing idiotic laws to the point that we are no longer thinking why the law was passed in the first place. If we did, we would also be able to calibrate the importance and significance of the law. When you can keep an ultra idiot like Pat Robertson on the air who a few years ago talked about a threat to the US from Canada there must be a lot of ultra idiots around. Reference: The break up of Quebec from the rest of Canada.

Revealing enough, our military cannot even provide security on their own military bases. This is proven by different accounts over the years, including the recent mass-murderer psychiatrist who killed 12 people and injured 30 in Texas on the military base? How can one even believe that the military can provide security for people in Afghanistan and Iraq?

When the military, politicians and police say they are going to provide security—or that they have secured an area—what they really mean is that they are occupying that area. Whenever "security" is mentioned one should immediately exchange that word with "occupying." This world will be much closer to the truth and it will be a profound eye-opener when the same "professionals" who state: "We need to provide security for the Afghan people," said what they really mean: "We will occupy Afghanistan."

Security is only provided and granted by people who decide to live in peace and respect the rights of others.

To monitor our growing population in the US, the question is: *"Who is monitoring our safety and security personnel?"* The percentage of crimes committed by personnel hired for security and safety is probably as bad or even worse as in the general population.

This couple walks into the White House and crashes the party for the prime minister of India. We can not even keep the president secure at the White house, how can we even think about providing security and safety for another country and what about you?

19
The Importance of Democracy and Freedom

We have gone through and finished the fight between labor and capital. The final fight to create lasting prosperity and freedom will be between the people of the world and their governments.

One of the primary reasons that democracy works is that the people are looking for peace and prosperity while leaders of government are looking for power and influence. These fundamentally different goals explain why democracies around the world are creative powers leading to peace and prosperity, while dictatorships lead to destruction, poverty, misery and crimes against humanity.

The reason why so few people vote in the US is that they feel that their vote doesn't make a difference. They have no choice within the two-party system as it has developed into a dictatorship. The election of President Obama was a huge exception to this rule. It represented a major slip by the power structure. This slip was fundamentally based on racism as it now manifests as an attempt to destroy his presidency!

In economics when you have only two suppliers competing in a market, it is called an oligopoly and it has been proven it will gravitate very quickly toward and act the same as a monopoly. It is the same in politics. If you only have two parties, they quickly discover that it is in their interest to work together. The two parties will, over time, develop into a dictatorship just as private enterprise will manifest as a monopoly.

These two parties may appear to be competitive, and at opposites; however, they will have the power to decide what the people may vote on. The self interest of the two parties, with regard to expanding their power, influence and privileges in society overall, becomes the most important determinate of what is being proposed to the voters.

Their "fight" and their actions, goals and purposes will always be justified on moral grounds, even if they are fundamentally destructive. The only thing that matters as it is manifested through their goals, objectives and purposes is expansion of their powers and privileges. They will always be justified on moral grounds and presented as if it is a benefit for the people. The dynamics of any organization as the individual identifies with its goals and aspirations are driven by desire for self realization. As such, the individuals in that organization would have no idea that the organization is fundamentally destructive to the society. They will be completely unable to see it themselves because they are being automatically indoctrinated. If they want to make a career within that organization, they have to align their desire for and path to self realization with the mission, goals and aspirations of that organization.

It is man's desire for self realization that causes him to loose his objectivity about the effects of that organization's actions and their goals and purposes. In fact, it makes him blind to it. That's why you can have millions of people causing incredible destruction to millions of people without realizing what they are doing.

Destroying freedom causes an incredible increase of human misery and even deaths. Conditions such as anorexia, obesity and other psychosomatic diseases are rooted in the preoccupation of the self, induced by boredom, caused by over "protection" and too much "safety and security".

To pass new laws, a 75 percent majority should be required and the laws should only be passed temporarily with a time frame for review. Abolishing laws and regulations should only require a simple majority. The fact that a new law is passed with only a simple majority—with 51 percent—violating the opinion of the remaining 49% is obscene.

Laws passed should not go into effect until a second vote has taken place before a new term for the politicians. This means you can pass a proposition for a law in one Congress but passing and implementing the law must be done with the next Congress and with the same majority. That is, a general election must take place between the first and second vote, and both must be passed with a 75 percent majority. That way the people would have the opportunity to make their opinion count. Laws must be passed one by one (no more riders), meaning, multiple laws cannot be grouped together. This should not include legislation with regard to the economy as swift action is needed to deal with up and down turns.

The government should not be allowed to spend money on advertising. Money given by the government to military agencies, organizations and businesses can also not be spent on advertising. In other words getting money from the government should not be allowed to be spent on advertising. Businesses that have government contracts should not be allowed to be traded on the stock exchange. When money is flowing from the government to the media, they also get control of the media. This path is being opened to promote political issues and to advertise for the government. This is a far more serious issue than legislation against monopolies in the private sector, since the government, its agencies, and the military is a de facto monopoly.

The internet should be kept very vulnerable. That way we will minimize the attack on it. If it is vulnerable, it will not be attacked.

The more a site tries to protect itself from hackers, the more important it is for hackers to break in. A site that doesn't try to protect itself will never be attacked. This is how everything is and works.

We need to minimize legislation and make it absolutely reasonable from all aspects of humanitarian considerations. If it is by any means possible, many government agencies need to be privatized and subject to competition.

We need to create a demand driven society by creating a base salary for all people whether they work or not.

The basic litmus test on the value of any organization is whether enough individuals, given free choice between different providers, would choose to pay out of their own pocket for services provided by that organization. If nobody is willing to pay for these services chances are that what is being offered is not needed.

Law enforcement and the police have to be changed from being a supply-driven organization to being a demand-driven organization.

This means that their actions would be driven by the request of individuals and organizations for their services. Example: If an individual feels threatened by another individual or group, that individual would contact law enforcement and ask for protection. An individual should have the right, if at all possible, to secure that another individual or group cannot contact them, interfere with their life, and/or be within a certain number of feet from that individual's home and work. If it is decided that the individual has a legitimate request, and after it is properly communicated to the individual or group or organizations that this is what they can or cannot do with regard to an individual, the violation of this ruling would be subject to adequate punishment. Example: If a woman is abused by her husband or boyfriend, she would be responsible to contact law enforcement if she truly wants to get out of the relationship. They would be able in front of a judge to get a judgment where no further contact should take place. The perpetrator responsible for the abuse would be prevented from contacting the abused or being a certain distance from the individual. What society needs to provide is a mechanism by which people can escape injustice, abuse and brutality.

The fundamental principle is the right to leave any situation without disastrous economic and personal consequences.

Why should all areas of the earth be subject to the same laws and security? Why not create areas with certain characteristics so people can go on vacation or move to as to the degrees of freedom they want in many aspects of life? We could create different areas such as highly regulated and controlled areas with very little personal freedom. Then create other areas where those same things are minimized and people can go and choose to live in those areas. This way we are giving people a choice. It would be extremely interesting to see what areas of the world would be the fastest growing and the most prosperous where most people want to live.

Protection of the individual should only be by individual request. Unless somebody asks for protection there is no purpose.

What we have now is what I call "objective protection." That protection assumes victimization and need for protection without any subjective (subject) request. A proactive law enforcement and justice system is inconsistent with freedom for the individual.

The "dictatorship" in America and the apathy of the American people are being sustained by the "Stockholm syndrome", created by the justice system of draconian sentencing and the criminalization of the people through legislation.

The Stockholm syndrome was coined after a bank robber in Stockholm, Sweden, took the bank staff as hostages. The Stockholm police did not go in to capture the perpetrator, but rather decided to wait him out. After about four weeks in captivity, the victims started to sympathize with their captors. Violent opposition grew against the police and the society by the hostages. It went so far that when the captor got arrested, one of the women who was kept hostage worked tirelessly to get him out of jail. She was able to help him escape from jail and they went on the run away from the law together. This woman was a very well adjusted career woman. She would be a very unlikely person to fall in love with and to identify with a bank robber. Since the Stockholm incident, research found that people in captivity will very quickly start to identify themselves with the captor. The consequence of Stockholm is that when we as human beings are exposed to overwhelming power, the desire for self realization, safety and security is projected and experienced within the framework established by the captor or overwhelming power with potentially disastrous consequences to the society.

Western democracies are not even democracies anymore since such a large portion of the GNP is managed by the public sector.

Given that humans are mostly economic beings they will vote for parties that benefit them. As an example, if 50 percent of the GNP is managed by the public sector or government, 50 percent of the voters are no longer free to vote for the party that supports government reduction. As government grows it is becoming a self sustaining monster that will inevitably gobble up and get in control of the whole society. The democratic system is unable to stop this from happening. It will require an unbelievable position of idealism on the part of the individual citizen to take a long range perspective and vote themselves into economic uncertainty by voting against their own economic "provider". This dynamic situation is totally contrary to everybody's long range benefit. In the future, it might be possible to change society into a free society again by enlightening the population to the complete fallacy of believing that they are privileged by the economic benefit directly or indirectly they derive from the government. In other words, a person would not bite the hand that feeds him or her. This means that if the 50 percent of the GNP that is managed by the government 50 percent of the population is dependent for their livelihood on grants from the government. If that is the case, you DON'T HAVE DEMOCRACY ANYMORE! The percentage needed is possibly much smaller to destroy true democracy. Democracy is no longer functioning anymore because people are no longer free to vote their consciousness, but rather for that which benefits them short term economically.

The other way to solve this problem is to institute a base salary for all citizens so no group feels privileged by the financial support from government.

There is a distinction between democracy and freedom. Democracy is no guarantee for freedom.

The reason we have all these "rights" movement, gays, blacks, women is rooted in the lack of freedom and oppressiveness in this country. They are forming because the natural freedom to be has been taken away from them.

The dictatorship of the mindless majority manifests in how the bureaucracy and elected officials are able to manipulate the people for their own interests. They are creating the problems they are elected to solve.

Out of the $380 billion in transfers to "poor people", only 20 percent goes to the poor the rest goes to the bureaucracy that is injuring the dignity and character of the poor.

The "poverty industry" creates poverty as the justice system creates criminals.

The politician is trying to please what they think is the majority. He reflects the reactions of a "mob," meaning the majority. A majority that reacts irrational by the "mob" syndrome and through the mass media manipulation that distorts reality and objectifies truth of other human beings through its reporting. For example: Dan Lundgren's reaction to the interview with Richard Allen Davis in reference to the Son of Sam Law that basically states that you cannot make money from your own murder case.

The Importance of Democracy and Freedom

You can always see that freedom is restricted and a dictatorship established as the precursor for war. An example would be the Desert War and the subsequent killings of the people in Waco, Texas. Government and mass media objectifies groups of people to declare war on them and then they present them as threats to society. Government feeds the media and the media feeds the government's objectives. Democracy itself doesn't work that well. Decisions are made almost on a random basis. Elections are decided not on logic but on emotion. That's another reason that individual freedom should be maximized and the power of government should be minimized. There is no really weak group in the society. If they are weak, that's nature's way of maximizing survivability. Like women and children they have been given powers other than muscles and are perfectly capable of exercising the powers they have been given. Destroying the natural relationships between men, women and children is injecting a tremendous dysfunction into society and ultimately extreme unhappiness for all. If men, women and children are given the opportunity to exercise their powers in a free and natural setting they will have the right powers.

The government, society, parents, or any authority for that matter is not "right" and the only way we will have change is to have people in the society who are independent and have the strength to oppose these authorities even if this independence is putting their own lives in jeopardy. It is the misfit that moves the society forward with new ideas. It is the "loner" who is the inventor and entrepreneur as well. If we create a too restrictive and authoritarian system of upbringing we will be in danger of creating those personalities into criminals in order for them to express their independence and opposition to the system. Chances are that these independent people will not subordinate themselves in any shape or form to the laws and regulations of that society.

Hence, the "well-meaning" has destroyed the individuals that represent the future and the evolution of that society. This will lead to catastrophic consequences both materially and morally!

The Gulf War syndrome—through the power of suggestion—is a typical example of thousands of people who believe they are sick. Social- and welfare-support systems fuel this belief by promising money to its converts. This is a revealing example of how the system promotes what it is supposed to prevent: Illness! Meanwhile, politicians and government agencies create "high profile cases" to defraud the public with distortions for self-preservation to expand their influence and power in society.

Evidence from the Justice Policy Institute is irrefutable that the crime rate drops significantly more in states that do not have a three-strike law than states that incarcerate criminals for life!

There exists an imperative need to extend Society's Law of Imperfection to individuals. This law connects perfectly to quantum physics and freedom's essence because it proves beyond any reasonable doubt that we do not live in a deterministic society. Since nobody is perfect, society must create degrees of freedom that relate to individual imperfection.

If, under existing legislation, we randomly investigate any individual long and hard enough, we find that they can be prosecuted for a criminal act. Do we want to live in a society like this?

20
Dynamics of Organizations

Self-organization happens spontaneously in an open system where that system reaches absorption limit. Any increase in input will automatically be dissipated into the environment. However, it has brought all the components of the system into the same stage—all "equals inside the system"—and we get a self-organizing system. That is the limit of absorption. In other words, we get spontaneous organization when "everything hits the wall." When you have an open system and you fill it to saturation. When something is full, it becomes organized (when it is at the absorption limit—before that point, it can be chaotic.)

Politicians must constantly pen new laws and regulations to justify their existence. This, in turn, reduces freedom and makes everybody a criminal. In other words, if everybody was monitored 24/7 and investigations were conducted in everybody's personal or business affairs, all of us would be criminals!

Any organization amplifies what serves its self interest and minimize what does not. A good example would be the CIA and other intelligence organizations in their assessment of weapons of mass destruction in Iraq before the war! These organizations make intelligence information as dramatic as possible to satisfy the perceived need of the government's goals and objectives. They will basically tell the government what they think they want to hear.

A person's opinion is formed by their self interest being aligned by the organization for which they work. The more people in agencies who are involved in analysis and suggestions for tactical strategy, the more confusion and lower the quality of recommendations will be.

Quality and recommendations as it relates to number of people involved

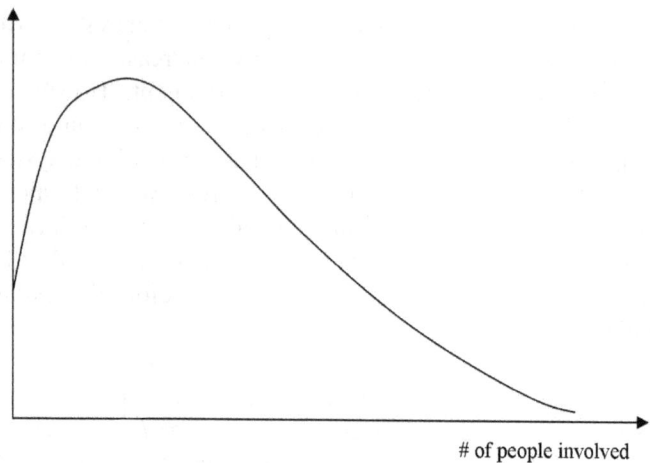

Figure 16
Quality of Recommendations

Each person, over time, adapts unique opinions and recommendations to justify their positions in the organization. These positions, however different and outlandish they may be, will always support the expansion of the power and influence of that organization.

People are always discussing international strategy from a moral point of view and make recommendations on "moral" grounds. The real US or other countries' strategies are based on self interest. The US case includes open markets for US companies, defense investment, weapons sales, access to resources and power. It would be in the short-term self interest of the US that North Korea has nuclear bombs. The result:

- More defense spending in the US and more weapons sales.
- More power to the US as an ally to other countries.

It divides the world and makes it weaker compared to the US The result is increasing power and influence for the US government domestically as well as internationally that's based on people's fear. These benefits must be considered during tactical and strategic discussions. A discussion among people without these considerations is a discussion among well-meaning idiots.

Even when it comes to emergencies like 911, our government is doing the wrong thing. When people called from the world trade center to the emergency dispatchers, they were told to stay put and wait for help rather than following their own instincts to get out. Had this happened many more lives would have been saved!

A lot of people get rich owning companies with government contracts and they are:
- Inherently fraudulent and corrupt.
- Companies with government contracts should not be allowed to trade on the NYSE or any other stock exchange.

Companies with government contracts are funded by the American people. It is wrong to transfer wealth from the American people by the government and its derivatives to a small group of individuals in the private sector. These are businesses and institutions funded by the American people.

Criteria for evaluating an organization's validity as a positive creator or a negative destructor for humanity are (This is needed since an organization, by definition, cannot evaluate themselves objectively):
- Does the organization prevent something?
- Can what the organization does be done by the private sector?
- If what the organization is set to prevent is allowed, would the consequences be more positive for society overall?

If the answer is "yes" to these three criteria, the organization needs to be taken through a rigorous analysis to justify its existence.

Individuals will always self justify as will organizations, only on a larger scale. Because we are searching for self justification and meaning in life the only way to do it is to fabricate a moralistic underpinning for self justification. Every individual and organization will always seek to maximize their power and influence in society because it's a bigger self realization and self actualization.

Government organizations are not operating in a free market system! They were initially set up with good intentions to be creators and to create is infinitely complex. However, they have evolved to become destructors because that is infinitely simple. By virtue of lacking a "customer", a government organization will always evolve into a destructive "NO" organization. Traffic police and planning commissions are examples. A private enterprise organization always has to be a creator in a free enterprise system. A private enterprise organization must always be an open system and get its energy for creating from its environment as well as from its internal organization. Because it has to constantly reinvent itself—confronting infinite complexity everyday to prosper and stay competitive.

Once you legislate, you destroy some part of your ability for self realization and personal growth!

"Please give up your seats to the elderly!" "Don't eat on the bus!" These are signs on the bus and good examples where you as a responsible and free individual could have exercised your own free will to do good and be altruistic and feel good about your actions. However, where the signs are put up your choice has been taken away and you can no longer do what is right out of your own conscientiousness and another opportunity for personal growth has been taken away! You may think this example is dumb and trivial but it highlights an extremely important principle as to legislation and enforcement takes away your opportunity for personal growth, sense of achievement and meaning and purpose! This goes to the core of who we are as human beings and are systematically destroyed by today's overzealous governments!

Government organizations will always evolve to their lowest energy state and always justify their existence by claiming more power on moral grounds.

FEMA is a typical bureaucracy that does not work well as evidenced during the New Orleans floods. What truly works is decentralized decision making and power. If any decision has to be made on the top, you lose motivation and the potential of the people executing that decision. In other words, an organization needs to set up goals and allow the people of the organization to perform.

60 Minutes, 8/7/1999. FBI translator tells Congress that she was told not to work so hard so they could get a larger budget and increase their staff. This is an example of an organization seeking to increase their size and influence regardless of whether it makes any sense.

Any government or anybody interviewed about a problem they are set to solve will automatically magnify the problem out of self interest and self justification. You cannot trust them!

The larger the organization the less moral responsibility it feels and the more pulverized the individual responsibility for the organization's acts. Moral responsibility only exists in the individual, while large organizations "brainwash" their members into believing that expanding power and influence on behalf of the organization is the right thing to do. Further, the organization will always find a moral justification for its actions. Wars, killings, torture and genocides can only be performed by large organizations where the individual responsibility has been diminished. Large organizations will always find a moral reason for their actions. Nations will believe in the absolute morality of their actions!

When a person joins an organization they will automatically identify themselves with the goals and aspirations of that organization. The desire for self realization makes them do so.

Over time the individual's self realization and personal goals and aspirations will align themselves with their organization. Any organization always seeks to expand its power and influence in society as proof of their worth and of the individuals who work there.

Any organization that is not subject to external pressure from a market, from a customer and competition will always, over time, gravitate to its lowest possible energy state and least common denominator that fulfills their self justification.

In other words, almost all organizations are established as progressive, creative and facilitating "yes" organizations. Over time they become destructive, "no", obstacle organizations because of the previously mentioned forces.

Hence, all organizations not subject to external forces that keep them creative "yes" organizations, need to be subject to zero-base budgeting and closely monitored. Otherwise, they become a huge negative force and a drag on society. They actually create the opposite of what the organization was originally intended to accomplish.

The city and county planning commissions were established right after the Second World War to make sure that all the GIs and every US worker gets a piece of land and able to buy a house. The purpose was creative, to say "yes" and help people buy a house. However, what they were originally formed to do is associated with infinite complexity and high energy input on behalf of those planning commissions. Over time, they have evolved into "no" organizations that today are preventing people from getting permission to buy a piece of land and build a house of their choice.

Morality has gone from a positive one of trying to make good for the individual to the morality of protection of land.

If an organization is large enough it can even choose a moral reason that looks good on the surface but in reality is destructive and will continue to prosper even when closer analysis shows that that organization is destructive and should be abolished.

One of the reasons a free democracy—with all its imperfections that it should have—works so well and is so progressive throughout history is that a true democracy and its leaders are forced by voters to create and do good. These dynamics are only true for organizations. They do not apply to the individual. A "free" individual would automatically do good and say "Yes" and be creative as self interest is the motivating force. It is only the mechanism of destroying personal responsibility as a member of an organization that allows organizations that are not subject to external pressure for their survival to gravitate toward their lowest energy state and become destructive.

Why is there a difference between an organization and an individual?

Because personal responsibility is diminished as soon as an individual joins an organization! Organizations can't feel any personal responsibility. The individual, as a member of an organization, has a desire of being aligned with the aspirations and goals of the organization through the desire for self realization. Hence, an organization behaves completely different than an individual.

The more incompetent a government organization is, the faster it will grow, and the faster the money pours into it.

If the organization is in charge of security and safety it can use fear as leverage for more funding and influence. The larger the gap between the imaginary reality caused by mass media and the true reality, the greater the idealization of the importance and purpose of the organization, the more support the organization will get. Example: The purpose of an organization is idealized by the legislatures. When the organization is not performing, politicians pour more and more money into it. Since they are emotionally and politically invested in the success of the organization and they have nobody to restrict their purse.

No amount of people in a group can make the group any smarter or more well-informed than the smartest and most well-informed person in that group.

Sadly enough, putting hundreds of idiots together does not create intelligence.

The more people are involved in something, the less truth and reality will evolve. In fact, only two people discussing something may move away from the truth. Reason: Once more people get involved, what one person says will become the truth for another person. When information has circulated enough entirely different information will emerge as the "truth".

The larger the organization and the more participants in the discussion the farther away from the truth the final results of the discussion will be.

There is an inverse relationship above a certain point between the number of people engaged in the analysis of something and the quality of the results coming from that analysis, especially if that group is isolated from the rest of the society and its input. The other strong driving force behind this relationship is the desire for self-justification by the organization. Then the mass media comes in as "the great magnifier of nothing."

Due to the complexity of the world right now, more decentralization and freedom is necessary. It is impossible to manage a "complex and complicated" world. The leaders cannot simply inform themselves enough due to the complexity of the world. What people are saying publicly and privately are very different. In fact, it usually is just the opposite. The sad part is that it is public opinion that guides policy. Public opinion is supported by the mass media and amplifies an opinion that is not grounded by a reality but by a belief. This is a belief that the individual needs to conform to any opinion they think is expected of them. Ultimately, this leads to the stupidification of a society.

People would say in public and by being interviewed in the mass media what they think society expects from them rather than their true opinion.

Establishing a Homeland Security Department cannot be stopped by any politician even if they wanted to because they are hostage to the idea. They have no choice other than to create it. If they go against it and there is an attack, the politicians will be blamed for it since they did not create the office that may have stopped the attack. They cannot decide against its creation. This dynamic principle is prevalent in all government doings and will have no end until all freedom is gone and the country is in bankruptcy.

As firefighters are setting and causing fires, so do many government agencies, creating what they were established to prevent. The justice system with the police is creating criminals; the welfare system is creating welfare recipients. For example, firefighters setting fires: The Colorado fire is symptomatic of the dynamics of government agencies creating what they are supposed to prevent.

The collapse of the World Trade Center in 2001 created a protective cover over a 10-story cellar structure where probably hundreds of people died from suffocation, lack of food and water caused by the continuous use of water to "control the fire" after the collapse. So, it is not what you do that is important but that you are doing something. Especially, if what they are doing is media-friendly. The people who ordered the fire trucks to continue to pour water on the rubble from the 911 collapse should all be fired.

It is a structural dictatorship of government agencies manifesting itself with groups of government people to be considered more valuable than other people and the proof is that the people have accepted this structure. People who are living in fear are attracted to dictators and strong men with the idea that they will protect them. Old ladies are attracted to bully police figures and strong men will be a good example!

The US government has created a monopoly or more accurately an oligopoly. It has destroyed a truly democratic process by instituting a protected, two-party system. This is destroying the US as a democracy. Leaders of government have a tendency to choose ideas and courses of action of what they think people expect and what is "popular" while in reality they are working for their self interest. They assume that people in general are stupid. That is how we get the most stupid decisions made by the leaders of states.

The paradoxical goal of the US is to make the world into a giant prison and to destroy as many people who are against American "freedom" as possible!

There have been more than a million people killed in traffic accidents since the first nuclear power plant was built in the 1950's. No people have been killed by radiation from nuclear power plants during the same time frame. The benefit to society can be arguably higher through the production of pollution-free electricity than from any other energy source. How can this stupor of not producing nuclear power prevail?

"When nuclear waste or extreme hazardous material is being moved by the railroads, the policy of the government is to not inform the communities it passes through until one week after the event?

"There is and has been repeated advertising for an event conducted by government and their agencies as seen on TV and in print after the event happened? Does the government in its all mightiness believe they can even reverse "the arrow of time"?

"The police are tightening security after an incident has happened"?

Wisdom of the drug lord ...
Example: You have one manufacturer of a pain relief drug used by cancer patients. The government cannot even control the use of that

drug which is legal. What is the purpose of trying to control any drug supply, especially when the US has spent $3 billion to start a war in Columbia to try to control the supply of drugs? The law against drugs not only destroys the moral fiber of America but it is also destroying the moral fiber of Latin-America.

When the entire political system on the federal level plus the political mass media can spend months and months on one pardoned Mr. Rich by President Clinton, there is a manifestation of no true purpose in the society. Just the sheer waste of resources is obscene. "Let us stop all pardons so we have a society where there is no forgiveness" was the conclusion in the mass media after months of deliberation. It is horrible and unconscionable!

When an agency is being criticized for not performing up to standards, the immediate and automatic response from the agency in question is that they are short on staff, resources and money. When the criticizing body is politicians responsible for the allocation of money to the agency and the criticizing has been made public by the mass media, the politicians are forced to increase the funding to minimize discontent or criticism by the voters.

The reason why people are giving massive support to the president for war and the reduction of freedom is threefold:
- They are acting on emotions.
- They are afraid of being looked upon as traitors.
- They are projecting an opinion for what they think other people and the government expects of them.

It is in the government's interest to make the people miserable so they can appear as saviors when they solve people's problems. Even if they were not involved in the solution they will make sure that they will appear to be the solution. Politicians are always blaming private industry. For example, during the electricity crisis in California the politicians positioned themselves in such a way to be the solution to the problem. In fact, it was they who created the problem in the first place. But they manage to get credit when problems are solved. That is just but one example of how the government deceives the people out of self interest. If it hadn't been for the unreasonable politically popular restrictions put on electricity generation in previous years and "water conservation" and, if we had left it to the private enterprise system, the electricity and water crisis would not have happened.

It is in the self interest of law enforcement to perpetuate and expand drug use.

The strengthening of law enforcement implies the desire of the government to manage the people more closely that reduces the freedom of the individuals and non-government organizations. The difference between the management by an independent organization and the government is the opportunity to escape from the management of an independent organization by quitting. This is not possible when you are managed by the government. Freedom has been taken away even if almost half of the country opposes the law and the management of it. The only way to escape is to vote against the law and the management of that law.

There was "nothing wrong" with Clinton when he was ridiculed because government as we know it has outlived itself. Anybody in the president's office would have been attacked the same way. It is a system that is no longer working. The next to be ridiculed is the Congress, state, county and city governments. The largest ridicule is going to be against the military brass and the people in the "justice" system. This is also a manifestation of the legislation of morality, its foolishness and unreasonableness.

Support programs that you have to qualify for based on poverty, perpetuate poverty by rewarding it. Support programs need to be for everyone, regardless of income. Any organization acts like a business enterprise, creating a demand and need for their services and products. In so doing, it creates what the organization was initially created to prevent.

The only way you could have understood the impeachment process of Clinton was on the background that the law was more important than anything else. The protection of the law was more important than the impeachment.
Barbara Battolino on Today show 8:10 am November 11 1998
Accused of the same as President Clinton—lying about sex under oath—she thinks that the president should resign because she has lost

her license to practice law and got punished. People find the law to be "holy" even if the law is wrong and rather would like to see other people punished than trying to change the law. This is another example of people saying and meaning what they think is expected of them under pressure of an authority/interview by mass media.

To not allow housing development is pure and blatant discrimination against the homeless by current home owners. Renters are homeless. The real motivation to prevent housing is economical. It will increase the price of homes, but they are using environmental concerns as a justification for not allowing development. Current home owners—most bureaucrats and politicians are in the group—have chosen the "morally" acceptable reasons to pursue their own self interest. These bureaucrats and politicians, rather than living in a brand new, beautiful house for a million dollars, have chosen to live in small shack houses built in the 50s, infested with asbestos, rather than giving others the opportunities to live in new homes.

A house does not pollute. In fact, here in California where we have housing, the flora and fauna where you have homes is much richer than areas that have not been developed, especially when it comes to hilly areas. As an example, in the San Francisco Bay area if you look at the map you can build five entire Bay Areas in the area between the Bay Area as it is now and the #5 freeway on rolling unproductive barren brown hills. People are driving around in cars are saying to themselves, "My God, there are so many people around and there is nothing to develop. The reason for that is that housing is around the streets and highways. This may come as a surprise that less than 10 percent of San Mateo County is built, that's on the peninsula, mind you. So since we can't have any more housing developments, we have hundreds of thousands who have to live somewhere in any event and not getting the opportunity to own their own homes.

What is good for the environment? To create the best possible environment for 90 percent of the people where they are staying 90 percent of their time outside work, namely at home or to preserve barren hills for less than 1 percent of the people to spend .001 percent of their time?

We think there is no space and we drive along the highways because there is a lot of housing along the highways. That is where we build homes. Put your hiking boots on and walk past the homes into the forest. You can walk from Marin County in the Bay Area to the Canadian border without seeing a person or a house, or get up in an airplane and you will find that the current build out, even in California, is miniscule (less than 3 percent).

Any organization has the potential to become a negative organization, including the Mormon Church, Christians, and Jews. The key question is, "Why do you have to organize?" One of the major answers has to be that a person, who belongs to one of these organizations, wants to impose their beliefs on others, not through logic or merit, but through power. Reference Adolf Hitler. "Not as being against Jews, but as he believed in absolute power."

It is really only one organization that is needed the most. That is an organization to preserve freedom. Everybody is talking about how scary it is with terrorism and crime. However, if we are able to solve that problem, there will be no freedom left. By solving the problems of the world we are also destroying the diversity and the dialectic process and, ultimately, freedom is a lost cause because it is a sign of freedom that imperfections can and will exist. There is no surprise that freedom is being lost when everything is stacked against it.

It is understandable that we as humans want to make things perfect. However, perfection is not an absolute concept. It implies certain values and opinions. It assumes that we have achieved absolute knowledge so the pursuit of perfection destroys freedom. To have freedom we also have to accept imperfection.

The year 1997 saw "usefulness" of current politics break down in a laughable and impossible quagmire of idiocy. That is the prosecution of the president and the ensuing debate. It took up all the time of many journalists who could have spent it doing more productive investigations of real problems.

Because the politicians have nothing to do, they are creating work for themselves, even attacking the very foundation of affluence. Example: Businesses.
Why should we still live in a government-controlled system as it is manifesting today, considering continues increases in taxation and other threats when that system failed in the eastern bloc?
Organizations and governments always end up choosing destruction since destruction is infinitely easier than creation. When the

organization has gathered enough power it will sell the idea of destruction as a virtue. In other words, the organization will turn destruction into a virtue.

Organizations cannot be creative by nature, only destructive. Only individuals can be creative and organizations can only be instruments of creation in as far as they are controlled by creative individuals.

The society today has made what the military and the police do into a virtue. Why do these organizations become destructive? Because it is a lot easier! You can destroy something in seconds that may have taken years or generations to build.

The government was formed to make people's lives easier and more organized. The government's strongest force in society today is in making people's lives miserable and stressful. Government prevents the average person from the opportunity to own their own home. The police were supposed to help the traffic move faster and smoother, while today, they have become the biggest obstacle to smooth traffic flow.

Military was established to protect and defend. They end up killing women and children in Waco, Texas. The legal system was set up for justice, but is now processing the blacks and others in cooperation with the police. This creates an entire class of people with no voting rights and no hope as a modern class of "Les Miserable's," worse than in France 100 years ago. All this destruction has been made into virtues in the modern society. Making a whistle blower or snitch a hero and the acts a virtue? Blackmailing people to testify in court against family and friends a virtue? Foreign policy today is all about destroying somebody else. All because it is infinitely easier to be destructive and make destruction into a virtue. Even just working in the defense industry kills thousands through exposure to hazardous substances. Ref Beryllium metal, 20/20 program April 19, 2000.

The zero-tolerance policy in schools is creating many more victims than any mass shooting has ever done, creating thousands of children, disillusioned and being treated as criminals by involving the police in even the tiniest of infractions. Are there any more sure fire ways to create criminals than by treating someone as if they were one?

Since every profession has a built in desire to maximize its importance, any victimization has to be made very serious and dramatic both to increase the power and importance of the therapist but also of the justice system to maximize the punishment for victimization.

The victim is manipulated to believe that what they have experienced is very important and damaging to them that make them really ill by suggestion of authority, meaning by therapists and the justice system. Example: My own experience as a boy that I had gotten mumps manifested itself as swelling on the side of my throat and fever. I believed that I had it because somebody told me that I had it, but it was not true.

Rewarding victims monetarily and emotionally opens the door to false accusations by claiming to be "a victim." This creates a society of victims. Being a victim is being rewarded. In contrast, we should give awards for achievement and self-reliance.

We are creating a society of power abuse by the weak and intimidation of the strong. Laws and regulations only change the opportunities for abuse from one group of people to another. This is creating a society where control is transferred to the group of a least common denominator meaning to the weak and undeserving.

Planning commissions and local governments serve their own interest in issuing building permits: City and planning councils will mostly act in their own self interest, however justify their actions on moral grounds or generally accepted principles. They will be opposed to the idea of cheap and easily available housing to all citizens since this will automatically reduce home prices and reduce their own affluence as homeowners. They are acting out of self interest. What is more important? For the maximum amount of people to maximize their well being and life style 99 percent of the time, or to prevent this from happening to the benefit of a small fraction of people to minimize their driving time to get into nature less than 1 percent of their time? Amazingly, both goals can be achieved at the same time by allowing parks, recreational areas and wilderness to be "fingers" into the developed areas. This will secure easy access to nature and parks for everybody and cheap housing for everybody. Idiots are driving down the road and say "It is so crowded here, so there is no more space." Of course it is crowded there because housing and development is done along the roads and highways. However, if you get up in an airplane, you find that there are vast areas which can be both preserved and developed, just two to three hundred yards from the highway or road. Fundamentally, the housing and development cannot be stopped in any event. So why not speed it up so everybody can live decently and cheaply?

Politicians and the police are victims of their own legislation and government. Government has become a self-sustaining monster where nobody is really in control of regulation, policies, power structure and procedures. It's the fear of change that prevents people from making the right decisions.

The biggest problem with governmentally funded agencies is that they will fight to grow their influence and power. But there is also no incentive to stop their growth other than budget constrains. And if their organization is large enough, it will also represent a political power block from the sheer number of voters and other influences they have from the society at large.

There is also, unfortunately, the news media's interest to perpetuate the large government organization since many are set up to prevent the exceptional and the unwanted from happening. They are established to weed out the society's imperfections. This is exactly what news is: The exceptional, unusual and imperfect. In this way the news media is acting out of self interest to perpetuate the myths through perpetual self-justification. Example: The more legislation, the more crime, the more news, the more moral legislation, the more scandals.

It's in the interest of any organization to create what they are to prevent in order to expand their power, importance and influence in the society. "Destructive organizations which are set up to prevent something will market themselves as any other positive/creative organization that is providing a benefit to the society. The difference is; one organization benefits society the other is destructive to society.

Politicians identify a problem, pass a law, and decide that we need a new agency to solve the problem. The next step is to set up an agency to put the law into reality. The law makers forget that the people who are hired to implement the law are also imperfect. As many as 80% of the people hired would not perform but rather talk to each other by having meetings, spend time on the internet, and talking to friends on the phone. The initial people hired to form the agency think that they should be managers and propose that they need more workers to be able to handle the workload. Assistants, junior mangers and clerks are hired but they are also imperfect and now a lot of time is being spent on "training and managing" people. The agency is criticized and the response is "we need more resources to be able to do our job". Politicians are "invested" in the success of the law and the agency and there is no incentive to save money. So the additional resources are given to the agency. This is how it grows! The less successful the agency is, the faster it will grow and "gobble up" taxpayer's money and society's resources. The lack of success creates the need for more funding!

The law of government bureaucracy is: "The less successful it is, the larger it will grow."

21
Well-Meaning Idiots and
The (Sub) Conscious Conspiracy

The communists had useful "idiots," Western democracies have "well-meaning idiots." Well-meaning in the sense that legislation of morality pushes the western democracies into the dictatorship of the majority. That democracy and freedom are the same is a widely held misconception. For example, Hitler had the support of 87 percent of the German electorate in 1939. So, what is freedom? "Freedom is the right to be different from the majority. It is the right to live differently and to have different values." In fact, the concept of freedom only has importance and significance for the minorities since the majority in a democracy elects a society that fits them. This is assuming that the majority knows what is best for them, which we have seen previously and will see later to be false.

In a democracy, freedom must be defined as the rights of minorities. Perversely enough, a law can be passed with simple majority vote, however slim, with far-reaching effects on everybody; even if almost half the voters voted against the law. The primary purpose of the US Constitution should be to protect the people from the possible tyranny of the majority.

Why is freedom important? To answer this question we need to establish certain fundamental assumptions about man and society.

First, a changing and evolving society is desirable. Evolution emerges out of a dialectic process of divergent opinions, values and lifestyles among people and groups that is ultimately based on a pluralistic society. Evolution implies a difference from what is to what it will be. In general, the impetus for change comes from misfits who are not content with the state of society. The more divergent the opinions and values of a society, the more vibrant and faster the society will evolve. In fact, plurality has value in itself. If this is true, legislation of morality and values is inconsistent with a pluralistic and rapidly evolving society.

What is the perfect society? Is the "perfect" society a completely homogenous society that shares the same values and beliefs and, preferably, people with similar intelligence? The desire to create the "perfect" society implies a set of values to be more valuable than others. The very attempt and subsequent success of an individual or group of individuals to impose their values on everybody is fundamentally inconsistent with freedom and a pluralistic society. The success of such an endeavor will create a dictatorship where everybody must conform to those values. To be enforced, society must be defended by destroying people who do not fit the mold. Earlier, we agreed that a pluralistic society is more desirable than a conformist society. This is a fundamental paradox. We cannot create a "perfect" society unless we destroy freedom. The "perfect" society must be an "imperfect" from any individual point of view. We have seen and will see later that "imperfection" in itself is the most desirable state for society to secure tranquility, stability and progress.

Variety is also the foundation of a strong society through its flexibility and ability to respond to change. In fact, a touch of "chaos" is desirable to create an exciting and fast-evolving society. An "ant hill" or a "bee hive" is a "perfect" society with perfect division of labor. It has pre-established goals and values with a single purpose for survival. However, the ant hill and the bee hive do not change or evolve except for maybe getting larger as they mature in an unconscious stupor.

Man is multifaceted in his intelligence. He has the ability to solve new problems based on previous experiences. He can choose creativity and transform matter and combine ideas and knowledge into new ideas and knowledge. He has emotions, such as anger, sorrow, happiness, sadness, fear, courage, love, hate, remorse, guilt and sex drive. That is the nature of man. He needs to live in a society that accepts those facets. A society that accepts and is tolerant to human expressions and facets is a "Natural Society."

What are the goals of "man"? Power, influence, control, wealth, family, friends, knowledge, create, children, sex, security are some of the goals and desires that can be summarized into one word, self realization!

Are some of "mans" goals better or more moral than the others? Or shall we make the assumption that man has the right to pursue all of them? Would it not be totally unrealistic to deny "man" some or all of them? Is it even desirable to do it? Should not the essence of freedom be the ability to pursue all goals? Would not that be the basis for happiness to fully realize yourself?

What is an organization? An organization is a group of people organized hierarchically with a common set of objectives. In general, the larger the organization, the more power and influence the organization has. For people in an organization to achieve maximum self realization the ultimate goal for every organization has to be to maximize its influence and power—whether private or government—through growth.

What is the nature of "man"? Man is fundamentally good. Given the opportunity, do we choose what is right and good or, evil and "bad" when given complete freedom? Your answer may be both. However, we must make an assumption about "mans" nature and structure the society according to the assumption we chose. The most compelling proof that "man" is good is the fact that society does function and billions of people live in peace with each other. You experience this fact everyday. In addition, "man" has lived in relative "peace" for thousands if not millions of years. If you've read history, you may object to this idea. However, history is recorded as the news media reports news. The more perverse and uncommon the event is, the larger the story. Thus, what is recorded in the history books does not reflect the real history!

Throughout history war has been started for greed, envy, revenge, religions, ideologies, respect, protection, and security. The ability for a nation or a group to engage in war is based upon the powers of the leaders and the homogeneity of the beliefs and values of the people. The more totalitarian and less pluralistic a society is, the greater the danger that war is being used by its leaders to consolidate and exercise its powers to sustain its privileges.

Freedom always is restricted and often the establishment of a dictatorship is the precursor to war. War is destruction. There are no winners materially. The only objective a war can achieve is to further consolidate the powers of the leaders on both sides while it runs its course. The winner wins nothing other than recognition.

The idea that wars or the exercise of brute force by one country against another is justified for economic reasons–such as US attack on Panama—is a complete fallacy. The only reason for that attack was to gain respect, exercise power and gain more popularity domestically. These reasons justified the killings of thousands of innocent people. There is nothing to benefit "man" created by war; only destruction. The act of war and the use of force between nations have only one goal. That is to try to gain control, respect and power consolidation by that nation's leaders. One nation's leaders "feed" on other leaders for its own powers and expansion of their purpose and influence in the nation they are governing. We the people are constantly being sold the idea that the world is a threatening place and complex. Therefore our leaders expand their powers and privileges in the most self-serving way.

The "cold" war was a perfect example. It served the leaders in the Soviet Union to consolidate their powers and privileges. It served the US leaders the same way. They loved and hated each other. Each one gave the other an important purpose. Ever since the cold war ended, the leaders of the US and Russia have been scrambling to fill the void. Do you think that the war on crime, drugs, and poverty happened by itself? Now, also terrorism has been added! Isn't it interesting that both the US and Russia are heavily engaged in fighting terrorism after the cold war? Russia is fighting it domestically, the US in the Middle East. The driving force behind both of them is the same! New enemies of the state had to be created for the government to sustain its powers and to continue to consolidate its privileges at the expense of the rest of us. Do you think they would be able to confiscate half of your earnings through taxes unless they brainwash you into the idea that you need them?

The most used idea by the government to make you accept its privileges and your taxation is that you need protection and security. There is no protection! The whole legal system is based on the principle of punishment after the criminal act has taken place! Nobody can be jailed and prosecuted for something they have not done. So, there is literally no prevention of crime other than the punishment's assumed preventative effect. The idea is that somebody who is in jail cannot commit another crime while they are in jail. There is no mechanism in place to prevent anybody to kill you at any time. This is the truth. It's also proof that man is fundamentally good since violence and crime is as uncommon as it is. This is an absolutely true statement statistically!

In order for society to give its citizens any protection at all, they would have to accept the physical presence of a "protector" 24-hours-a-day plus likewise surveillance of its citizens by its government. In fact, protection is impossible. With no protection there is no security. "Despite this fact," society functions very well. So what is the foundation of the legal system? Revenge! It does not protect against rape, murder or mutilation of victims since the act has to have happened before the legal system can do anything. Does revenge and punishment work? Yes and no, if the punishment is experienced as justified and reasonable it works. If not, it does not work. Then punishment becomes humiliation. Anybody exposed to it will become hateful. What does hate lead to "yes revenge"! This is what I call the "punishment revenge cycle" in the criminal system. This is a system that creates exactly what it was meant to prevent. The criminal system punishes people that in turn become revengeful. They are not given a chance to succeed in life since many of their opportunities have been taken away. Much of their freedom has been taken away even after they are out of jail and through with probation.

However, the criminal has the same drive for self realization as the rest of us. The only avenue for self realization for a criminal is to become a worse criminal because we structure the system this way and tell them so. This self realization is fueled by revenge on the society. The result is continued criminal acts. An even greater perversion exists in the relationship between crimes and the severity of the punishment. For example, if a convicted rapist commits another rape—the convict knows that if he is caught he will be severely punished, with life in jail—chances are that he will kill his victim and any other possible witnesses to the crime. In his mind he has nothing to lose. The system of punishment creates even more serious crimes than otherwise would have taken place with less punishment. The system of severe punishment has exactly the opposite effect of what it should.

The act of punishment also restitutes a human being from the "natural" punishment that guides us. This is our ability to distinguish between right and wrong and the feeling of guilt through the acceptance of personal responsibility. By punishing an individual we take the guilt feeling away since it already has been "paid for." The only feeling left after punishment is revenge. The "natural" psychological mechanism to prevent another crime to happen again has been destroyed. In fact, society increases its odds tremendously that criminals will do worse and worse crimes by processing the person through the criminal system.

The proof that I am right is witnessed by the explosion in crimes. These crimes closely correlate to the increased criminal prosecution. "Crime is down the last year," you would say, not true! If you adjust for changing demographics–baby boomers are getting older as the largest group—you will see crime goes up. It is inversely correlated to age after 35. If you adjust for prison population explosion, crime is sky rocketing. New laws, of course, contribute to the "explosion" since more and more people willingly or unwillingly break one of these new laws. One of the consequences when more and more people are forced to break the law is a general decline in the respect for the law. A principle can be established. The more laws we have, the less respect for the laws. The legal system also moves toward the principle that you are "guilty until you are proven innocent" and that you can only do "what is explicitly permissible."

Principle: Any organization creates exactly the same problems as they were set to solve. It even creates a problem even if there is no problem. Any organization will do anything to carry out their "mission" and to justify themselves.

As an example, there is no incentive in the criminal justice system to solve the crime problem; only to solve crimes and prosecute criminals. The justice system is like any other organization. They want to expand their influence and power in the society through greater and greater self-justification by actually creating what they were set to prevent. The crime problem is, of course, in the interest of government elected officials in particular because it feeds their influence and importance. This is also an example where the desire to create the "perfect society" by trying to get completely rid of crime and violence has been created into a much larger problem by pouring more and more resources into the problem. Crime and violence are a natural part of any society. The crime rate would have stayed small had it been treated as such. There is also, unfortunately, the news media's interest to perpetuate and support large government organizations. Why? Many government organizations are established to prevent and eliminate the exceptional and unwanted. Their goal is to "weed out" imperfections in the society. This is exactly what is considered news. The exceptions, the "unwanted," the perverted, and the imperfect! The news media is acting out of self interest to perpetuate the "myths" about government organizational self-justification. It will actively "sell" the need to solve "big" problems. The biggest dilemma is the power of the news media to paint a reality out of the exceptional. The population is brainwashed by the media into believing that the exception and the unnatural are the real realities and will act and vote as to what this illusionary reality represents to them. For example, the more crime, the more news, the more moral legislation, the more scandals, the more interesting news. Is it possible that a large portion of the western population is suffering from reality delusions where the news being reported has become the unreality replacing the real reality? This also ties into the agenda of what politicians raise as important issues to resolve and legislate. We are getting an iterative process going on between the mass media, politicians and government agencies that is not founded in reality but on the exceptions to what is normal. In turn, they pass laws and set agendas for society that is, under the best of circumstances, counter productive to the affluence, tranquility and well-being of the society and, under the worst of circumstances, it creates a horror regime where everybody ends up as victims of legislation and misuse of power.

The US not only has more than 3 million people in jail at any point in time but over 50 million people have criminal records and countless other lives are left in ruins. Then, the war against crime, drugs and poverty has become a war against its own citizens. This proves that there is something wrong with the system, not with its citizens.

An example of media influence is the stereotyping of young male blacks as drug addicts and violent criminals. This stereotyping has been so effective that anybody is petrified when they meet two or more of them on the streets after dark. They have become the "favorite criminal" to be victimized by the justice system. "We might as well do something wrong since we are already being treated as unwanted criminals. If we have not done anything wrong, chances are that we at sometime in the future in any event will be accused and convicted of a crime whether we did it or not!" This has become the "mantra" in the African American youth community in the US, a modern holocaust effectuated by the government.

We are creating a society which is exactly the opposite of what we all really want. This is exemplified with the movies we are going to and the dreams of what we want to be and want to experience. What is the purpose of parks? It is to be used and enjoyed by people! A typical example of idiocy is the government promotion of the idea that veterans are bound to have psychological problems from their war experience. The opposite is true.

Are the idiots going to inherit the earth? When the police and the guards in prisons commit horrible crimes, then the idiocy of the justice system has reached a new high. Ref: More killings committed by the police than actual murders in the society.

A solution

- Any elected politician has to completely get out of private investments not only themselves but also their closest family.
- Direct elections. If a person gets 2 percent of the vote, that person gets 2 percent of the votes in Congress.
- Every government organization shall be subject to "zero base budgeting" every year and be evaluated on the original intentions of the creation of the organization in the first place. The organization needs to defend its existence before elected individuals in Congress.
- Establishment and ratification of the International Court that is elected by the nations of the world to prosecute crimes against humanity.

It is a fundamental principle in nature or society that every positive action or situation has a negative action or situation. By trying to remove all negatives we will also have automatically removed all positives. We should allow negatives to exist. We should be careful when removing them because we are also reducing the positives!

Examples:
- Outdoor grilling creates smoke which pollutes
- Driving cars leads to death and pollution
- Love and hate.

Any increment of information and experience leads to higher levels of wisdom and the ability to make right decisions. Any expansion of individual freedom leads to more creativity and the desire to give and do good. Taking responsibility for your own actions under freedom maximizes rewards coming from the sense of achievement.

If freedom is taken away, we also have destroyed the sense of achievement. Since good is stronger than bad, over time, rewards achieved by doing good and the misery created from being bad and evil experienced under freedom on a personal level, will develop the individual to become a better person.

By punishing an individual you are destroying guilt feelings. Guilt is a much stronger punishment of the individual than external punishment. It develops the individual into a person who is creative who gives and wants to do good. The need for self preservation moves a human being toward creativity and to choose to do good. Personal growth can only be achieved when you are free!

- The dumber the person, the simpler the argument will be, the greater the chance to be elected for public office.
- You have the right to your own body!
- Religion is to elevate "not knowing into a virtue."
- The very essence of conformity and uniformity within each nation creates polarization between nations. It is a threat to world harmony and tranquility. Strong nationalism along with strong religious beliefs creates violence and mayhem worldwide.
- Passing laws that throw people in jail is easy to do when the people passing the laws are removed from the people they affect. People who the laws affect are only statistics. The results are that the people who are affected is automatically dehumanized and objectified.
- There is only one way of doing something right. There are an infinite number of ways that something can go wrong.
- The people who are screaming about more law are the people who need it. They are the people who should be locked up. Please try this experiment. Will you change your life if there were no laws? If you say "no" to this, then you don't need the law. In fact, the law is damaging you!
- It is a fundamental desire of government or anybody to seek other organizations or individuals to become dependent. This dependence gives the dominant player power.

A principle that should be immediately adopted is that an agency should immediately lose government funding if the problem they are asked to solve increases annually.

What is the purpose of government unless it benefits people and individuals? If government doesn't benefit anyone, the government exists for its own purpose. It will inherently be detrimental to people. The problem is that under the disguise of helping and protecting one group of people, it abuses another. This constellation allows the government to pursue its interests at the expense of everyone.

What you are prevented from having, you desire more!

One essence of human life is to strive for what we do not have. Legislation highlights and promotes what you want, especially when it relates to one of man's most desirable and important conditions: freedom. All legislation is experienced as limitations to a person's ability and opportunity for self realization. Freedom is the very foundation that makes self realization possible. However, the desire for security and protection that is an illusion makes man pervert his own ability to experience freedom by accepting reduced freedom through legislation and regulations.

We are sacrificing freedom on the altar of security and protection.

It is a complete mystery how millions of dollars in penalty to a corporation through lawsuits paid to another party is supposed to benefit society when that money could have been used to correct the problem. Another solution is that the financial outcome of such a law suit should be used to correct the problem.

Punishment and the desire for protection and security is emanating from deficient morality in that society.
The lower the morality is in society, the harsher the punishments, and the stronger the desire for protection and security.
When the legislators consider that a criminal act could be committed by themselves, the harsher the laws they pass for those crimes and the more money and resources they spend on the protection and the security against those crimes. By passing the law they are admitting, implicitly, that they are lacking the moral fiber themselves to not commit the crime in question.

All well-meaning government programs do not work because there is little motivation for people involved to make it happen except for expansion of power.

Distortions of reality and its consequences

Example:
- Killing by 6-year-old boy.
- Legislation by exception to what is normal.
- Passing laws to deal with the abnormal and unusual.
- Projecting this incident on the population.

One of the most stupid and obvious examples of the so-called subconscious conspiracy is the very high danger for fire during hot and dry weather in California. Continuous radio and TV reports tell of how dangerous fires are. It is like announcing to any crazy person out there: "Set a fire, now!" This is the perfect time for it." Why is this in the self interest of the media and the fire department? A fire is great and romantic news. The fire department gets something to do and the opportunity to look needed and great to the community.

These "grief and trauma" specialists are teaching people the exact opposite of what they should do to serve their self interest. Telling a person to constantly talk about it and even writing it down every day flies in the face of everything logical. This solidifies the trauma in that person's mind and causes preoccupation with it. A person needs the opportunity to work through the trauma themselves that will make the person stronger and more self-reliant.

The dog mauling case in San Francisco is typical of the media and how the law generalizes the killings by dogs. Now every dog owner in the country lives in fear of what dogs might do, including being prevented from renting a house or apartment. The landlord also can be considered responsible if the dog of a tenant attacks somebody.

A father is stabbing and trying to kill his teenage daughter. For a father to commit an action like this, chances are that he was subjected to blackmail by his daughter. Possibly she threatened him as a sexual child abuser and other horrible accusations. The father's action is a direct result of government regulation and media propaganda.

When a parent has an impossible child or teenager, and the parent wants to put their foot down, they will be charged with abuse. Bad "children" are even taking advantage of their parents by claiming abuse.

Pointers

- It is a mistake to declare a moratorium against oil drilling in the ocean. Oil drilling causes very little pollution! Burning it does!
- An oil spill does pollute, however, the clean up will do much more harm to the environment!

If it happens, leave it alone but stop it as soon as possible, the oil spill will disappear within one year with minimum impact on the environment. Oil is not the same as gasoline! Oil is made from plants; have you ever used Vaseline or mineral oil on your skin? It is pure refined oil! An experiment was done in Norway by the Oceanographic Institute in Bergen in the early seventies, one of the most prestigious in the world; they poured the oil straight from the well on top of the water in the aquarium and let it sit there for weeks. They could prove no damage at all! To pour the oil on top of the water in an aquarium is much more severe than any oil spill in the ocean! An oil slick in the ocean will cause death of sea birds; small rodents may also be killed when it reaches shore. However, the deaths are not caused by poisoning but from the oil attaching to feathers or furs that will destroy their natural protective oil layer and the oil will also impact their mobility leading to death. These deaths are of no significance to the environment as it is too small to have an impact, but it does look heart-breaking! The pictures are then used by the mass media and the politicians to fuel the hysteria about the oil spill in the Mexican Gulf or anywhere else for their own benefit. It is a fraud!

22
Crime and Punishment

There is no protection, because the entire justice system acts after the crime. It prevents nothing, except for preventing repeat offences by imprisoning people. However, this book proves that violence against people through the justice system accelerates crime. The justice system is creating criminals.

Criminality was so uncommon 100 years ago that horrible outlaws became legends. The "Wild West" was much safer and had less crime than modern-day overprotected cities. One can only be prosecuted and punished after the crime. This means that punishment hasn't prevented anything.

Why did we pass the "3-strikes-you're-out" law? Because every time someone is punished, they become worse criminals by a mixture of revenge and the same desire for self realization that is in all of us. However it is being expressed with a negative sign, since the individual has been led to believe by the justice system that they are negative to society. Their path to self realization becomes destructive rather than creative. If unjust punishment does not work to modify children's behavior, how can we possibly believe that it works for adults? The proof for it is the explosion in crime. What more proof do you need?

When violence is committed by the legal system—from kidnapping (put in jail) through murder (execution)—how can we believe that this system can produce anything but more horrible violence? The question becomes: Why is this system retained? It justifies big government control of the people. We believe that violence in the home and abuse against children lead to violent and abusive individuals as adults. Then we try to "cure" the violence and abusive behavior by continuing the violence and abuse of the same person through the justice system. Now we call it punishment.

On this background alone, the whole system is totally illogical. The bottom line is, by trying to create the prefect society and to fix a "small problem" by legislation and punishment we are creating a much bigger one. We can use an infinite amount of resources to try to cure something completely. In the process we are creating an even worse problem.

We have to accept risk and allow pluralism to exist to minimize the problem. We can only sustain society by building upon individual responsibility. Through freedom and responsibility the individual is forced to grow intellectually and morally. There is no other choice since protection and control are impossible. Society is only as strong as its individual parts. We must create a society that maximizes intellectual and emotional growth. This can only be achieved when individuals are forced to make choices. This state of being can only exist in freedom. We must take the chance to believe that man is fundamentally good.

Laws and regulations give powers to certain groups of people who will be used for intimidation, blackmail and abuse. By passing laws and regulations, we shift the opportunity to misuse power among different groups of people. For example, women use the sexual harassment law to blackmail and intimidate, whether the accusations are true or not. Accusations by children of sexual abuse by parents, even if it is not true, are planted by therapists in children's minds.

The government has legislated away the power of parents to punish and reward their children. It has assumed that role by establishing boot camps where children and teenagers are severely beaten. In fact, a 14–year-old Florida boy was beaten to death in a boot camp.

A loving parent usually shows mercy in punishing a child. Society would be much better served by legislating parental rights. The system is not perfect. Mistakes will happen. Overall, society will improve and produce more well-behaved children by returning the rights back to the parents. In March 2005, a 16-year-old girl sliced the throat of an older woman. The discussion of whether she should be tried as an adult or child dissipates the effect of punishment both on the girl and the society at large. Instead, the 16-year-old girl needs to be spanked until she screams for mercy. She should be told that if she ever commits violence again that she will get tenfold what she just got. This will immediately change her behavior and communicate to everybody else that if they do the same, they will get the same.

Children are disrespecting their parents because they don't have the power to punish them. If you cannot punish, you cannot effectively reward.

Real punishment only truly exists for "21 days", because after this time frame, it becomes a habit and does not matter anymore. It has been proven that human conditioning takes "21 days". If you put a person in jail for more than 21 days, they become used to prison life and it no longer has a punishing effect. As each day of punishment is experienced as the same, time perception will be only one day. For example, if a person gets a prison sentence for 15 years, this experience will just be another day because every day after the 21 days will be the same. What works are 3 to 21 day prison terms!

If you analyze abuse severity between private individuals on one hand and the justice system on the other, you will find that government incarceration of an individual for months is a much higher level of violence against an individual than a beating by one private individual of another.

Whatever is being legislated, an immediate and opposite reaction takes place in society. Legislation creates what it is trying to prevent. For example, legislation of morality/protection of women during the last part of the 20th century has all but destroyed romance and relationships between men and women. Romantic song and respect for women in the '70s and before has disparagingly evolved into songs about abuse, rape and degradation and is the direct cause of homosexuality and lesbianism.

Today, parents cannot discipline their own children, who can be taken away from them and abused in foster homes and by government. This is punishment without compassion. THIS DOES NOT WORK!

It is human to make mistakes. It is a foundation of freedom that cannot be created any other way. We must allow mistakes. Taking it away creates a horrible dictatorship.

Rather than having maximum crackdown and enforcement of DUI on Christmas Eve and New Year's Eve, society should consider making it legal. These two days out to the year the laws should be relaxed. People who may drive home after drinking on these days are the most responsible people. Real threats are those who drink and get really drunk and drive on a regular basis.

In fact, I suggest that society allows driving under the influence if you are 21 years or older up to 1.0 and 1.5 level from 7 pm to 5 am on weekdays and up to 2.0 level on Friday and Saturday nights as this will reignite the arts, entertainment, entrepreneurship, romance and sports. What about a "couple" of beers at the ballpark or after golf without the fear of being arrested when you are driving home? There is reason to believe that the increase in fatalities will be minuscule while allowing the rest of us to have a lot more fun! Personally, I drove at least three times a week during the eighties with a level of above 1.5 and never had an accident. The DUI law is purely made on emotion and not on reality. Identifying the really dangerous drivers need to become the basis for who keeps their driver's license and who do not. This needs to be objective and not based on incomplete statistics. If we want to minimize traffic accidents, then we should use objective criteria—how many accidents a driver has per year would be logical. Then, people with a high accident rate should lose their license not if they drink and drive. With a system like this, we will see a great drop in traffic accidents! (If we calibrate DUI accidents with how many accidents happen because its dark and people are tired in the evening, we will find what the real statistics are and the statistics will show that DUI isn't as bad as we'd thought)

A 24-year-old man was charged with murder after his baby dies from "shaken baby syndrome." Before it happened, Child Protective Services (CPS) monitored the couple for child abuse. This monitoring and interference would be experienced as a violation by the parents and focusing the baby as the source of their troubles leading to the killing of the baby. This is a typical example of how government prevention creates the crime.

Crimes against humanity are the most serious. Other crimes need to be far less punishable than crimes against humanity. For example, preventing people from buying a house, having a job and a family is a crime against humanity.

What is a bigger crime? Is it mass murder versus murder of an individual; mass abuse versus abuse toward one or a few; theft through taxation and confiscation versus stealing from a business or individual?

It has been proven scientifically that higher stress levels in humans increase cortisol levels that kill brain cells and make the brain shrink. Science has found that high stress conditions are experienced in prisons and wars. There is no greater crime against humanity—except for killing—than to take away ones ability to think and enjoy life.

Real security and intelligence investigation are impossible from the impossibility of monitoring enough communications to be meaningful. It does not matter what can be done when the bottle neck is in the monitoring and in the interpretation of the information. Hence, security and safety provided by government is impossible!

When a person is murdered there is no more justice. That person is dead. There is only the remaining family and friends who want to commit another crime against another individual in the name of justice. This individual may not even have been the perpetuator. This does not create more justice, but rather injustice.

The stronger the dictatorship the more immorality and looting happens if oppression is removed. This is what we see in Iraq and when there are riots in the US. We do not have this in Scandinavia.

Negative legislation to "protect women", has completely changed the male attitude toward women over the last 30 years. This manifests itself as more violence in televisions, movies and games against women.

The universal language among living things is love, not hate. Anybody who has been around animals and owned a dog knows this. Animal behavior proves that love and goodness are much stronger drives in nature than attack and hate. We only create hate and violence as a reaction to hate and violence!

The justice system not only removes some of the most independent and intelligent people from society, but also intimidates the rest of the population with its inhuman sentencing. A free and democratic society with great impetus for growth must have a very gentle justice system for people to be free to stand up against government abuses.

Now the US prosecutes entrepreneurs, business leaders and "intelligentsia" just like Mao Tse Tung, and Khmer Rouge did. More than 250 cases exist, so far. This is the stupor of asking for perfection in an imperfect world.

Crime is fundamentally (unless caused by insanity), extreme opposition to authority, rules and regulation. Criminals are revolutionaries without really knowing it.

Crime and Punishment 191

It is always a human being involved in any security effort. But with a human being there it is no security and safety. The selling of security and safety to the public is a fraud unless your intention is to break the human spirit.

When a woman can accuse a man of rape even if she changes her mind after the start of intercourse there are three important consequences:
- Any woman who wants to get rid of her boyfriend or husband can accuse him of rape.
- What really happened cannot be proven by the boyfriend or husband.
- The law creates an incentive for the male to kill the woman if she accuses him of rape.

These consequences are in the interest of the government and justice system to produce more criminals and also for the media to get more "good" stories.

The Justice System is an adversarial system to benefit the attorneys on both sides—prosecutors who try to convict without regard to guilt or innocence. The system is maximizing the need for defense. The justice system under this framework is inherently inhuman.

CNN march 22, 2007 at 8:40 PM PST. A mother receives a two-month notice from Child Protective Services that her 7–year-old son will be removed if she cannot reduce his weight. Is it the child protective service's plan to take away the child, to put him into a foster home, and starve him? How callus and abusive can society get?

An example, Patty is now on disability payments. She needs to prove within three months to Social Security that she is actually disabled. Otherwise, she will owe the government $11,000. She has no choice other than making herself disabled and to become a prostitute.

Do you believe that the US population is more stupid and destructive than that of Holland and Switzerland? In countries like these, the amount of drug use–which is legal—is just a fraction of what it is in the US The only reason we have these draconian drug laws causing incredible misery is that it's in the self interest of the US governmental industrial complex.

To arrest and punish somebody for a tragedy or for something that was done at a moment of "insanity" is to assume that punishment prevents others from doing the same. This implicitly assumes that humans are by nature "monsters." This undermines humanity itself. It creates a dehumanized, brutal and callous society if these humans are being punished. In fact, punishment actually creates what it was meant to prevent. The "moral compass" in the individual is being destroyed by the justice system!

There is a profound relation between taxation and crime. To maximize revenue for the government, it has to pass laws to enforce tax collection. Doing so creates crimes.

The Max Factor Heir supposedly drugged girls who voluntarily followed him to his home and were "raped" by him. What really happened was that these girls--he supposedly took advantage of made videos of the sex act--had hurt feelings because he did not continue to have sex with them. They ganged up on him with the support of the "magnifiers" (news media) that scared him and he escaped to Mexico. Now the "victims" had to substantiate their stories even more since they were put in front of the magnifiers. They will tell the magnifiers whatever the magnifiers want to hear. The heir gets 125 years in jail. At the same time, President George Bush is in Africa talking about human rights. There is no country in Africa that would put anybody in jail for 125 years for having sex with somebody. If 125 years in jail is not cruel and unusual punishment and a violation of human rights, nothing is.

An alternative scenario to the Scott Peterson case

The criminal justice system and ultimately the politicians and people of this country may be the true criminals in the Scott Peterson case. Chances are that when Lacy Peterson found out about his mistress, she threatened him with divorce. She said that she would take the house and prevent him from ever seeing the child. Scott snapped and hit her. She responded by trying to call the police to get him arrested for wife abuse. Screaming at him, he hit her again. Now in fear and frustration, he snapped again and hit her over and over again until he realized that if she was able to call the police he would get years in jail. At that moment, out of feelings of frustration and helplessness, he kills her to avoid the other punishment. This is a typical case where society sets up absolute morality, legislation, standards and punishment. Then it applies it to an imperfect and fragile relationship between humans. Therefore, the criminal justice system killed Lacy. In other words, fear of punishment caused the crime. The more severe the punishment is in society, the more severe secondary crimes are to cover up.

Another Example: Rape

A young lady goes voluntarily with a young man she met at a bar to his house to have a nightcap. The young man gets her in bed. He has sex with her. She is a virgin. He destroys her virginity. She suddenly regrets the act and accuses him of rape. In his mind he immediately gets a feeling of enormous fear, considering the punishment, and kills the young woman.

Society has a choice to balance the punishment toward criminal acts against the possibility of precipitating new and even more violent crimes, and the need for the criminal to eradicate witnesses and cover it up. In other words, the degree of punishment directly correlates to the severity of the crime.

If the punishment for rape was a lot less, chances are that he would not have killed her. The mass media and the distortion of reality and the hysteria it has created are actually creating the continued victimization of the victims as well. It has created a complete distortion of the real severity of different crimes. The mass media, in cooperation with the justice system and government, in their self interest make otherwise "minor" crimes into serious crimes to maximize profits and influence!

Rape didn't really exist in Norway until it was created out of self interest by the criminal justice system in recent years. I know because I grew up there and I did not see one case in 25 years until I moved to the US in 1978. Now, you have rapes there just like in the US In other words, today Norway has "learned" from the US You cannot prosecute people on hearsay. You cannot punish somebody without having objective proof of the crime.

60 Minutes, July 21, 2002. There is at least one criminal complaint a day involving border patrol agents in Arizona involved in drug smuggling and murder. What are we trying to prevent when the ones who are set to prevent crimes are the creators of the crime? The idiocy has no limit! In the same 20/20 TV program, they show one segment where people have been put in US jails for life without parole. For example 19-year-old boy molests a 12-year-old boy. The next segment shows Romanian children sleeping in the sewer system that runs in the streets as the ultimate horror???

1/25/2001 A 13-year-old boy is convicted of murder and sentenced to life in prison without parole.

Is God subject to legislation by the Congress? If the economy is going sour, that would make them flock around God.

There is a tendency among the best, bravest and most independent men to get in trouble from time to time and sometimes do wrong. By making the definition of freedom too narrow, we destroy many of these men by putting them in jail. It is also a subconscious way for the "group man" to get rid of the competition for the female by incarcerating them. We have destroyed the barnstormer kind of person who is full of it, but has the possibility of creating great things.

The future of society is being decided upon by drug and alcohol infested activist groups suffering from paranoia and fear of change and the future. They elevate themselves on issues they don't understand by choosing "no" to evolution and creation.

Looking at statistics to determine if a law is paying off can lead to a completely wrong conclusion. For example, if we prosecuted and executed all people who are arrested for drunk driving, the statistics will greatly improve over time. So we can conclude that the law for arresting and executing drunk drivers is successful.

Government is passing laws against the importation of women from foreign countries. The unforeseen consequences are possible for unjustified incarceration of well-to-do individuals who bring a woman they love to this country. Then, when she finds out about the laws she

Crime and Punishment 195

may decide to engage in blackmailing the person who brought her into the country. That person might lie about the relationship when it goes sour. So one person always talks the truth even if they can hardly speak English? The person with money is always the guilty one. I do not believe these stories at all and neither should you!

Ninety percent of lawsuits in the country are filed by people who are envious. Society has fallen so deep that they have made envy a virtue and the best opportunity to make a lot of money. A whole subculture has been created between law enforcement and criminals where they need each other for self realization and self-worth. They are living in a symbiotic relationship.

Injustices committed in this country by the government and the legal system is such that it creates an environment of violence and disregard for humanity. For example, George Will, columnist and commentator is so callous that he does not care whether a couple was burned alive because they killed somebody.

The Republicans have been able to undo affluence built up during the '90s in less than a year after they got into power manifesting with the power crisis and further lack of development of infrastructure to increase power supply, housing, water and transportation.

The police kill more people through chases, arrests and incarcerations than murders among the people, so much for their "serving and protecting".

What is taking place in the US justice system is worse than a holocaust in Germany during the Second World War. They have elevated a conviction of a criminal to a "250-year-sentence" that buries a human alive. This is personalized by the intimate and direct interaction between regular citizens and those convicted. Does this make a conviction of "burying someone alive" into a time of joy and relief for the rest of the population? We have been conditioned by the media that the victims should feel happy, joy and relief. This is a complete perversion of the human intellect. It is more human to kill somebody in a gas chamber than putting somebody in jail for life without the possibility of parole. In this respect, what is being done to humanity in the US now is worse than the Holocaust. For example, somebody who has not hurt anybody and does nothing wrong other than being a drug addict, gets 20 years or more in jail.

If law enforcement is so important, how come other countries that has much less law enforcement has less crime and violence? Nobody should dare go on a cruise since you do not have the "terrific" preventative law enforcement as you have on shore in America.

Very few people in the world are forced into anything. For example, UNICEF claims that 1,000,000 young girls are forced into prostitution in the world each year. This is a completely untrue claim! I know from growing up in a small town in Norway with a lot of freedom that some girls choose to be whores. Passing laws to prevent this from happening will replace freedom with incarceration and much more abuse of humans. The only thing that drives UNICEF, the government and the mass media is their own self interest and self-survival. "Horror stories" are backed up by a few examples of individual abuse which is then projected on the entire group. They don't even want to talk to hookers who are perfectly happy being whores. What drives the whole thing the most is: "If I cannot have sex with these prostitutes, I don't want anybody else to have it either."

What you are calling assault and violence in this country is at most tiny infractions. These are cultivated and nurtured by your justice system into something serious out of self interest. It is ridiculous what is being classified as a serious assault. Just pushing or hitting a person is magnified into serious assault and can put you in jail as a felon. In reality it is a natural human interaction in 99 percent of the cases with no lasting bodily injury.

By suppressing small infractions we create the possibility of a much bigger explosion. For example, rather than having a little fight here and there between lovers, micromanagement through legislation makes both parties—especially the male forced to control himself un-naturally–to cause continuous build up of anger and resentment without any outlet. Put this in combination with the authority that he feels is naturally his as a male. This has been taken away from him within a generation, and has created the possibility of even murder by an otherwise well-balanced and intelligent human being.

Crime and Punishment

Any reasonable person who has not completely lost his ability to realistic judgment by propaganda understands the way the system works. There is no relationship between the crime and the punishment. The relationship has become completely blurred and unreasonably skewed. Reasonableness has been lost.

The legal system with endless lawsuits and court cases to get "closure," is taking the possibility of otherwise meaningful lives away from everybody involved. Their whole lives are wrapped into these cases in the most traumatic way to satisfy the self interest of the legal system and all the "support" structure around it. Psychologists, therapists, sociologists and media feed on all of it. In other words, all the support staff involved feeds on human misery. When the reality is seen by the people involved they will turn against it when the real truth is revealed as stated in this book.

Nothing in this country is left to individual judgment (freedom). Everything is being legislated down to the smallest item. If it violates anybody's inconvenience or stupid opinion, we have a law against it. This is taking meaningful and productive lives away in the name of democracy. In other words, it has become the dictatorship of the majority.

"A society without laws is a society in chaos and violence!" This was said by a congressman during the impeachment debate of President Clinton. What is the cause of real violence in the world? It is the law and the government itself. There are 3 million people in jail: children are taken away from their parents with the smallest of accusations. Marriages are being destroyed! If the congressman's logic is correct, more law and execution of it creates less violence. It does not, it creates more violence! More freedom creates fairness and more happiness. However, the ultimate law society is a dictatorship. So dictatorship is the ultimate government. Looking at the impeachment debate, the congressman who made the quote did not even bother to follow and listen to the debate. Do they expect the rest of the country to listen? This was a truly sickening experience.

The investigation of Clinton by Kenneth Star created a crime by investigating the president in a sexual matter. Would not you agree, Mr. Star, that if you had not investigated the personal sex life of the president that no crime would have been committed according to your report? Did not your questioning and investigation create the crime of perjury and cover up? While without your investigation it would have been perfectly legal to have sex between two consenting adults. In fact, the president did not have sex he had "blow jobs". It also would have been legal for those two adults to keep it a secret.

A crime cannot be prevented without committing an even larger crime for its prevention. There are two kinds of punishment. External— one is jail time and fines is imposed by somebody else externally or— internal when somebody is punishing themselves by taking responsibility for their own actions. External punishment, since the past does not exit, creates a paradox that an even larger and more abusive crime must be committed by preventing the crime. In fact, crime prevention cannot exist without destroying freedom. We can't have crime prevention. That's impossible!

The centers in the brain responsible for sexual arousal are the same ones activated by the punisher when punishment is exercised and of the person who is being punished. If this is true, then the idea of punishment is driven by sexuality. If the person cannot express themselves sexually with a consensual partner, this person finds sexual satisfaction through exercising power and punishment. Victims who subordinate themselves to this power and punishment get the same sexual satisfaction. In most people the feeling of power to punish and the submission to power is enough for sexual arousal and satisfaction for both. This constellation is what is behind the feeling of love for another person. The love between the sexes has been diminished and destroyed by weakening the male to be like the female. The natural state of affairs is that they are two opposites, just like yin and yang, and brought together to create a harmonious whole. Simply said, opposites attract.

The mass creation of new laws and legislation is creating an impossible complexity in the society. Police codes of silence to not snitch on each other have perversely been made into the primary tool for convictions for the rest of us. While the police code is not to snitch on each other, that which they think is immoral and not right convicts the rest of us.

Legislation within "women's causes" has destroyed female ideals and made many of them into cruel and calculating individuals. They become even thieves who cannot be trusted. Many women are manipulating the system to create an "easier" life for themselves at the expense of their ex-husbands. In reality, women get everything: the house, kids and money. A man on average income will not be able to reestablish a new life for himself after a divorce involving children. These men are doomed to never having a "life" again. That's obscene!

When "Unabomber" Theodore Kaczynski gets this kind of PR as somebody very unique, how do we explain that we have more than 3 million people in jail? Many times, what keeps a person in the system is not the original crime, but parole violations. The parole system sets people up for continuous problems with the law for minor infractions on purpose! A minor infraction, such as being drunk one time, puts the person back into jail again.

It would be very interesting to find out if outrageous behavior like stealing among kids—if left unpunished by the society would have a vaccinating effect on the individual. Do these individuals become more honest and trustworthy as adults compared to children who are not this way when they grow up? We will probably find out that kids who are really rough and rambunctious will grow up to be even more trustworthy than those who are better behaved as children.

We are all victims of the policies, rules and laws established by the government. What the legislators obviously don't understand is that they also are victims of their own laws.

The sexual harassment law is a typical law which creates the crime.
- Creates the allegation.
- Creates the cover-up.
- Feeds the legal system.
- Feeds the politician.
- Feeds the press.
- Creates income opportunities for the "victims" as an incentive.
- Creates opportunities for blackmail.
- Destroys lives.

The fact that something is wrong doesn't mean that it has to be criminalized and that a law has to be passed. To pass a law to try to prevent something that is wrong makes it even much worse. Legislation violates human dynamics. It violates the humans' natural morality and law. Legislation has proven that it makes it worse throughout the 20th Century. Laws need to be evaluated objectively based on the end result. For example, when somebody sues for sexual harassment the objective is revenge and monetary gain for the "victim." If the current trend continues, with the exponential growth of laws, rules and regulations, and nothing is done about it, society will eventually self-destruct.

The idea of being proven guilty without reasonable doubt makes everybody into liars. Everybody knows that everybody is lying. So the truth is supposed to manifest? The process is completely flawed in the first place. That is why many guilty people get off the hook and many innocent people get falsely convicted.

Example: CBS 48 Hours May, 15 2000
It is a typical example of the average person who tells whatever they think is expected of them as a witness.

An Article in San Francisco Chronicle on page one May 17, 2000 reports a puzzling rise in murder rates. When you read the article, you find that the largest rise is in metropolitan cities, especially in areas where police work is most oppressive. How can murder rates increase when people get older and less criminal?

Why are the increases in crime the fastest in areas with the most "justice" and law enforcement?

We also have the three strikes law where thousands of people a month are thrown in prison. This is another proof of how government pressure on the citizens creates crime, especially murders.

With all the laws, the only difference between somebody in jail and you is luck. We all should be in jail. I guess that would solve all of our problems! Research has been done showing that everybody is a lawbreaker. So, if we have a fair and just system, everybody would be in jail. It is only the imperfection of the system as it exists and selective enforcement that prevents jail for everybody!

The system of revenge for victims is creating a system where everybody is a victim. The reduction of freedom is a violation and obstruction of the human spirit. How can you run a country with clear underlying principles to create consistency and fairness? When an "abused" wife goes to the police with a case, it will magnify the abuse many times over. Going to the police may be the single most important factor that potentially makes the abuser into a killer. Most laws passed cannot and should not be implemented, due to complexity and implementation problems.

Entering information about individuals into computers accurately prevents those individuals from buying weapons. The data base for background checks must be accurate and complete to work. This is impossible to accomplish. Do you think that any government agencies are going to be any better, more accurate and more motivated than what you are?

This is the endless spiral "of increasing punishment" and legislation. The first legislation makes it always worse through unintended consequences. The only thing to do is to pass more legislation and make the punishment even more severe until we have created a completely micromanaged and inhuman society. The external pressure on the individual has reached a point of complete anxiety, stress and fear. In that condition, a human will act with unreasonable anger, brutality and violence. Or, they will give up completely and slide into depression, drug abuse, and alcoholism.

A CBS 60 Minutes Sunday May 7, 2000, dealt with the third strike law in California. In January 2005, somebody broke into my home early one morning and attempted to steal my wallet. I woke up and saw a black man standing over me screaming, "Give me your wallet." I resisted and got into a struggle. When I realized that it was not worth it, I gave him my wallet and he ran off. In the afternoon I got the contents back, excluding the cash, by another black man, who I rewarded with a finder's fee.

On Thursday night January 27, 2005, my business was burglarized. A laptop computer, radio and a cordless drill were stolen. Both instances were reported to the police. Through my contacts in the community, I learned who the perpetrators were. I decided not to report it, but instead put the word out if ever I heard of another incident, I would report it. Looking at the program "Slavery in America" I could see obvious parallel of that time and today. If a slave did something wrong or tried to escape they would be burned with an "R" on both sides of the face. One ear would be cut off. If they were caught four times they would be castrated. If I had called the police and it had been the third strike, the perpetrators would have received 25 years to life. In fact, the punishment today is much worse than it was of slaves 200 years ago. However, the police and justice system today has replaced the slave owners as the controlling and punishing force in the black community.

How can people get 25 years to life for petty theft? You can see in the program how prosecutors and politicians smile gleefully when confronted with the horror of a human being locked up for life. This is just like Gestapo guards who laughed and had a good time when they were killing thousands of Jews. Just ask a concentration camp survivor. At least the Jews who survived German prison only were in jail for five years or less.

The more a parent tries to prevent a child from doing something—especially when the child is extremely bright and independent the more desire the child has to do it. How can the government think they can do what the parents cannot do better?

All laws that "favor" women against men have created deep-seated resentment and anger in men. This anger manifested itself in the mobbing of women in Central Park in New York City, June 16, 2000. When society violates natural laws between people and, the internal morality and sense of justice has been destroyed by unnatural and wrong legislation, the result is what happened in Central Park. I am completely convinced that what happened in the park is just the start of something much uglier and profound for society. When you create an inhuman society through legislation that creates the "perfect" society, you create inhuman people. One interesting part of the New York incident is how you can actually see reporters and politicians full of glee. They say the exact opposite pretending that they are shocked when they actually loved the incident. One reporter wrote; "All the ugliness of human nature." A person who says that is really ugly. How can the reporter say that the woman was caught and brutally attacked when she was not? Nobody was hit!

The interesting thing is that the police and justice system itself are becoming victims of their own zealousness. The "death penalty" of Gary Graham in Texas is a good example. How can the government stop the execution of this man since that state already executed more than 130 people in a short period of time? If they stop this execution they need to admit and feel guilty about all the others they have killed. This example shows how injustice perpetuates itself in the justice system due to the dynamics of the system and ultimately of human nature.

The legal system assumes that people are bad and need to be controlled. If true, mankind is bad and should be allowed to be that way. It will be more in line with our true selves.

If society is making the consequences of calling 911 for a domestic fight too severe, they will get very few calls even when it would have been appropriate. Punishment again will have the opposite effect of what it was supposed to accomplish.

What are the consequences of fabricating sexual abuse? Teachers and others are constantly being charged with sexual abuse by children and others. Their careers and lives are being ruined. By having strong punishment for false accusations it is going to be almost impossible to get a child/student to admit that they falsely accused somebody. The question is: "How many sexual abuse cases will there be if society dropped the legislation against it altogether?" To answer this question, society must access what the real psychological damage to a child/student is from sexual abuse. If they are not getting counseling, we need to use the principle of allowing something to happen in a free society to minimize the prevalence. One scenario would be to severely punish for false accusations. If so, the accuser would never admit that they lied. This leads to a complete travesty of keeping the law. In conclusion, society must eliminate laws that have to do with accusations without proof.

Counselors and therapists on their path to self realization need the confirmation that people are severely damaged by incidents in their past for their careers.

They truly need to persuade the victims for their services, so their self interest, in a well meaning way, wants the person to be a victim and stay a victim in a dependent relationship to the counselor. In fact, this desire to "help" people is so strong that they will cultivate—in an otherwise healthy person—the belief that they are actually a victim and will need continuous services and counseling. Either way, they are extremely damaging to the people they counsel. There is one fundamental observation in my life. I have had conversations with other people who have lived strong, independent lives. They agree that no personal problem can be solved by being an introvert with contemplation and counseling. The only way you can bring yourself back after trauma—with no or minimum damage—is to engage in the act of giving to other people.

Child support: You pay it so your ex-wife or girlfriend who divorces or splits from you can go and fool around with other men.

A 48 Hours Program on Oct 7, 1999 is a typical example of how the environment of severe punishment promoted by the mass media creates the actions of the killing of a 14-year-old little girl across the street when he hit her in play. Because of his fear of punishment he attempted to silence her and hide the body.

Principle: Reduce punishment in the society to allow natural violence to exist to minimize irreversible and severe violence created by the fear of punishment.

A Date Line July 20, 1999 program is a typical example of the justice system involved in a domestic situation. Doing so creates far more problems than it solves. A woman is being taken to court by her daughter. A "not guilty" verdict is handed down by the jury and ends up breaking up the family.

There should be no law based on "morality" as these laws destroy personal morality. The individual's sense of meaning and purpose is demolished. Legislation that is needed is to protect the individual's freedom and establish game rules among people, businesses, organizations, government and their interactions.

It is not about creating the "perfect" society but rather creating the "imperfect" society.

Example

Two boys at the ball park drink too much and get into a fist-fight on the way out of PacBell Park in San Francisco. One boy hits his head and accidentally dies. The mass media blows up the story as "the magnifiers" of everything. The media leads to a national movement for making pocket shots illegal. It strips away the freedom of everyone else to buy whatever size bottle they want for a drink. Not only might this devastate the liquor industry, but will cause thousands of people in the industry to lose their jobs. This is another example of one incident that is used as justification for taking away the freedom of choice for millions of innocent citizens.

This is typical because nobody will stand up against legislation that reduces rights in the society that is perceived to be harmful. The right to harm yourself needs to be a fundamental right. Otherwise, you might as well outlaw soccer, downhill skiing and football. In other words, activity associated with danger should be a personal choice, legislation against it is wrong. Ultimately, it violates your rights to your body that is the last domain of freedom. When you lose the right to your body, you lose all rights and freedom. Society has already taken away your rights to your children. Reference: The kidnapping of more than 400 children by authorities in Texas from a so-called cult is an example. We can also talk about what a cult is. I would argue that nationalism and patriotism is a cult that has the power with the support of religion, to persuade people to die for cult values. Every national state is fundamentally a cult. In the end we have minority cults that are deemed illegal and unwanted. We have large majority cults— nationalism is an example—where the nation's values are considered to be highly desirable. An unwanted cult is by definition a minority group that has different values than the majority.

In a commentary on TV by Protective Services in Texas, when asked by the interviewer on TV, "Wouldn't it be very abusive to take these children away from their parents", answered: "Children are extremely adaptable so they have probably adapted to their new situation." If children are adaptable to any situation, including being taken away from their parents and this is the highest level of abuse. Why should the children be taken away from the parents in the first place, if they are that adaptable? "Duh"!!

You have the right to act and as long as it doesn't directly affect other people to do the same. It's okay, as long as it is not directly destructive to another person's ability to achieve happiness. Just the simple act of living affects other people. It cannot be that one person cannot affect other people in some way.

Example

Children belong to the parents until they are 18. After that, they belong to themselves. If that right is taken away, children have been taken away from parents. The passing of legislation against child abuse has caused an incredible increase in child abuse and killings. An example would be an 8–year-old child threatening their father by calling the police on him and putting forth a lie about the incident. "If I don't get that new bicycle, I will call the police right now and tell them you have been systematically sexually abusing me since I was 1 year old." This may be completely untrue, but through the mass media the child may have gotten the idea that they can use this accusation to gain power over their own parents. In this incident, should the parent out of fear buy the bicycle and just walk out of the room with their tail between their legs, completely controlled and humiliated by their own child?

It is the taking away of authority and power from the parent that creates and drives the anger behind most child abuse and child killings.

Example

Another example of how legislation and punishment create a much larger crime is the known fact that most adult arsonists are people who recently had a run-in with the law. In revenge toward the society and their "unjust" experience decide to reap their revenge through fire. The anger is directed toward the children when the parents feel that their natural authority has been taken away. The rights to reward and punish are essential for parents. Otherwise, child rearing has no meaning. Parents must have the right to educate by what they think is right, reward and punish their children.

Parents in this country believe that the child should be prevented from getting experience and information.

Society tells people who had certain kind of experiences in childhood and early adulthood that it is bad for you. This becomes a self-fulfilling prophecy inevitably leading to major psychological problems as an adult. When society with all its power to persuade tells someone they can't be happy, we believe it. It is that belief and persuasion that makes the person miserable, maybe for the rest of their life. In reality that same experience could be looked upon as a bad experience. At the same time it may enrich their lives and make them better. In the final analysis, it's the belief about your experiences that determines your mental health and well being. Growing up in Norway and as a 21–year-old if I would have told anybody that I was a victim and could not function as an adult because of some homosexual abuse experience when I was 5 years old. Every adult around me would have said, "Shut Up! You are not an adult if you can't handle it, grow up!" Because of that my "bad experiences" made me into a stronger person, more proud, because I could tell myself that it is not one experience that I could ever go through that would take my sanity and my ability to be happy away from me. That is what makes you an adult in the first place, the ability to accept and overcome both bad and good experiences in your life.

More than 1000 college students commit suicide every year!

To be heterosexual, means yin and yang. You see this in the animal kingdom. Yin and yang are equal, just different. Equality, true heterosexual equality is the recognition and cultivation of maleness vs. femaleness. Traditionally, this would be the dominant male and the submissive weaker female. If those two natural roles are taken away from the male and female, we are becoming homosexuals or lesbians. The male becomes a female. The female becomes the male. We are destroying the male and female relationship and everything that goes with it—love, romance, caring, commitment, and sex. Love is no longer driven by two opposites trying to create and strive for something that is complete and harmonious. It actually is neutral. It's like putting two magnets together with the same pole. You must put the negative to the positive to attract.

The loss of power by women was temporarily caused by the Catholic Church. All throughout history, men have been wooing and trying to win the hearts of women. We can see this in our literature and stories all throughout the ages. If all this time women have had no power, then why would it have been necessary for the men to earn their good will and hearts rather than simply taking them by force? This would have certainly been possible if women were without any power what so ever! So why is it that today we have to create all these laws to protect the women? This constellation of winning the heart of the female is one of the most powerful sources of inspiration for both sexes throughout history. The fact that women just recently got the right to vote in western society does not mean that women didn't have an equal or greater position of power in the society in the past.

You could argue that women didn't have the right to vote because they didn't need it!

Women's fight for the right to vote was not fought by the vast majority of women. They were perfectly happy with their existing position of power. The right to vote was fought by a tiny minority of women who were denying their own femininity and womanhood. Of course, the male always wants to please the female, so we passed the laws for the right for women to vote. I am not proposing that the woman's right to vote should be taken away from them but the idea that women need special protection and legislation is not working.

Everyone is talking about women's rights. The passing of laws to promote artificially women's rights are inherently discriminatory against women, as it is based on the idea that women are too weak to assert their rightful position in a free society. The legislation, not only is discriminatory against women, but it is destroying the very fabric of the relationship between men and women, but also woman's natural position in the society. Women are perfectly capable of taking care of themselves in a free society and gain their position and power through their womanhood and femininity. The explosion in crimes against women and deteriorating respect for women in combination with the destruction of marriage as an institution and of romance and love combined with the explosion in homosexuality and lesbianism proves my point. The perceived necessity to protect the "weaker" sex against men is causing extreme unhappiness today among both sexes. It is this very "weakness", sexual attraction and child bearing ability that naturally gives women their position of power in the society. This has been destroyed over the last 40 years. While laughter, thrilling courtship, and cultivation of the female were the relationship between the sexes throughout history, today it has been destroyed. The loss to humanity and both sexes are incalculable!

The justice system should not be proactive but reactive. Nothing is a crime unless somebody reports it as such. Nobody should be put in jail unless there is proven that this person has committed serious physical harm against another person and it can be proven without any shadow of a doubt that it might be repeated by that individual and it is a wish of the victim that the person needs to go to jail. And if that's so, the jail sentence should be minimized to 21 days. Any jail sentence longer does not manifest in that person's mind as additional punishment. It has been proven that 21 days is what it takes to create something into a habit. So a person who is sitting in jail for 21 years will only perceive the punishment to be 21 days.

Major point

As long as the system is experienced as being unfair, then we become vengeful, manifesting itself in criminal behavior. This becomes a self-fulfilling prophecy. The major producer of criminals is the justice system that was set up with good intentions by well-meaning people trying to prevent crime.

An excellent case of how the police and prosecutors create criminals and/or the coercion of guilty pleas is the Central Park Rape in 1989 on prime time on Thursday Sept 22, 2002.

Anybody associated with the justice system should get the maximum punishment for crimes, times three. They should know better than the average citizen. If you can't trust them, then who can you trust? Prosecutorial power should be completely removed from law enforcement. An adversarial system should exist between prosecutors and law enforcement. Law enforcement should be treated like any other witness. It should actually be considered a hostile witness because they have an interest in every case and a deep-rooted desire for self-justification. Today, it's a cozy camaraderie club that causes incredible injustice.

Jail is the ultimately crime against humanity. Jail is the worst kind of torture. It has been proven in Sweden that after 30 days, there is a 30 percent drop in mental ability as measured by IQ when somebody is deprived from normal stimulants.

The use of maximum security prisons is the same as burying people alive! They lose their IQ and drift into insanity in a short period of time. If this is not cruel and unusual punishment, nothing is. People who support this kind of punishment and justice are personally trampling on the constitution. Society needs to recognize criminality as sickness; treating and rehabilitating need to take place and must be carefully managed. People who are not notorious criminals need to be shown tolerance. Society needs to allow "moments of insanity" and mistakes to minimize crime, damage to society and individuals.

Justice system compensation should be based on drops in the crime rate and how few people are in jail.

In a TV special, "The Lottery," was the sickest speculation and the lowest emotions of humanity I have ever seen. It was about ritually stoning a person each year as a sacrifice. This was aired 9/29/96 on NBC (KRON).

Injustice example

On Sunday Jan 4, 2009 CBS 60 minutes showed a college student who was sentenced to 18 years in jail for driving drunk and killing a 7-year-old girl in a car accident. Judge sentenced student to 18 years to justify her draconian and inhuman action (judgment). She was forced into this action by her own words during her campaign speeches. Now she doesn't have the wisdom or strength of character to reverse herself before the public eye. The judge is doing speeches to justify her action. This behavior is typical when human beings do something they know is wrong, they persuade themselves and others that the action was correct. This female monster of a judge has no choice than to do public speeches of self persuasion and seek the approval of others for her actions. This desire for self justification gets stronger the more abnormal, perverse and draconian the action or opinion is.

There was a case where an adult pretends to be a guy on the internet communicating with a teenage girl bullying her until she commits suicide. This one unusual incident is going to be handled by Congress to create new legislation?

OJ case: Judge gives him 10 years for being arrogant and stupid.

Joe Walsh's 6-year-old boy, Adam, found murdered. Joe does a press conference being responsible for *America's Most Wanted* TV program. It doesn't work to have laws on the books that punish the parents of innocent child victims. According to Joe's own philosophy, he and his wife should be arrested for gross neglect since the boy was kidnapped while in their custody. What drives Joe to be the host of *America's Most Wanted* is his feeling of being particularly responsible for the kidnapping of his son. If Walsh were punished for his neglect, his sense of responsibility would go away. His driving force for being the host of *America's Most Wanted* disappears. This is a good example of why many of the crimes being prosecuted today should not be on the books.

People who have nothing to do are the busiest and never get anything done.

The act of purchase becomes a psychological substitute for the act of actually creating the item.

There is nothing that will unify humanity more than a catastrophic environmental threat that threatens life on earth because it goes into the core of why we're here.

The same set up that was created to make sure that the United States stays a free and just society paradoxically can also evolve this society into a much worse dictatorship than almost anywhere else. Freedom, reasonableness, and justice are annihilated. The reason for this danger in the United States is that there is no institution in 100 percent control. Well-meaning legislation and enforcement can create a monster through rules and legislation where everybody, including the president, is a victim. Nobody except the people can change it! It's impersonal—not human. That's why the United States can become the worst Dictatorship ever, because the construct of law and enforcement are no longer subject to individual human control.

"Because you have division of power"...

The US Constitution has in itself the best and the worst for mankind. The largest threat to freedom and prosperity, represented by the Constitution is the division of power. It is the greatest guarantee for freedom and, paradoxically, the greatest threat because nobody within the two-party system has the power to change it. That is why the election process needs to change into direct elections!

The system has the possibility to become so huge and uncontrollable that nobody is really in control of it anymore.

The sad part of the way the government is set up is that everybody has become a victim of laws and regulations—everybody, even those in government. We have created a monster that just grows exponentially.

Even the president is a victim of a monstrous construct of the human imagination. Laws, rules and regulations are created by the well-meaning, and nobody can control it. It has become so large and all encompassing that it has taken on its own life and cannot be stopped. Everybody is a victim.

This is worse than a one-person dictatorship because it has no hope and is beyond humanity. That monster of laws, rules and regulations, have no compassion because it has no hope.

The ultimate multi-level marketing scheme in the United States is illegal drugs. By virtue of being illegal, drugs are extremely expensive. If somebody becomes a drug addict, the only way they can sustain their own addiction is to recruit others to become drug addicts to sell drugs to the new addicts to sustain their own addiction. If a drug addict is not entrepreneurial, he will steal or become a pimp. If it's a woman, she will become a prostitute. So the foundation for a lot of the "crimes" in America is a direct function of legislation and punishment against drug use.

There is only one more perfect multi-level marketing scheme than drugs and that is traditional religion. The reward for joining a church is eternal life, a free ticket to paradise. Since it's built on belief—meaning no certainty—validation of the belief has to come through the recruitment of others.

Corruption only exists between private enterprise and government because it is only in that interaction that a person is not subject to the inherent transparency and the dynamics of free enterprise.

Well-intended government regulation of private enterprise most often leads to artificially high profit and turf protection. Legislation creates walls around existing industries that become so high that competition cannot enter. The intentions behind the regulations were to protect people and prevent what actually happened but created the opposite.
Example: The seaman's labor unions in Norway of the 50's, 60's and 70's caused so many salary increases and reduction in work that the shipping industry was allowed to expect of their workers, that companies had to move most of the industry out of Norway. This is an example of sawing off the branch you're sitting on.

Example of government gone amok

President Bush in a speech on Tuesday 28, Oct 2003 said: "It is the threat of freedom which creates terrorism. There are only evil people in the world!" A remarkable statement made by a President of The United States!

At least on three occasions when I was growing up, "lose" girls had sex with multiple partners in the same room as we looked upon the acts. Was that "gang rape"? The definition of gang rape, whether its gang rape or not, is defined by the girl who is having sex. The definition is made by the girl, based on her interpretation of the event after the fact. The so called gang rape could have been a completely voluntary act on behalf of the girl. There is a tendency for this to happen between the ages of 14-18. What is it with this country that has made sexuality into a mortal sin and being prosecuted just like murder? Sexuality is one of the most central drives in human beings. It is a means to experience pleasure and is a motivational force for achievement in all aspects of life.

What harms one person is not absolute. But belief in what is harmful or not harmful is. If this culture promotes that sex is harmful, then it will be experienced as harmful. I suggest that we start treating sex as not harmful, but as natural as eating and just pleasurable.

In California, if you are a victim of domestic violence it is mandatory to go to counseling.

December 22, 2009. On Bay Area news:
The Oakland, California police arrested between 100-150 low to medium level drug dealers after a "long investigation." This is the police's "cash crop of sub humans" to justify their jobs and to give them some appearance of purpose and meaning. Of course, they did not arrest the high level drug dealers because that could actually reduce drug use and the number of people involved in the Oakland drug trade. By arresting low and medium level drug dealers and allowing high level drug dealers to continue with their drug trade, new lower and middle level drug dealers will be recruited. The others are in jail. At the same time, to make sure that the drug trade is not slowed down and

stopped even temporarily. On the contrary, when the low and middle level drug dealers are released from jail, the number of drug dealers has now been greatly expanded so that even more drug dealers and users can be processed through the legal system. It is also worth noting that the arrests were done two days before Christmas to maximize anger and animosity among the people who are being arrested. When they get out of jail they are angry and revengeful. An increase in violent crime is secured. It is also the perfect time to create as much anger and opposition as possible among the general population, especially among family and friends of the people arrested. This will secure as much increase as possible in violent crime and the recruiting of criminals. It is appalling!

"How can you, middle class, overprotected, suburban sofa philosopher, decide how urban ghetto people should be punished and live? You do not know anything! You are just theory and you have no real knowledge and experience preparing you for making those decisions!"

Principle: *Any act between people where no intentional permanent physical damage has occurred. All parties involved are free to walk away from the act, no crime has taken place.*

Principle: *Any self inflicted act is the sole responsibility of the individual.*

Effectiveness of prisons (Wikipedia)

Meta-analysis of previous studies shows that prison sentences do not reduce future offenses, when compared to non-residential sanctions. This meta-analysis of one hundred separate studies found that post-release offenses were around 7% higher after imprisonment compared with non-residential sanctions, at statistically significant levels. Another meta-analysis of 101 separate tests of the impact of prison on crime found a 3% increase in offending after imprisonment. Longer periods of time in prison make outcomes worse, not better; offending increases by around 3% as prison sentences increase in length.

Effective rehabilitation programs reduce the likelihood of re-offense and recidivism. Effective programs are characterized by three things:

first, they provide more hours for people with known offense risk factors (the Risk Principle); secondly, they address problems and needs that have a proven causal link to offending (the Needs Principle); and thirdly, they use cognitive-behavioral approaches to behavior modification (the Responsivity Principle). Providing rehabilitation to people at lower risk of reoffending results in a 3% reduction in reoffending, while providing rehabilitation to people with a high risk of reoffending is three times as effective, resulting in a 10% reduction in subsequent offending. Risk factors for reoffending are: age at first offense, number of prior offenses, level of family and personal problems in childhood and other historical factors, along with level of current needs related to offending. Those individuals who had many personal and family problems in childhood (particularly 19 or more), started offending before puberty, and have committed multiple priors are more likely to reoffend in the future, according to longitudinal studies internationally.

In support of the Needs Principle, programs that specifically target criminogenic needs (causal needs and problems), see a 19% reduction in reoffending. In support of the Responsivity Principle, there is a 23% reduction in reoffending after participating in programs that use cognitive-behavioral methods to bring about changes in behavior, thinking, and relationships. When all three principles are effectively applied, the impact on offending is a 26–32% reduction, compared to a 3–7% increase in offending found with imprisonment alone.

Residential approaches—whether in prison or some other live-in option—tend to be less effective than non-residential approaches.

These researchers found that effective programs delivered in the community were followed by a 35% reduction in reoffending, whereas effective programs delivered in residential settings (such as prisons and halfway houses) were followed by a 17% reduction in reoffending.

One very likely reason for this is that for teens and adults, mixing with antisocial peers increases the risk of offending. In prison or residences inmates spend a great deal of time with other people immersed in criminal pursuits and beliefs, whereas in community-based programs there is more opportunity to mix with people involved in constructive, law-abiding activities. Antisocial peers in prisons and residences can form a very powerful pressure group, subtly and not so subtly influencing the behavior of other inmates.

**Prison population
per 100,000 inhabitants**

United States of America	756
Russian Federation	611
New Zealand	186
Australia	157
United Kingdom	148
Netherlands	128
Canada	107
Italy	104
South Korea	104
Germany	95
Turkey	91
France	85
Sweden	82
Denmark	77
Japan	62
Iceland	40

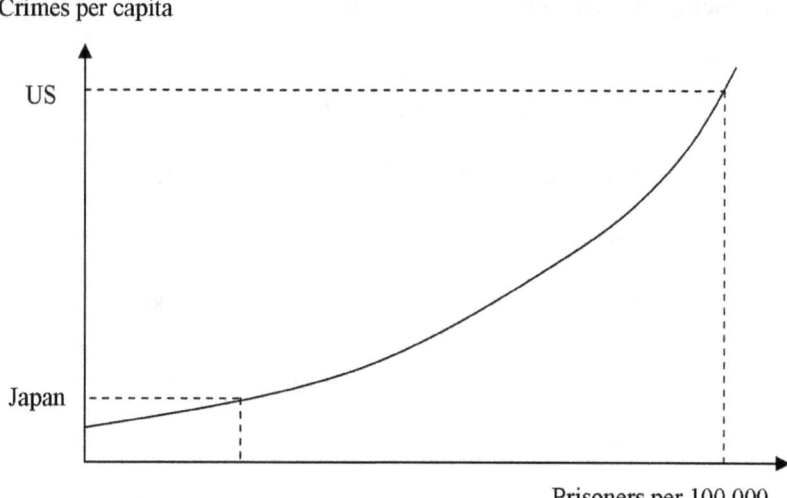

**Figure 17
Prisoners and Crime**

Pointers

- Solution to the crime problem is to allow "crime" to exist.
- Legal system should be conflict resolution oriented rather than geared toward prosecution.

It is programs like *America's Most Wanted*, *Cops*, the break-in of homes, the Waco incident, the war against drugs, throwing citizens in jail with three strikes and you're out laws. This is what fuels hatred against government. These programs can also provide the evidence for crimes against humanity. What is being shown is similar to the actions of Hitler's Gestapo—even their uniforms look similar. This is exactly what the people of Norway experienced during the Nazi invasion—the kicking down doors and the arrest of parents in front of their children. We saw the same tactics being used in Iraq, as well. As a child, growing up in Norway, I have memories of stories told about my grandfather being taken into Nazi custody, and my father hiding out in

the woods, repeatedly eluding his potential captors as an insurgent fighting the Germans.
- Someone who unsuccessfully accuses someone of a crime should get the same punishment as the accused would have gotten if proven guilty.
- The fact that a human being can handle psychologically the process of aging and death. They can also handle anything else psychologically that is hardly of any importance in comparison.
- The victim, of course, will support the doctor's findings and make what happened to them as serious as possible so they can get the attention. But he also acquires power by getting the victimizer punished as severely as possible. The way we have set up society, reap as big a reward as possible by being the victim. To hell with anybody else!
- The legal system creates drug addicts and homeless people who in turn feed social workers, psychologists, therapists, prison workers and police.
- The medical profession creates illness and drug dependent people as well as "disabled people" who also feed social workers. The only way to break this vicious cycle is to create a truly demand-oriented and natural society.

Ponder the following:
- Domestic Violence: It's 50/50 between men and women killing each other. Women are as violent as men. In fact, most fights are started by women with their pushing and prodding
- There are a lot of unfaithful alcoholic women in today's society.
- Women's shelters are breeding grounds for women to take advantage of laws in their favor at the expense of men.
- Experience with women that once they had a few drinks became completely unreasonable monsters. They are vicious. If you haven't dealt with a drunk out of control violent women whose is out to get you, you haven't experienced anything at all. It's absolutely a terrifying experience, especially, now that in light of all the domestic violence laws that you have no means to fight back.

The criminal system today drives mothers and fathers to kill their own families. Does nobody ask the question why?

- People are killing themselves and each other because of government interference. There is no other variable in the history of humanity that can explain the explosion in suicides and murders.
- The powerlessness and humiliation by the interference of police and social workers creates what they are set to prevent. The interference creates hopelessness, murder, abuse and violence. The interference also undermines the individual's sense of responsibility.

I have personal experience where the police were...
- Falsifying my testimony
- Falsifying the charges against me.

If they can do this against me, a white immigrant with a good education, what are they doing to Blacks, Hispanics, and other ethnic groups? With only two police cases I know intimately, in both cases, human rights were perversely violated by the police and the justice system. I ask this question. Was this just a coincidence? I want you to write to me about your case!

- Using plea bargaining is putting the justice system and ultimately justice out of effect. Another proof that the system isn't working. Innocent people plead guilty. Guilty people get off. Prosecutors use snitching and blackmailing to get witnesses for prosecuting criminals. In the military, a man becomes a hero when he is tortured and still not snitching on other prisoners of war and not revealing military secrets to the enemy. I was raised in Norway to never snitch on anybody as a most important human virtue. Even as kids we were told to honor this principle!
- The legal system sets people up to never admit that they have lied. Ex: Case against teacher for statuary rape against student. The Karen Cross case is a good example. A student lied and bragged to his friends about having sex. Their case escalated into the courtroom where of course the student would not admit that he had been lying. The 15-year-old did not even understand how serious his accusations were.
- We are horrified by fundamental Muslims. We think what they are doing is horrible when they cut a man's hand off for stealing a "cookie," But I would rather have that done to me than being locked up for life, if this was my third strike.

- Ref: Emotional Intelligence Book, by Daniel Goldman. Findings: Kids are much less emotionally developed today than before. Cause: Fear among parents to let kids out to play, looking at TV. Focus needs to be on rebuilding families. How can you, when the leadership of the family is undermined.
- Inside Edition Oct 7, 1996 Lisa Papas Case
- Your kids can be taken away from you if you forget to use a seatbelt. If you crash, you'll get a felony conviction up to 12 years in jail. Prosecutors can also use children to testify against their own mother.
- As the past fades away out of reality, the punishment needs to be reduced accordingly. In other words, maximum punishment can only be given immediately after the crime has been committed. A sliding scale needs to be established, based on the amount of time it's been since the crime has been committed.

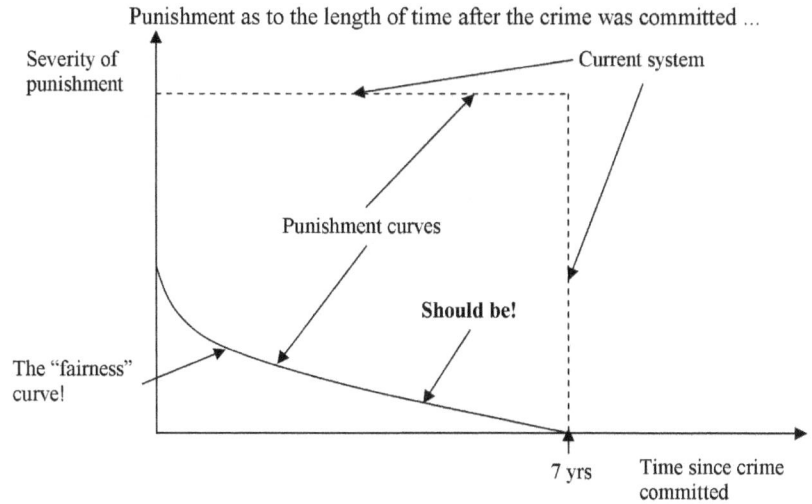

Figure 18
Fairness

- Because we have taken the right away from the parents to discipline their children we have set up government agencies and boot camps that are allowed to discipline the children. Who would be the right one to discipline the children? I believe the parents who love their children are the right ones to

discipline them. Instead of allowing the parent to exercise a small amount of discipline in the early stages of a problem, the society forces the parents to wait until the problem is much larger. Society then must use more heavy discipline and abuse to try to correct the child. The child is also put together with other difficult children when they are put into boot camp. They may form relationships with other children to form alliances against the parents, government and society.
- Why would the police increase the security after an attack??!!
- We have made the divorce law so one-sided for women that they have the tendency to lead to ferocious senseless violence committed by men. If a law is perceived to be unfair, it will lead to extreme violence.
- Who are the victims in the society? Somebody is victimized in a short moment. Then we destroy the person who did the "victimization" by throwing the person in jail—maybe for years—and take his children and job away.

The heroes of humanity in history have almost always gone through tremendous pressure, hardship and many times brutality and injustice. However, the adversity the hero experienced cultivated the best in that individual. They ended up as the best of what mankind can produce. Set this up against the lawsuit pettiness and idiocy of the modern society and victimization of today's suffering in fear of facing reality and trauma, and the belief that it will cause lasting damage to their psyches and inability to live normal and productive lives is laughable. It is self-deception boarding on negative self-hypnosis rooted in a choice to be a victim as to the means of finding life's purpose. Being a victim, actually experiences a purpose in life. What we call in the modern society, trauma that justifies us to stamp ourselves as victims is nothing as compared to what the heroes in history went through and were able to overcome. Most of what we are prosecuting people for is pettiness. It's all self hypnosis and deception from the mass media that makes us believe that what happened to us is that important.
- One of the most important parts of American culture has been destroyed by passing the DUI laws. It has destroyed the nightlife and clubs—the breeding ground for great entertainers and musicians and fun for the rest of us!

Crime and Punishment 223

- If you look at history and use logic, you will find that the vast majority of crime has been committed by leaders of governments or bureaucracies. If you define real crime as destruction, murder, and disability of people and theft of property, you will find that over 99% of all crimes have been committed by governments and its leaders during the 20th century. Crimes committed by individual citizens are negligible as compared with government and its leaders.

The principles that can be formulated from these historical facts are: the real criminals throughout history have been leaders of governments and religious organizations. If crime and destruction shall be minimized in the future, government and its leaders and religious organizations have to be controlled by the people.

23
Observations

1

Food for thought for antiabortionists (If thinking is possible among them): Logic and the yin-yang principle states that, if you cannot perform abortions and use stem cells from embryos, then we cannot condone medical interference favoring child birth. Both positions are anchored in a fatalistic world view. Making embryos live by human interference disturbs God's creation.

2

At which point do people say that the government is wrong instead of them for punishing what they do. You can conceive of a society that is wrapped up in legislative values that by definition makes us all criminals. The question becomes: Where is the crossover point? The US has gotten to that point a long time ago. Is the government right, or are the people right? If we make acquiring wealth, knowledge and sexuality into crimes—considered a sin in orthodox Christianity and the primary guidelines for US legislation, everybody should be locked up. There cannot be a question of being caught or who is living in peace and freedom.

3

There is no hope for people who are poor in America to ever advance themselves. What happens here will eventually happen everywhere. There is no hope because the poor can never buy a house and live a life of purpose, achievement and dignity. Our government is creating the nightmare. In fact, the federal government is the worst and most discriminating landowner in US history. The endless, rolling, hills around the San Francisco Bay are sitting there barren. There are hardly any trees growing on the hills. Less than 10 percent of these hills could immediately solve the housing problem and tremendously increase the area's biodiversity. Instead, the most fertile and productive land in the world—San Joaquin Valley—is strewn with housing, 100 miles away from the Bay Area. They are track homes built by a few corrupt contractors in collusion with corrupt politicians. These homes are so far away from cities that you need to drive for two hours each way. This driving "clogs" up the freeways and is spewing out pollution four hours a day that fuel global warming. At the same time, to build on agricultural land reduces the world's food supplies. It destroys the opportunity for poor people in the Bay Area to live a decent and hopeful life.

The greatest idiocy emanating from federal land not used for housing is that people who own homes in the Bay Area can only afford little "shit homes" built in the '50s filled with asbestos. They cost one million dollars when the same people could live in new, large, modern homes for the same money.

4

The Roman Empire's demise was caused by Christianity making knowledge, wealth and sexuality into sins—leading to the dark Middle-Ages and the "Barbarian" invasion!

5

When we talk about hostility or threats from other nations, we are threatened by that nation's leaders, not the people. When we say that we have a dispute with Iran it is not with the Iranian people but with Iranian leaders. US leaders decide to have a dispute with the Iranian leaders, not the American people. Wars between nations are caused by leaders of nations, not by the people of nations. So who do we need to control? WMD can only truly exist in the long run in democracies!

6

A marriage contract should be treated the same as a business. The contract needs to identify the head of the family and the distribution of property and income. In addition, agreement needs to be made with regard to:
- Rewards.
- Punishments.
- Philosophy about children.

The trend of societies is to limit everything that is pleasurable and enjoyable. This includes sex, drinking, smoking and everything else that could be considered enjoyable and pleasurable. What powerful forces and human perversion is behind this trend? Why are we going around punishing ourselves? It doesn't make sense!

Child labor: Is it better for a child to steal and beg for survival and become a prostitute rather than working?

Look at straight versus gay men. A lot of women are attracted to gay men:
- Straight men are raised to be distant, disciplinary and dominant.
- Women are comfortable around gays because gays are frivolous, like themselves.

- Societies break down as promotion of gays and lesbians stems from destroying the male by suppression and dominance of modern society. Women find maleness and dominance in government, rather than in the male, as it was in the past. As such, they seek protection from government rather than from the male.

Rehabilitation programs don't work unless they are voluntary. If they are not, it violates the principle of freedom.

The fact that many women today get the custody of the children when they divorce their husbands and choose to raise the children without fathers proves the women's desire to keep children for themselves and to exclude the father. Those decisions are made on purely egotistical grounds without regard to the child's desire to have a father. Women are driven by having "dolls" when they are young. But they get a rude awakening when the child grows up because the child needs the male for healthy emotional development.

The female is the custodian of culture. (Yin)—She makes the continuation of traditions, the arts, cooking, and music. She is normally the driving force behind it. She must have her nest!

The male is the custodian of morality. (Yang)—morality, achievement, ambition.

The role of women

"*A wife who is in competition with her husband, or who has just enough mind to detect his faults, is the extinguisher of genius.*"
~Goethe

It was one or maybe two generations who could afford to have women at home. The upper class was able to keep their women at home without working. When everybody's affluence increased due to the industrial revolution, the sign of affluence was the opportunity to allow women to stay home and to not work as a status symbol. It was also an expression of the man's love so she did not have to work and have money and time to beautify herself. Dissatisfaction among women in this arrangement is grounded in the inherent desire for self realization, the desire to work and achieve. In fact, doing nothing is the ultimate deprivation from living and the ultimate punishment.

One of the fundamental constants in human relationships is dominance and submission, in marriage, government, business and other organizations. Not allowing the relationship between husband and wife to be a relationship of dominance and submission is not natural.

Subordination = submission

To be a subordinate means to be submissive to something.

Any organization of human beings would not function without the ability to exercise dominance and to be submissive. And a marriage is the smallest organization within a society, and the same laws which apply to any organization needs to be allowed in the smallest of organizations. Why do you love your dog? The dog is submissive and the dog loves you because you are dominant. If you are not dominant with you dog, the dog will stop loving you. At least a real dog—like a German Sheppard or Pit Bull would stop loving you. Either he will be submissive to you or he will eat you.

Very few marriages would fall apart, if they have great sex together. Today, through legislation the power has been taken away from the male and made him into a sissy. And the female has been made into a man. If the man's opportunity to be masculine, meaning dominant has been taken away from him and the female has been persuaded that it is no longer desirable to be feminine, sexuality is destroyed. A house and money is not going to keep a couple together. Not even children. So in order to create happy marriages again, we need to restore masculinity and femininity. That is yang and the yin which is needed for harmony and love. A whole generation's opportunity to be happy in marriage has been destroyed in the last 40 years.

The social experiment "to make the male into a female and make the female into a male" needs to stop because it is completely perverted and not normal. It would not exist without legislation and the destruction of freedom!

For an organization to exist, one person has to be willing to do what the other person tells that person to do, and that is an act of submission. The person who tells another person what to do is an act of dominance.

Neither the dominant one nor the submissive one should feel bad about being one way or the other. It actually causes a feeling of respect and admiration and love. The US has a president—in order for this country to work. We have to, at some level, submit to his authority and dominance. Otherwise, it will be completely dysfunctional. What's wrong with being a female?—that's why we have in the wedding vows "Do you promise to honor and obey him?" That sentence is the most important one in the wedding ceremony as it is a great aphrodisiac and an expression of love. You get married because you are getting a WIFE. And you want a wife because you want to have children and sex with her. Not like it is today, you take a wife because she's going to be a good business partner. Do you believe that getting a business partner is better than becoming husband and wife?

When people react violently to this opinion, they actually know, deep inside, that I'm right. Those people who react this way, they try to force everybody else to be a certain way, but in their personal life, they act entirely different. This is manifesting itself over and over again among so called Christians and right wing politicians. Doing the exact opposite in private what they are trying to force others to conform to. The American people are ready to throw up over the hypocrisy of it all.

In other words, bowing and curtsying need to be restored!

The female gains her power through her femininity and carrying the children. The male gains his power by providing protection and safety and materially for the female and the children. What we can call true morality (not sexual morality, if that even exists)—the custodian of true morality is the male. The female is the custodian of culture. So if we want "moral" children, they need the attachment to their father. The father gives conditional love. This injects ambition and competitiveness into the children, as well as the idea of fair play. The mother gives unconditional love. The mother through her unconditional love injects into the children, culture, traditions and nurturing. Both parents are needed for healthy development of children.

When you look at the stages of a boy's development, according to psychology—the way it was taught 30 years before we had a strong political influence on it, and it might have been a lot more objective back then. The stages of a boy's sexual development, is as follows: He discovers his sexuality by playing with himself already from the time of two years old or younger. He is capable of achieving an orgasm already as an infantile. Then his sexuality from about 5 years old to about 8 years old is directed toward girls. From about 8 to about 11 he is in many ways homosexual and has sexual relations with his boy friends. The girls are rejected at that age by the boys. From about 11 his interest in girls starts to become dominate again. And by the time he is 12 or 14 he can be hysterically in love with a girl. Normally at a distance but it develops very quickly into sexual playfulness. He is immature; he may have his first real sexual relationship from the time between 16 and 21 as being the most common.

Same sex sexuality among girls is much more prevalent than it is between the boys and it lasts a lot longer into becoming a teenager. At the same time, girls when they are about 14 are in many respects ready to find and have long term sexual relationships. And they are seeking out boys who are at least 5 to 6 years older than they are and are rejecting boys of the same age. The boys of the same age are rejected because they are completely immature and not ready for their affection.

A 17 year old boy gets 10 years for having consensual sex with a 15 year old girl!

It has been a catastrophic decline in "boys" motivations and performance in school over the last 30 years. This is understandable, as boy's motivation is driven by the ambition where his number one goal is to find a wife and have a family. A man's ambition is not driven as much for himself but his ability to take care of someone else. This ambition is instilled in him by his father, and too many boys grow up without fathers. Legislation and culture has over the last 30 years undermined his ability and desire to start a family by the continuous promotion of hostility against the male and to make it a virtue among women to leave their husbands and boyfriends. It was therefore great to see and touching that a school in Berkeley CA, is going to welcome boisterousness, desire for exploration and masculine energy in their students. This is a very important step in the right direction for the US to foster a new generation of entrepreneurs and scientists.

Medicine

What is pain? It is the body's ability to heal itself by increasing the blood flow to that part of the body that has been hurt. When we feel pain, the mind focuses its efforts on that area that has been hurt. Hence, taking "medication" to reduce swelling and pain will slow down the healing process. This is also an example of how the mind creates the healing process.

Almost all over-the-counter drugs do not cure illness, but rather treat symptoms. Symptoms are, to a large extent, a manifestation of the body's natural defense and immune system to mobilize to fight off illnesses as effectively as possible. For example, a cough is the body's natural reaction to get rid of bacteria and mucus from the lungs. If you take a cough suppressant, bacteria and mucus stay in the lungs and aggravate the illness. There is reason to believe that the prevalent occurrence of pneumonia in the US is a direct consequence of people taking cough suppressants.

Another example is when you get a fever. A fever mobilizes the body's immune system to produce white blood cells to kill viruses and bacteria. If you take fever-reducing medication you are hampering the body's ability to fight off infectious diseases. Fever also makes bacteria and viruses more vulnerable to the attack from the white blood cells. Generally whatever you treat—suppressing or stimulate—by taking "medication" or symptom reducers, makes the body want to compensate from interference. What you have treated rebounds even stronger when the medication's effect wears off. The surest way to get chronic headaches is to take headache medicine. So, what some call medications—which are few—and by definition cures a disease, is not in reality medication but symptom reducers. It is extremely important to understand and make this distinction. On the other hand, natural medicines and health enhancing products are designed to work with the body to strengthen its own chemistry to fight off illnesses, boost the immune system and contribute to the overall health and wellbeing of the individual.

The conditioning and dependency cycle of medication. Taking medications for anti-clogging for heart disease over time destroys the body's ability to anti-clog. If you stop taking the medication, chances for clogging of the circulatory system are greatly increased.

Taking pain killers makes the body even more susceptible to pains and headaches when you stop taking them.

Principle: The body is bouncing back to the other and opposite extreme when you stop taking the medication.

It's also been proven that if you take allergy medication you will be much more allergic after it wears off!

US Doctors sometimes tell people that there is something wrong with them, even if there is no problem! If you look long and deep enough, you can find something wrong in anybody. This can have an enormous effect on the person who has the "problem." It may completely destroy their lives and cause self-inflicted imprisonment and no participation in physical activity or careers. Suppose the doctor finds out that you have a slightly elevated blood pressure. The doctor prescribes medication. The side-effect of blood pressure medication is muscle pain, calcium build up in the muscles and joints, manifesting itself as a pain similar to arthritis. Doctor tells patient you have elevated blood pressure and that you need to avoid physical activity. No physical activity has proven to compromise the immune system and speed up the aging process. A compromised immune system increases the chances to get cancer. The person pulls back from physical activity, and stops working because of pain. The likelihood of a premature death greatly increases. The quality of life has been destroyed. The best medication would be to change diet and exercise. Both would increase the quality of life, extend life expectancy and foster a desire to continue their career.

It is more important for the medical profession to prove that they are doing something through X-rays, blood samples and intravenous feeding than actually curing a disease.

Notwithstanding what I said about medicine above: "Modern medicine does a lot of good and you need to seek medical treatment if you get sick. You also need to go for check ups. However, you need to educate yourself, be critical and seek multiple opinions before action is taken!"

24
Who are The Real Criminals?

As the ruling class in a feudal system suppresses its own people for its own benefits, so do modern western societies. Government human service agencies will justify their own power and existence by producing "victims" who need their services. It makes these people happy by giving medical services, food and shelter to the people. Government needs to continuously create a purpose for them to justify their existence and is using "morality" as an excuse. However, the result is the erosion of freedom.

The government knows that to preserve its power, influence and privileges, it can only be justified by having a threat to the society. No wonder when the cold war dissipated, government turned around and declared war against its own citizens by declaring war on drugs and crime. Of course, when you declare war on something, you also have to have an enemy. The government is a master at creating them. It is obvious that former California Governor Pete Wilson was out to take revenge on the state's people. He knew he was not going to be re-elected, so he took revenge under the disguise of morality by punishing undocumented immigrants in the most inhumane way. Wilson denied them access to education, medicine, and California driver's licenses. He passed laws to create another class of "Les Miserable's". Do we live in France, 150 years ago? If you haven't read the book or seen the screen play, you should. It would be an eye opener.

Protection and security were the arguments of organized crime and the mafia to "tax" people. It is a direct parallel to the government and what is happening. In fact, "organized crime" and the mafia were the formation of government within another government. There is very little difference between them. Of course, the government in power will diligently fight another government within its borders. The question is: How can we create a society where both are prevented from taking advantage of the people? A major difference is the election of politicians to "serve" the people. However, if the election process is flawed, self interest among politicians becomes the stronger force. The interest of the people suffers.

If unemployment benefits are taken away, why are we paying such a high tax rate? The primary purpose of taxes originally was to protect people from misfortune.
Are we paying taxes for protection? There is no protection, only punishment. So we pay taxes so the government can continue to punish us? How perverted!

High taxes on cigarettes, alcohol and luxury items are how the government under the moral guise of reducing consumption makes money off of people's misery.

Some countries even monopolize alcohol, drugs and cigarettes to make sure they control the profit. They use the disguise that the money is used for the common good for all of us! It actually supports the government. The government rips us off to benefit themselves. If most of the money went back to the citizenry in tax reduction and/or the welfare system, then a justification could possibly be made. This is not the case in western societies. The money goes to support the government. In that respect, they behave exactly like the mafia did in the 20s and 30s. They are telling you that you need protection. The result is the loss of freedom.

Most criminal acts are not done by individual citizens, but by governments. Governments of the 20th Century have caused more death estimated to be at least 250 million people and incredible more suffering for hundreds of millions more. This is without any comparison to what has been committed by individuals. If war and killings are good, let us be honest about it and say it. "We like to have wars and kill people and destroy as much as possible of what is built by man from time to time so we can gain satisfaction from it."

War elevates the importance and power of the politicians. That is why war is irresistible.

The reason why very little happened after Katrina and why we had a disastrous response is because the American people have become a nuisance and necessary evil to the government. The people have become somebody the government cannot trust. They demonize the American people to be rapists and robbers, and fundamentally criminal in nature. Their response emanates out of the belief that humanity is fundamentally evil and needs to be oppressed and micromanaged. Otherwise people will commit unspeakable crimes against each other.

Law and order after the disaster was more important than to help and save people.

In the swearing in of the US president he states: "I promise to protect the government of the US!" There is no mentioning about protecting the people. This is conspicuously absent. No, you are not elected to do that. You are elected to serve and protect the American people. This pledge explains why the government has become a separate and ruling class in the US

A new feudal system is being established by politicians and bureaucrats where position of power and privilege are being inherited by the children of politicians & bureaucrats. If that is so, we have a "de facto" feudal system and nepotism.

The real criminality is the police beating of a 64-year-old black man by four officers in New Orleans, and the police looting the city including stealing cars from a Chevrolet dealership.

It was government who created weapons of mass destruction in the 20th Century. Now humanity has to deal with criminal acts against humanity in the 21st Century committed by government. Governments continue to create and foster conditions in the world so weapons of mass destruction might be used. They feed on each other to expand their own internal powers in their own countries, using the possibility of war and aggression from other countries to expand and solidify their power and privilege in their own countries. As an example, the cold war fed the dictatorship in the Soviet Union and they fed the expansion of power by the US government. Now we use sanctions against nations, proven to solidify the existing power in that country and turn its people hostile toward the US and other sanctioning countries. How perverted and dumb is that unless the goal is to create even more tension and potential for conflict!

The free capitalistic system regulates itself. The only thing regulation does is to create a false sense of security and make people more stupid. Legislation creates criminals and, of course, all this is in the government's interest.

Spending money on weapons of mass destruction seems to correlate very well with the impoverishment of the people in those countries engaged in acquiring them.

Lack of freedom and dictatorships seem to correlate well with countries that spend money on these weapons, like North Korea and China.

The US government gives amphetamine pills to fighter pilots. The pilots who were involved in the friendly fire incident in Afghanistan were high on amphetamines. Reference: Nova PBS, Tuesday Jan 7 2003. Unmanned Armed Vehicles (UAW) technology used for attacks in Afghanistan with no warning in the nighttime kills everything on the ground, complete slaughter, taking no prisoners, no chance for the target to surrender. No defense, no law, just slaughter of innocent people and they still continue to do it as I write this in 2010.

Another proof that governments are only supporting the idea of governments without regard to the well being of people is the singular focus on the establishment of a government in Iraq by the US government. It's actually self-serving of the government. It ties into and helps to create the "new feudal system."

Leaks of government secrets and the need for them in a democratic society prove that secrecy is inconsistent with democracy and freedom. Ms. McCarthy leaked information about secret prisons in different countries recognizing that leaking was needed for democracy to persist proves the point.

Complexity is invented by the government to make the people feel too stupid to make up their opinion about issues. It is another way for government to increase and consolidate its power. This destroys democracy and freedom creating complexity by too much analysis that reduces the likelihood the best decision is being made.

The idea of secrecy of information by the government is completely unproductive with regard to the end results we are trying to achieve.

To keep information about possible terrorists and terrorist plots secret from the population means that rather than mobilizing all the people of the world to find who and where they are and the ability to prevent the plot is greatly diminished.

When parents are forced through legislation and punishment to care for their kids, the government has reduced the parent to just custodians of the child and as an extension of the government interest in raising a useful idiot as a citizen. Because legislating laws to take care of children destroys love and compassion toward the child.

Politicians talked about getting the world to go against Saddam Hussein. It is not the world but the governments and the politicians of the world who wanted Saddam Hussein, not the people of the world. The reason the US is the greatest superpower in the world is not because it has that many people but because the US has built the most Weapons of Mass Destruction.

Heard on TV: Somebody got 1,300 years in prison! That is a sentence going back to before the crusades and the Viking age. People who want people punished this way are no better than the criminal who did the crime in the first place. This is especially true when they want somebody to die, even if the person who allegedly committed the crime might be innocent. If that is not cruel and unusual punishment, then what is?

In San Quentin prison when a person dies before their sentence is finished, that person must be buried on the prison property with no markings other than their jail number. This goes on until such time as their sentences have been served thereby depriving their families for the right to give them a proper burial. In the example above, the family might have to wait 1,275 years (until the year 3285!) before they can give their family member a proper burial according to their values. Is this a just and compassionate society? **In fact, it is insanity!**

Peter Newfeld, founder of the Innocence Project, tried to get statistics from the FBI about the percentage of innocent people in jail. This has been met with reluctance from the judges and police to release evidence to the Innocent Project. The most likely reason for this reaction is that a proof of innocence undermines the power and legitimacy of the justice system. Obviously they don't care about justice.

The driving force behind wars is to make everybody in the government, defense and the justice arena more important. They elevate what they do to something meaningful. The threat of terrorism is increased by conducting wars. That is exactly what the government wants and why today's wars are fought.

Systematic torture has always been committed by governments! In fact, the plea bargaining system is based on torture as it is a way of coercing somebody to plea guilty with the threat and use of punishment. The same system as was used in the "dark middle ages"!

Who are The Real Criminals? 237

Through legislation the government makes everybody into a criminal to rule the people. Legislation also leads to dummification of the people.

The government is doing the same as Emperor Constantine did in 315 A. D, editing the Bible into the "King James Edition" as a political document to consolidate and preserve the power of the Roman Empire by making all the people feel guilty. The people must seek forgiveness for their sins through the Church controlled by the Emperor. All people would be sinners according to this edited Bible by making the three most important aspects of a person's life into sins, namely:
- Acquisition of knowledge
- Acquisition of wealth
- Having Sex

The same is happening today and will lead to another dark ages and unspeakable suffering by the people!

Dec 25, on Christmas day at approx 8 p.m., as I go for a walk on San Pablo Avenue, I look over into the parking lot of Bank of America. I see a police officer hand cuffing a prostitute. He has her lean over his car with her butt in the air. The only thing missing was a cane for spanking. I ask myself, "When will this perverted masturbation trip condoned by the government with the support of the church stop?" The policeman did not even pay for the pleasure.

If you notice, governments never find or kill the leaders of terrorist governments or the leaders of terrorist. Why haven't they found Osama bin Laden? The reason is that the leaders of governments believe that if they do not kill them, they will protect themselves personally against the terrorists. The end result is hostility against the people ruled by these people manifesting itself in endless killings of the people within the movements to "fight terrorism."

Sept 25, 2003, Man in Oakland, California refuses to stop for DUI checkpoint leading to a police chase in which two people are killed and a six-year-old child is severely wounded.

Individual punishment is a reductionist treatment and view. This serves as the foundation for punishing the individual. What is needed is a holistic view of punishment in the society.

When you have laws against abuse they will create the abuse!

The primary laws needed are laws that prevent government from abusing its citizens.

It is estimated that over 250 million people were murdered by governments in the 20th Century!

Source: Rudolph J. Rummel, *Death By Government* (1900-87)

"Democides" - Government inflicted deaths:	169,198,000
Wars:	34,021,000
Famines associated with war and mismanagement:	<u>55,108,000</u>
Total:	**258,327,000**

- Almost the size of the entire US population was murdered by governments during the 20th century! This number does <u>not</u> include the number of prisoners during the 20th century and people who was disabled!
- Murders by individuals during 20th century (US approximately = 1 million x 5) 5 million worldwide. This is a very rough estimate as good statistics are not available. However, the level of magnitude between government murders and murders by individuals is fairly accurate and shows that murders by individuals as compared with government murders are insignificant. Out of total killings of humans in the 20th century less than 2% were committed by private individuals while over 98% of murders were caused by governments!
- Murders by governments are continuing into the 21st century and are still going strong as I write this book in 2010!

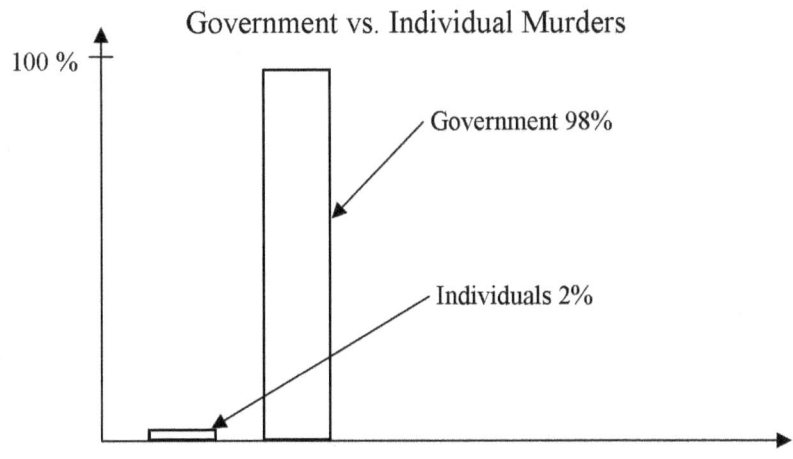

**Figure 19
Government vs. Individuals**

The government should be sued for fraud and discrimination as the tax laws discriminate against renters and favor home owners with regard to taxes and write offs.

There is reason to believe that the Iraq war was planned just after the first "Desert Storm War" in 1991. The strategy was to start an embargo of Iraq to cause increased discontent with Saddam Hussein so that when the US government would go in later, it would be seen as liberators of the Iraqi people. This strategy has cost more than 100,000 lives, especially of innocent children during the embargo years. Now it is costing countless more in the second war. The strategy has not worked—manifesting itself in increasing anger by the Iraqi people against the US occupation.

How can government get away with this kind of genocide while an individual killing one person gets a death sentence and somebody who steals for the third time gets life? This does not make any sense. This is a complete injustice toward humanity.

It is proven through history that any aggressive act of war leading to occupation of another country has never been won. As of March 2007, 51 percent of the Iraqi people thought it was OK to kill Americans. Iraq has about 20 million people. To win this war the US government needs to kill more than 10 million Iraqi people, which is almost double of what Adolf Hitler killed of Jews during the Second World War. This may be avoided if the US bribes the "enemy" with US tax money and that is what is going on today in 2010.

One of the primary reasons that an extended attack does not work in any society is that the people of that society are willing to die for the right to create their own future. The more pressure, the more the people of that country turn against their occupier. This has been proven throughout all of history. It is only people with no background in history who would use embargo against a country as a tool to achieve anything. It does the exact opposite. When a war is declared by a nation who's not oppressed by another nation or people—and that war is not declared by the people—it is declared by the leaders of the country and the war is executed against the leaders of the other country. An aggressive act is never supported by the people only defensive wars are supported by the people. Wars usually are not fought between people, but between governments.

When Bush said that Iran is an "Evil Empire", it is not the people who are evil. What he really meant is that the leaders of Iran are evil. That is a huge distinction. There was never a cold war between the people of Russia and the people of the US it was always a war between the leaders of those countries. "Ordinary" people will never be hostile against another people unless they are victims of government propaganda.

You can ask yourself, "Why did we have the cold war and what were the consequences?" It was in the self interest of the US and Soviet governments to have a cold war because it elevated their power and influence within their own countries and solidified their power structure. In other words, it was in their self interest.

When the cold war ended the government had to invent and create new wars to continue the consolidation of their powers and influence. The really sad part is that in the US, the government created wars against its own people. They manifest themselves in the wars against drugs, poverty and cultural wars. Now, also against immigrants! When that was not enough self-gratification for the leaders of government, they had to invent an invisible enemy called terrorism. This is just like Hitler did with the Jews. Now everybody can understand the dynamics of what has been happening over the last few years. The war in Iraq has created thousands of new terrorists, and millions of sympathizers all over the Muslim world. How can anybody be so dumb based on this simple logic doing what they are doing? Especially when Saddam Hussein would have been the last person in the world to attack the US, because he understood that it would mean his self-destruction. That's why Saddam killed every terrorist coming into his country because he wanted to remove any excuse for the US to attack him. We did not find any WMDs. We will not find any in most countries ruled by dictators. The reason is because a dictator is ruling by fear. A dictator will always seek to unarm the people and maximize the control over the military. A dictator will always live in fear of his own WMDs because he must give weapons to his military.

There are only three explanations why the attack on Iraq happened.
- Either incredible stupidity from US government leaders.
- They did it out of self interest.
- "Saddam Hussein is the man who tried to kill my father" said by George Bush in one of his "emotional" speeches.

Corruption only exists between government and private enterprise.

If the United States president is allowed to overrule international law regarding torture, we might as well never arrest the rulers of other nations when they do the same things to their people.

The safest places to visit on earth, are always the most desolate with very little or no government. A visitor who goes to those places that have been left alone will in most cases be completely safe, especially if Christianity has not been introduced!

As a rule, the less government and "traditional" religion, the less crime you will find!

By building up the Iraqi security forces we are arming Iraq which can lead to even more killing and fighting between the Iraqis when we leave. These weapons given to Iraqi security forces may even be turned on the Americans. Why does America believe that every problem in the world can be solved by violence and killing?

People around the world want peace. Only governments use war and instigate fighting and violence.

A woman walking on San Pablo Avenue gets stopped by the police and is fined for littering a cigarette butt. This person must go to court and pay a $10 fine. At the same time as she was being stopped by the police she was also asked if she could lift up her jacket so police could look at her bare breasts.

Oakland, California proves that police officers and the justice system do not work. Oakland has one of the highest murder rates in the country, the highest police density, and the highest percentage of incarceration. If those things work, Oakland should have the lowest murder rate in the country.

There is a direct correlation between how much government a country has and how many weapons of mass destruction it develops. To reduce and get rid of WMDs from the face of the earth we have to reduce government power around the world. Like in the US, North Korea, and Russia. An interesting fact that proved this point is reduction of military forces and military spending in Russia and the parallel reduction of government power in that country! After government became stronger again in Russia we can see a correlated increase in military spending!

To make 9/11 dictate government policy is ridiculous. Everyday 14,000 people die in the US, five times as many people as those who died in the terrorist attack. The more we "fight" terrorism, the more terrorism will happen both by "traditional" terrorists and the government to terrorize and destroy freedom itself. The 9/11 attack is being used by the government to consolidate its powers and privileges under the disguise of providing security and protection. The fact is terrorism would not exist had it not been for government actions and policies.

Two things that cause terrorism in the Middle East are:
- Injustice against the Palestinian people.
- Occupation by the US of Saudi Arabia, Iraq and Afghanistan.

Solution
Set up a separate state for Palestine and remove US troops from Saudi Arabia, Iraq and Afghanistan!

IT IS THAT SIMPLE!

Government leaders are selling the people through self interest that the society is so complex we need to leave all decisions to them. The fact is that the people very often are ahead of the politicians when it comes to making the right decisions. The idea of complexity is sold to us out of self interest by the government!

Intelligence reports about Iraq were not needed, only common sense. For Saddam Hussein to attack the US, he had to be on a suicide mission. If Saddam had attacked the US he would have assured a US attack on Iraq that would have destroyed his power. There is no way Saddam Hussein would ever have attacked the US "Duh!"

In fact, no identifiable organization in the world would ever attack the US. This truth forced the US with it's constellation of power to create the perfect enemy: the terrorists. This perfect enemy preserved internal political power of the US government and for the well being of the defense industrial complex.

If US leadership truly believed that Iraq had WMD, the US would have never attacked them. By attacking Iraq, the US would have given Saddam Hussein no other choice than to use his WMDs against the US He would have done exactly what we were trying to prevent because he would have been put into a corner with nowhere to go other than to use WMDs.

There were two primary reasons why we didn't find any WMDs in Iraq.

First Saddam knew that finding WMDs would have given the US an excuse for it to attack.

Second, a dictator who rules with fear among the people would fear that WMDs would be turned against his own regime. In fact, he wouldn't have wanted them because the fear is that the people would use the weapons against the government. He would not trust anybody but his inner circle. The only way a dictator can with some security develop and employ WMDs is to create an ongoing war against some enemy that is perceived in that country as a threat against them. This threat is always created by propaganda and by war.

Manufacturing and storing WMDs can more easily be accepted in a perverted way by a transparent democracy of checks and balances and by a people who trust and love their government. How can you trust anybody in the federal government when they or their families have investments in companies who are granted government contracts? For example, in the San Francisco Chronicle, Saturday March 13, 2004, on the front page, Section C, lower right corner. "Dianne Feinstein's husband Mr. Harold Blume has major investments in two companies that were just granted contracts for rebuilding Iraq". That's sad. If it is in both democrats and republicans financial interests to start a war, how can you trust them?

It would be very interesting to find out how many congressmen and their families have investments in companies who get government contracts.

There is a very little step between campaign contributions and the government opportunity to extort the private sector. This constellation also exists in the government's relationship toward lobbyists and lobbying. Blackmail occurs with the implication that you get favors and "protection" by politicians by being a great contributor. This constellation mimics the way the mafia operated in the past.

Money to rebuild Iraq is spent through the DOD versus US aide. DOD allocations cause a much higher danger to personnel working in the rebuilding than if it had been spent through other agencies. The reason the money is going through the DOD is that it is ultimately given to specific private contractors owned by US politicians and/or their families. It makes it much easier to circulate money into politician's pockets by running it through DOD. Any other organization would have much more oversight.

The largest serial murder of US citizens in recent years was the massacre of mothers, fathers and children in Waco Texas by the US government. The real criminals around the world are governments and government representatives through corruption. For example the Malawi government sells food reserves and pockets the money. This leads to widespread hunger and death among their people, a holocaust created by today's governments. There is no comparison. The real terrorists and criminals around the world measured by their criminal acts are governments.

Only large corporations like Enron and WorldCom closely tied with the government get away with hiding costs and bumping revenues since enterprises are subject to government regulations and interactions. In many ways they are protected by the government that gives them the opportunity to "cook the books" and allow managers to skim company revenues. Real businesses in a competitive environment subject to minimum government regulation will automatically be regulated by the free marketplace. It is when you mix politicians with individual businesses that real fraud occurs.

The whole charade about terrorism is about power and privileges. "Is the government giddy over the opportunity to destroy freedom in all aspects of humanity?"

The fact that Saddam Hussein was accused of trying to get nuclear weapons while the US used it to justify the Iraq attack is, of course, in the US interest to justify dismantling freedom and consolidating of their own privileges and self interest.

To attack or place troops in another country is by definition anti-democratic and anti-freedom.

If we have a terrorist attack anywhere on the planet, a task force should immediately be established by the U. N. to evaluate the crisis. The leader of that terror group should be granted the opportunity to present his grievances to the U. N.!

If the U. N. task force finds grounds for serious grievances, the U. N. would have the mandate and obligation to solve and defuse terrorism in that part of the world. This is the exact opposite of what's being done right now.

Pictures of the Twin Towers in New York coming down over and over again only have one goal—to satisfy curiosity and create fear among people. The terrorist attack has become an excuse to destroy freedom even more than what was already destroyed at the time of the attack.

Freedom is the only way to destroy terrorists. The lack of freedom and injustice are the reason we have terrorists. How can we defend freedom by reducing and destroying freedom? The Bush Regime was the opposite of freedom. President Bush couldn't even cover up how happy he was when the Twin Towers collapsed. That includes his cabinet and the military brass as well. Anybody who knows a little bit about human nature when they watched TV after the terrorist attack could see their faces glee over what happened.

 The government commits hate crimes, but citizens are imprisoned. It doesn't make sense! The US government is increasingly imposing American law and values on the world. How can this be consistent with the idea of freedom and tolerance toward diversity and pluralism? The news media and the government need to share the responsibility for creating an atmosphere of hate crimes against Arabs in this country.

 The US through its alliances with other governments cracks down on terrorism. This helps other governments solidify their powers and dictatorships. An example of government stupor is what was said "having an opinion different from the government is an attack on freedom." This surfaced in an interview between President Bush and the leader of Indonesia. The interview was partially censored.

 There is nothing wrong with the American people. It's bad government that's wrong. If you can't trust your own government then you have bad government that is extremely dangerous. Also, it is the opposite of the Declaration of Independence that states: "government of the people and by the people." This idea is being completely violated in today's America. What do you expect from a government that is at war with its own people?

 Imprisoning 3 million people and untold millions more who have been jailed is? Other world governments are going along with the US not out of a concern for people but to establish their own power and security. Government power is increasing around the world with the support of other governments, especially by the US. In other words, governments in other countries are being supported in such a way as to boost their own powers and privileges.

 The "two-party system" in America found out many years ago that they have more in common as rulers rather than servants of the people.

Who are The Real Criminals? 247

Does the bombing of another country make you feel better? The reason why the bombing is being done is to make you feel better. There is no logic, objective value or philosophy behind the bombings, just the lowest of human emotions, namely revenge.

The menace to the world is government that creates its own Ten Commandments:
- Weapons trade
- Wars
- Taxes
- Dictatorships
- Incarcerations
- Ridiculous rules and regulations to harass people
- Promotion of poverty
- Promotion of dependence
- Drug use and drug proliferation
- Broken marriages

Government leaders are full of glee for the opportunity to consolidate their powers on the back of the terrorist attacks. We can see how Chinese leaders aligned themselves with the US against terrorists. I ask why citizens are not given the vaccine against anthrax? Why only government employees? The government is in the business of protecting its own hide. The truth is that they don't give a damn about you! Wars are being started so people can elevate their own powers and influence. That's how simple it is.

If the US citizen cannot trust its own government, here at home, how can they possibly trust the same government abroad? Patriotism is nationalism. Nationalism is Nazism is Imperialism is Fascism. That is something that can be proved. This is the role the US now plays in the world.

The purpose of the drug war is for government to have a monopoly by taxing drugs and giving pharmaceutical companies big profits for tax purposes. How can a country that harbors WMDs deny any other country the same? How can you expect America to support democracy around the world when you don't have it here?

The whole idea of personal freedom and decision-making authority has been completely taken away from the individual. According to the Geneva Convention, soldiers should be treated humanely by warring adversaries. The reason for this rule is that wars are not between people but between governments. That even includes fighters in the military as they are treated as "innocent" of the war!

On Sept 10, 2001, the day before 9/11, George Bush had a meeting where he decided for the first time to go after the Al Quada movement to break it up. That act proves that he knew about the attack in advance. This was reported on ABC News "This Week" by Mr. Moran, White House correspondent.

The put options on the airlines in the stock market means that people make money when airline stocks fall. That volume tripled the last few weeks before the September 11 attack. This fact can be verified by accessing SEC records at the time. It is also possible to find out who profited from these put options. Why hasn't this investigation been conducted? It's a good thing we went after Martha Stewart for insider trading even the fact that I like her! Her case created a precedence so when we put the profiteers from the 9/11 attack to justice, they will be punished as they committed really obscene crimes!

When information about terrorists is given to and gathered by government agencies—if the information is not acted upon to prevent a terrorist attack—what they are doing is useless. It's a complete waste of taxpayer's money. They would probably not act unless they have terrorist names, the time and date and location where the attack will be, and not even then will they act as 9/11 proved!

Local governments are passing laws against begging and pan handling. San Francisco repeat offenders are fined $500 or put in jail for 6 months. This law is set up to satisfy the legal system's need to incarcerate more people. In its deepest sense, the law is de facto, introducing slavery, since the freedom to do nothing has been taken away from the citizen. These laws are a crime against humanity.

We as adults cannot even discipline children. But government can lock them up for years and subject them to horrible mental and physical abuse.

It is a manifestation of the great weakness of the US Constitution that sons, daughters, and grandchildren of previous, incompetent

Who are The Real Criminals? 249

presidents can be elected as presidents or to any other office. When top level politics have become a family affair it shows the lack of a truly free and democratic process.

On top of everything else, the government has been and is doing secret medical experiments and treatments on unknowing subjects, exposing millions of people to radiation and dangerous chemicals, even using uranium in ammunition. Politicians are rewarded by mass media with exposure when atrocities, disasters and negatives happen. That ends up becoming the driving force behind the negatives. Look at what governments have created over the last 30 years: "A bunch of overweight, victimized wimps!" Maybe governments are thinking they are doing the right things. Maybe they are getting horny from all the power they gain. What the government is all about is not illegal. But it is disgusting!

By all the creation of rules and regulations during the 20th Century, this construct of the human imagination is now destroying and punishing the people. But it also is a menace and is destroying everybody in society. This monster has taken on its own life and is making everybody into a victim. It's like we have created Hal the computer from *2001 A Space Odyssey*, making all of us victims from the president on down. It's an out of control monster feeding on freedom.

According to government principle and law, Hong Kong fraudulently achieved its affluence through tax avoidance and the free flow of capital.

Government and the justice system should help people solve their problems not cause more problems. The police have gone from protect-and-serve to prosecute-and-punish. They have evolved into destruction rather than of creation.

What incredible trauma the service men suffered who were kept in China. They had to endure living in a Chinese hotel next to the airport for 12 days. They probably will all suffer for the rest of their lives from the "China syndrome" while we throw people in jail for years for minuscule reasons. To top it off we put people to death in front of their friends and families without any regard for human dignity and life.

Politicians have no concept of creation and business, giving somebody who got the contract in San Francisco $20 million of taxpayer's money as seed money in the year 2000 to develop a marina restaurant complex on Treasure Island. This was a contract given to somebody who contributed over $50,000 to somebody's election campaign.

Justification to destroy freedom and create the "modern" United States has been allowed by its citizens. This is caused by the self interest propaganda by the government and military. Their goal is to make the world a hostile place surrounded by threats in order to "control crime". With the added "threat from immigrants", the American people have sanctioned a police state. The history of the 20th Century will be how the system destroyed freedom, committed genocide and was worse than what any individual criminal ever did. There is going to be no government leader except for maybe Gorbachev, Gandhi and Mandela who will be heroes of the 20th Century. President Obama has the opportunity to become a great president; I hope he sizes the moment!

On the Sally Jessy Raphael Show Sept 29, 1998, about teenagers and how the guards treat them. Guards are portrayed as heroes. At the same time, corrections are done through fear. Are we going to live in fear, and do the "right things" based on fear? Or, are we going to raise children to do the right things based on moral fiber and freedom?

Terrorism is a minor infraction and virtually nothing as compared to crimes of governments and its atrocities. It is time for the people of the world to be enlightened enough that ideology is the seduction of the masses by crazy, power maniacs fostered by their political systems. War doesn't serve anybody but the political leaders seeking to consolidate their powers. As we notice from recent history, when you have holocausts, governments are doing very little.

On the Sally Jessy Raphael Show August 27, 1998, woman is accused of child abuse for disciplining her child. There are only two solutions for the society.
- Parents give up their children to the government or,

- Abolishing the child abuse laws.
Legislation has destroyed the very fabric of the family. Why would anybody get married and have children in this country when you are risking that? The ultimate cruelty is taking children away from their parents. The real major abuser of children and their parents is the government. We are making our children crazy with all this unnatural legislation!

Antitrust laws filed against Microsoft and Intel was completely wrong! We are living in a global economy with global competition. The idiocy of government and perverse logic is manifesting itself in the prosecution of two of the most important and successful companies in the high technology economy. Filing lawsuits against these two companies put a wet blanket on these two companies that are responsible for the engine of growth for the world economy for the last 10 to 20 years.

The government is guilty of the same stupidity as it did with the banks regulation 20 years ago. To a large extent this prevented American banks from becoming world banks engaged in financing the world economy. That's why American banks never became world banks. The US government left the world banks to the Swiss. This stupor prevented the American banks from becoming world banks engaged in financing the world economy. The US government prevented American banks from dominating the world. If the banking system worked in the US, wouldn't it be logical to think that it would work in the rest of the world and could have spurred the world economy to a much faster growth rate? Now after the failure of the world banking system, the government did not allow the free enterprise system to work by allowing the banks to collapse but bailed them out on the back of the average tax payer! The politicians did the bail-out because they would have lost money as well! So, they bailed the banks out from self interest and the knowledge that they were responsible for the collapse!

Slow growth in the world economy and the reason that poverty and hunger in the world has not yet been resolved is from nationalism combined with regulation stupor of government of the business community and financial institutions. The proof that the free enterprise system works is the collapse of the financial system in the fall of 2008. It should have collapsed as the reason for the bubble was government creation of Fannie Mae and Freddie Mac creating artificial value and security in the housing sector leading to wild speculation in the financial sector.

The collapse of the financial sector was created by government interference in the economy and removal of risk from the banking system!

The sad part of progressives is that they act on things they don't really understand. The premise of what they are doing is wrong, causing extreme damage to the world. If we had allowed nuclear power to evolve naturally from the '50s, we would not have the problem of global warming today. Short-sighted, well-intentioned environmental activists have created some of the most serious environmental problems that we have today.

The free enterprise system is naturally finding the most cost effective way of delivering its products and services to the end user. Now we are developing solar homes for the consumer. We could have gotten there 20-30 years ago had it not been for the environmentalists' stupor.

"Governments are creating nuclear bombs, not the people!"

It is time for the world's people to take charge and throw out government as we know it!

The balloon of idiocy was blown up to its limits. Considering the Clinton impeachment, it was a great case exposing the (sub) conscious conspiracy. Everybody feeds on each other where the foundation is idiocy or nothing. The non-interest in politics by the average person is because the system is not working. Everybody looks to the Constitution. Why? We are looking at the Constitution because it was written more than 200 years ago when we were living in a more natural society. On the other hand it has to be wrong to believe that something that was written 200 years ago is the absolute truth. The Constitution should be rewritten today to make it even better.

The US military is terrified of the Ottawa process to ban land mines worldwide. Of course they would be terrified because it represents the first step to ban all weapons worldwide.

If we should have Child Protective Services, then divorce should be illegal. There is almost nothing that is worse than a divorce as far as trauma and abuse of a child. The only thing that is worse is when the child is taken away from the parent. The biggest and most horrible abuser is the government—today and historically. Protection from governmental abuse is the most important issue in society. This is also reflected in the US Constitution. So why does the US do the opposite of what the Constitution says?

Just when communism fell in Russia, the US government killed 70 women and children in Waco, Texas. I have never heard that the same killing of women and children was ever done in communist Russia.

The fundamental problem that makes it a dictatorship and destroys freedom and ultimately society is suspicion and envy of the fellow man. We create a society where everybody is miserable rather than allow somebody to succeed and be free. You must make political decisions from your heart since all news and information is slanted by special interests. All mass media news is fundamentally entertainment.

The internet has the potential to make many government agencies obsolete. It makes the capitalistic free enterprise system work even better. Easy access to information makes many regulatory organizations obsolete. For example, product safety, environmental impact of products and product evaluations.

The mass media will also be paid for by the purchasing of information by the consumers.

Example: Side impact crashworthiness of cars.

I am sure the public would be willing to pay for the testing if privatized.

The Clinton case will be looked upon in the same way as we look at the McCarthy era. This was a farce and entertainment.

Prime Time Live March 18, 1998. How good is government when it engages in slave trade of women for whore houses outside of Russia?

The fire in Alamo, Texas set by the Park and Forestry Department is a typical example of a government agency's action that was formed to prevent fires. Actually, it's in their interest to actually cause a fire. The truth is that there are many cases where firefighters have been the arsonists. The psychological mechanism is the preoccupation with the task they have been set to perform. When the task doesn't happen often and strongly enough, there is a strong incentive to precipitate it. These fires feed into agencies that enforce building codes for new buildings. In their self interest, they make more difficult building codes that increase their powers to justify what they do.

When Gene Kelly sings and dances in the movie *Singing in the Rain*, the police come and destroy his happiness. This is a typical example of destructive behavior. When police are symbols of destroying even an expression of happiness—like what they did to Gene Kelly—that should be a crime.

Has any individual in recent history forced sterilization on other people? The US government did exactly that until the early '70s according to government documents. How many individuals have incarcerated and locked up anybody for many years? It has happened a few times. Your government is doing that everyday to thousands.

The consequences of legislation are human tragedy and injustice. It's a waste of resources and it destroys the human spirit. Psychologists and psychiatrists are out to defend their own profession. In so doing promotes legislation against all sorts of behavior, especially making sexuality something that is completely beyond reason. Example: Boy wanted to have sex with an older person, mother did not stop it. Mother gets 12 years in jail. What is more abusive? The boy is losing his mother or having sex? This does not make sense at all!

60 Minutes, CBS, June 12, 2000. Every time government goes into business, like medical supplies it becomes totally corrupt and fraudulent. More than $1 billion fraud was committed in the medical supply business just in California.

The incompetence of government has become complete;
- A complete failure to increase the power supply in California
- No water

- No land for housing development
- The lack of maintenance of infrastructure such as highways, freeways, and public transportation

This is the basic infrastructure needed for healthy development of a society. In fact, the California government does the exact opposite of what they need to do. All of it is morally justified.

To find and create child abuse cases, the justice system creates work and meaning for the social system. Reference: Mother dragging boy through a department store, now thrown in jail, kid taken away from mother. An abusive act by government, far beyond what the mother did. This is another proof that a whole system thinks and acts on wrong principles.

The War on Drugs is a typical example. It shows that government is completely incapable of providing any creative and positive means of solving any problems of a society. Choosing to put people in jail is the ultimate destructive means of trying to solve a problem.

The idea all of these authorities have is that they need to "put the citizen's interests first!" This is what they are using as a moral justification while it is in their self interest why it is being done.

We have created a society where people are afraid of each other, rather than embracing and loving each other. The reason is that it is in the government interest to create that kind of society because the government powers and income and opportunity for taxation is driven by injecting the fear and need among people for security and protection. The government creates this state of affairs.

Ted Koppel July 20, 2000. Restraining Chains Used in Prison – This is a horrible violation of human rights and dignity.

The Middle East conflict can never be solved unless the people of the world get rid of nationalism, religious fanatics and racism which are the root problems.

Tragedy, shooting and violence by individuals perpetuates big government. That is why politicians and the mass media are full of glee when it happens. That gives them a sense of being needed with a purpose. It feeds the government self interest and mass media. The self interest of the social system and therapists are being fed as well, magnifying the psychological damage to everyone involved. Just start to notice how they are full of glee when tragedy happens. Don't let their attempt to act different fool you.

Example of crime by government:
Using Agent Orange in Vietnam during the Vietnam War causing millions to be poisoned by dioxins, which has been proven to cause birth defects, reduce brain development and cancer.

If you need proof of what governments are doing, turn on the news. There is the proof of wars and killings. In another 50 years, WMDs will symbolize shame and destructiveness. Future generations will look at our prison system as we look at the German concentration camps during the Second World War.

The knowledge among traditional "Christians" that what they believe in is naive, childish and immoral, and that they are trapped in their belief, creates an enormous hostility and overwhelming desire to be revengeful and to exterminate others they feel do not share their belief.

Christians, Muslims and Jews project upon their religions what they wish it to be, but not what it really is according to the Bible, Koran, and the Torah.

The Mormons are very clever when they send out their young men and women as "Missionaries" so they can be repeatedly humiliated for a year by non-Mormons. This creates a very strong feeling of "in" group versus "out" group. It seeks to consolidate their loyalty to the "in" group and leads to no moral consideration when they exploit the "out" group.

The founding fathers separation of church and state was not wanted for religious reasons. What they really wanted was—instead of filling in those gaps in knowledge with God—to explore those gaps scientifically and fill them with scientific knowledge.

If you pray for going to heaven, and if God exists and is almighty, he will observe that you are lying to him and not let you in!

What is the purpose of being a superpower other than controlling, intimidating and throwing your weight around? The idea of being a superpower imposes their views/values on other countries and gains advantage at the expense of other countries.

Politicians are playing a self-serving game with the countries' economies, stimulating it before elections when it is in their interest. The division of power yields a great temptation to slow down and speed up the economy in conjunction with elections as to what their powers are and what they control. It's the temptation on behalf of the ruling party in an election to manipulate the economy.

Nationalism and governments are mob like gangs with no respect for human individuals and human life. They believe themselves in the absolute right of territories and control of human life.

What is the US interest in another country? Is it economical, influence, prestige?

Dateline Oct 20, 1995—39th District in Philadelphia about police corruption. They investigate more than 1000 cases of police corruption. Why a national prison lock down the same time the segment was on TV (censorship)?

The politicians and the government create the economic crisis around the world because it is in their own self interest.

What really works is the free market with free flow of capital to foster an environment with high investments and high consumption. In fact, the governments of the world are like wet blankets to economic activity manifested by taxes, customs, regulation, restrictions and an enormous waste of resources. This is true both in manpower and in material for military purposes and in the bureaucracies around the world.

What the government does best, under the current paradigm, is to restrict private business and initiatives and freedom, while developing nuclear bombs and weapons for themselves.

So, you are passing these laws in order to create what you appear to claim to prevent, in order to justify your own position and career and to increase your own importance. You do it in order to create something to do which appears to be justified and important. It creates a society where you have to break the law in order to get ahead.

The fundamental problems are not created by the citizens but by the governments of the world creating nuclear arms, war and terrorists.

If we the people can get rid of the government as we know it world wide, we will also solve the biggest problems to human growth.

The US recruiting and training of Afghani and Iraqi forces to provide security for the people in those countries is completely misguided. The fact is that the US is militarizing those countries so that those trained forces can commit genocide and provide support for dictatorships later, as well as starting wars with other countries. This is exactly the opposite of what the US should do. The US is militarizing them rather than training, supporting and promoting a peace loving country with efficient agriculture and developing a peace economy in those countries. Nobody asks the question—what are these forces to provide security and safety—from what?

Maybe the answer is to prevent democracy to take hold in these countries. One of the reasons for training and developing local military forces in all these countries is to prevent unwanted groups in these countries from gaining power.

Conclusion: What is behind the training and development of military forces in these countries is obviously to prevent freedom and democracy from developing in those countries.

The definition of democracy should not be US value driven! From a purely objective standpoint, just looking at the numbers, there are more killings and incarcerations in the US than in almost any other country. Is that what the US is trying to export?

People in America always talk about "they". "Back then, 'they' castrated people who were homosexuals. "They" had strict laws against sodomy." They" did radiation experiments on the population. The question is who are "they"?

To the United States—what is wrong with you? You are killing and torturing people, and for what purpose? Another proof that morality is being destroyed by legislation and punishment is the violent protest against the Vietnam War but hardly existent with the apathy seen today with regard to Iraq and Afghanistan war and with other recent and current genocides committed around the world. Conclusion: Morality has been in free fall the last 40 years!

Who discriminates?

Do businesses? No—businesses will try to attract and keep the best people possible and pay them what they are "worth". The key word is "people". That includes all ethnic groups including women. A company that discriminates puts themselves at a competitive disadvantage.

Do private individuals? No! Individuals cannot and will not discriminate in a free society.

Does government? Yes! Legislation to discriminate is the basis for discrimination. All fundamental fights for non discrimination have been fights to change local, state and federal laws. The civil war was to fight laws that discriminate. All fights against discrimination are fights for freedom! By maximizing individual freedom we will minimize discrimination.

No individual or business will discriminate unless enabled by law. When passing a law against discrimination we are only shifting the criteria from one kind of discrimination to another set of criteria. To avoid discrimination, the laws have to be neutral and treat everybody in the society objectively. It needs to be based on objective criteria that do not incorporate elements of a person's ethnicity, values or religion. In other words, laws passed cannot or should not limit a person's freedom. When government discriminates it is "blind discrimination". To grant advantages and support to one sector of the economy discriminates against the other sectors. Government contracts discriminate against companies that are not supplying the government. It is inherently discriminatory to pass rules and regulations that are isolated to one sector of the society or favor one side of the economy over the other. Now, under the recession, all the economic stimulation to particular sectors is discriminatory again. Economic stimulus needs to be "blind"! Otherwise, it is unfair!

In a way, you can argue that all legislation is discriminatory. All regulations and laws are designed to prevent people from doing something. So by definition, legislation is to prevent something.

I'm not saying that we don't need laws and regulations. We need them just like you have rules for sports to make sure that the playing field is fair and to avoid negative consequences of an activity. However, regulations need to be minimized. It slows down the evolution of society and limits the creative process.

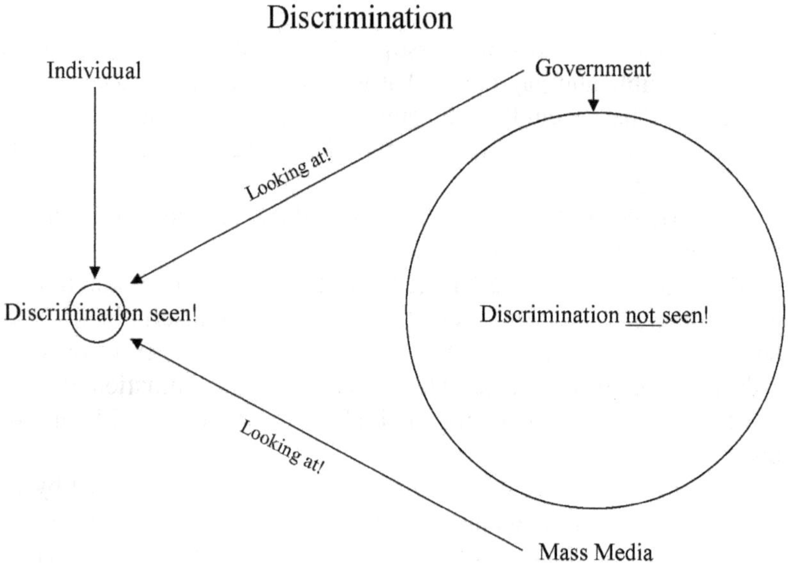

Discrimination

Individual — Looking at! — Discrimination seen!

Government — Discrimination not seen!

Mass Media — Looking at!

**Figure 20
Discrimination**

25
The Madness of War

Military spending is a crime against humanity. It is not needed. History repeatedly proves that any occupying force of another country will be defeated in the long run by simple resistance from people using light artillery and hand guns.

In a transition, countries should maintain their nuclear capability. They let the world understand that if they are attacked—and they can find the homogeneous aggressors—they will retaliate with nuclear force. In other words, committing an act of aggression by another country (or homogenous group) means suicide.

Spending excessive money on war and military must be regarded as a crime against humanity. This money and talent could be spent by corporations to create jobs, fight global warming, combat illiteracy, hunger and disease around the world. The money not being spent on positive development of the world is directly responsible for millions of deaths each year, not only through wars, but also through improper resource allocation.

The Vietnam War proves that wars can not be won. WWII was not won. It prevented Hitler from occupying other countries and the continuation of his regime. WW2 was a defensive war against an aggressor. That is why it was won! Winning can only be measured by the winner as economic exploitation after the war. Otherwise, it was only fought on ideological, religious, prestige, internal and political reasons to preserve ruler powers by creating the external threat of war. A war cannot be won. The reason for the war is only in the human psyche! By "winning" a war we can replace a government, but we can't force people to think differently. You can't change most opinions. Wars are fought by a nation's leaders, not the people.

War has become so complex. What happens is that the winner with the highest technology is destroying the lives of its own soldiers. While protecting their own soldiers against chemical warfare, they give them medication to neutralize reactions to the chemicals. This in turn has now been proven to cause birth defects in offspring. How stupid can the world be? Ref: Gulf War.

We are failing in Iraq because we treat other people as sub humans around the world. Their deaths are only statistics. Their killings are not even reported on our news. We dismiss that they are as advanced in their thinking as we are. When you apply military strategy that emanates out of politicians' imaginations, you not only alienate every person in Iraq but you alienate every person in the world by standing for the country of fear. Every superpower, throughout history, has never been able to occupy any country in the long run.

The number one policy in foreign affairs should be to avoid losing human lives. Attacking another country with killings or deliberately killing somebody is murder, regardless of whether the killing is done by an individual, organization or government.

International Organization to Control Destruction

When we have unrest of a certain character such as terrorist attacks and suicide bombings, the leaders behind the unrest must be allowed to put forth their grievances in front the United Nations and action needs to be taken to prevent further violence. The solution needs to be creative rather than destructive and cannot be punishment.

To defuse tension and the consequences of it, we must as a society engage in a conversation to allow the people to move their case forward!
- We must eliminate weapons and weapon production worldwide. We should use the United Nations with representatives from all the countries to verify this.
- Music and art already unifies the world. The next step is to become unified economically and politically. However, this has to happen with maximum individual freedom and freedom to do "right" and "wrong." This unification only happens under certain, agreed upon principles that everyone can accept. A democratic system, in addition to national democracies, needs to be established worldwide under the domain of the United Nations.

Fifteen years after 800,000 Tutsis were massacred in Rwanda by the Hutus. Rwanda has been able to triple its citizen's income. How? This was achieved through forgiveness of the perpetrators. Now, the killers and victims are living together again.

26
Economics

Humanity has been in a survival mode since the beginning, manifesting itself in the idea of owning property. Owning property in a society of limited resources means a higher level of security and a greater survival chance for yourself and your offspring. Today—at least in America—the basic survival need has already been met. Is the choice of pursuit made by people for what they really want to accomplish in their life?

People who choose their path based on interest, talent and passion are already liberated from survival shackles. People achieving this consciousness level decide to dedicate their lives to personal success not as it relates to money or owning, but as it relates to creating and giving.

There is reason to believe that a paradigm shift must take place in the western world from having and owning as the driving force to creating. In such a society, ownership and "having" actually become irrelevant. People choose and have access to what they need, so usage without ownership renders ownership irrelevant. At that point, people and families choose based on what they actually need, rather than irrational insecurity and fear that once drove people to own and have in the past. There is reason to believe that an ownership society becomes more and more irrelevant. What determines a person's living standard in a nutshell is that they have a place to live that fits their needs: access to transportation, entertainment, food, clothing, medicine and education. As long as that is satisfied without irrational fear of loss, the person will choose what is reasonable. For example, why own a stereo and records if you have access to it everywhere from satellite or the internet? Why own a car if you have access to transportation at any time with great convenience? Why having a huge house in the suburb when you are single or a couple? You can have a house with six rooms, but you may not want this hassle. You may just want a nice place with a living room, a dining room, and a kitchen because that is really all you need.

Making this paradigm shift liberates people into a much higher level of freedom to choose what they really want following their passions and interests. In other words, they live at the highest level of existence. They learn and create based on their unique talents and desires. A society like that would also become super efficient with regard to using resources and maximize well-being. The era has terminated where the industrialist or the financier are heroes. How they measure success is outdated. Chances are that we would see an explosion in science, art, technology, space exploration, politics, and philosophy rather than that of a human being choosing a path to security and mindless slavery to economics.

What happens is that modern society through automation and technology has come to the point where only a tiny fraction of the population needs to produce what the entire earth needs. The question becomes, "what does the rest of the population do when everything has been taken care of?"

We will soon witness an explosion in art and music, publishing, science, research and development, space exploration, public debates, politics, education, medicine, entertainment, romance, partying, traveling, creating, self improvement, body building, sculpting, fashion, beauty products, restaurants, bars and dance venues. In other words, humanity is moving forward to have a good time.

But this will not happen as long as we have fanatic ideologies and religious fanatics. It will happen only if humanity allows diversity and imperfection to exist. We must not try to impose our values on anybody else. The only thing we need to do is protect individual and collective freedom from government.

A person who is free, will chose to be good rather than bad!

The living standard is not only a function of material goods in your life. The living standard is the opportunity to:
- Create.
- Receive an education.
- Strive to achieve your dreams and aspirations.

This is the ultimate litmus test of how great a society is when these three are maximized.

Economically we need to make the "cake" larger. Nothing else counts. Money does not count except to be kept stable and serve as a tool to stimulate or slow the economy.

- The US needs to greatly expand vacation time.
- No resources should be used unless its validity is proven in the free marketplace.
- Each dollar is a voting ballot as to what society offers.

Anything else is mostly a waste of resources except for space exploration and fundamental scientific research. The debate is losing the primary point by focusing on money instead of output. Meaning the delivery and magnitude of goods and services is paramount. By creating a super-efficient economy based on supply and demand creates a much larger surplus in the private sector than what we now have. This also makes the economy super efficient with regard to international competition. The whole argument that we should spend government "seed" money in technology industries is a complete waste of money. The economy is a zero sum game in the short term. A super-efficient economy has a much larger ability to fund any technology or scientific research through the private sector than any government plan can ever conceive. The difference is that the investment decisions in R&D are made by businessmen who have proven by their success that they know how to manage money to benefit the most people. People who buy their products are the proof! An exception is fundamental research that should be heavily invested in by society and managed by the government. The build out and maintenance of the societies infrastructure should be privatized and facilitated by the government!

There is nothing wrong with being rich. However, we must create a dynamic society where no fortunes can be preserved by any individual unless they constantly prove that their creations can survive and prosper in a competitive environment.

Man's destiny is to be self-governed on the individual level. Ownership and power become irrelevant when man steps into the universe because it expands with the speed of light. There is literally unlimited space and matter for each individual. Consequently, ownership and power as we know it becomes unimportant. Ownership and power is only important during scarcity. Scarcity is also the foundation of value.

If every household in America each got 1/10th of an acre to build a house, how big of an area would it take if we assume that twice as much land is needed for infrastructure such as manufacturing, services, retail, educational facilities, hospitals, parks, roads, etc.? There are 115 million households; we would need 11.5 million acres for everybody to have a house with a garden and, another 23 million acres for infrastructure. The total area of California is 101,534,080 acres. 34.5 million acres are needed for development that is 34% of California. Answer: If we draw a line from San Francisco to Lake Tahoe. Take the area between the line and the Oregon border; the entire US population would fit on the land. The rest of the country will be "empty"!

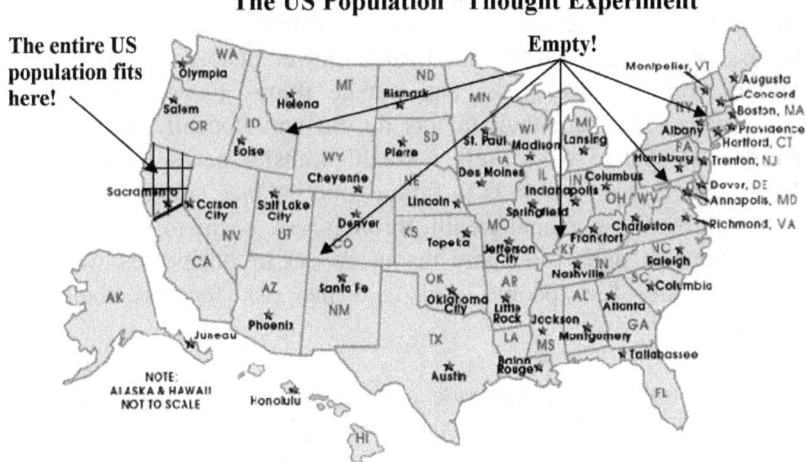

Figure 21
The US Population "Thought Experiment"

Ask yourself a question; if we did it, would you like to live there? Think about it for a while before you answer the question to yourself!

If we build "tall" cities they will be superefficient from an energy standpoint, and would be able to offer great entertainment and fun. It will be great centers of science, art and entertainment and will greatly reduce the need for cars.

Principle: If you are not engaged in directly transforming matter into "useful" products, construction of buildings, the machines for production and physical transportation of those products, you are engaged in mostly non-productive work. What you do is not needed in the wealth-creating process and in what is needed for the creation of living standard for the society. As a consequence, we must create the optimal system to minimize every endeavor that is not directly involved in this wealth creation. This can be achieved by creating a truly demand-driven society!

To make the capitalistic system work well, we need to have an excellent welfare system. This means we need to have a safety net. If you fail, it is not a financial catastrophe. Every person must have access to education, food, clothing, shelter, health care and transportation. These tenets must always be true for all citizens. This is necessary to unleash the capitalism's power. The safety net would allow people to take risks and pursue things for which they are passionate and where their talents lie. So paradoxically, to make the capitalistic system work well, a wealth transfer needs to take place. What society needs to do is to find a good balance between the safety net and creating personal wealth through new business ventures. Too much welfare pulls too many resources out of businesses. With too little welfare, few people will take the risk to start their own businesses.

In California the Employment Development Board and the State Board of Equalization were set up originally to increase employment opportunities in California. Rather than putting tax monies collected from businesses during a strong economy into a fund to bolster a weak economy, the state spent its money during good times to pay for more law enforcement and prisons.

This questionable move left no money during our present recession to create more employment and fund education. Now, collecting taxes from businesses during the recession is causing business failures and increased unemployment. How stupid is that?

In health care the capitalistic system does not work as there is no rational buyer. The decision whether to buy health insurance is a decision of life and death. Anyone would be willing to pay any amount to survive, even go bankrupt. It doesn't matter if insurance companies compete. The last dollar will be spent by the patient if free to do so. Hence, healthcare needs to be run by government on the fundamental level to create a fair, efficient and just system. Anything offered in society when the individual has no choice especially when the decision concerns the very survival of the individual—needs to be provided by the government as a basic platform.

- Food
- Shelter
- Health care
- Education
- Transportation

Otherwise, you have slavery. It is time for the US and the rest of the world to finally end slavery.

A slave is, by definition, a person who does not have any other choice than to offer his labor to someone else in exchange for his own basic survival.

The politician's income should be related to the growth in gross national product and to the status of the budget, whether it is a deficit or surplus. If the gross national product grows and shows a "profit" meaning surplus, the politicians income should go up and if the gross national product goes down with deficits, their income will go down. They should face the same dynamics as the private sector. The income of government employees, on the average, has to be 20% less than it is in the private sector. The reason for the difference is that employees in the private sector are exposed to higher levels of risk to which government employees are not exposed. So, the higher the income in the private sector, the higher the income would be among government employees. This would be calculated as the average between employees in the private sector and the average in the government sector. This needs to be the foundation for the government budget with regard to government employee income. Today it is obscene that the average income among government employees is $7000 higher than it is in the private sector especially when you take into account that the government is paid for through taxation of the private sector. So the employer, meaning the private sector, on the average, makes much less money than the employee, meaning the government sector. What we have today violates all reasonable fairness.

Today we have congressional hearings where leaders from the private sector are subject to cross examination and public accusations by the congress. It is like the little private sector servants have to go in front of the rulers and are accused of this and that! This is completely contrary to the idea of government as it was expressed in the American and French revolution. The government was supposed to be the servant to serve the people, not the other way around. This circus becomes especially aggravating when it is a cover for the politicians to not admit their mistakes. As an example: the leaders of Goldman Sacks, which may have done some wrong things, are being accused in public that they caused the financial collapse. While the truth is that the financial collapse was caused by government regulation and policy. The policy was, and it had good intensions, to make sure that everybody who wanted to buy a house in the US could afford to do it. Fannie Mae and Freddie Mac were set up to make this happen as semi- government institutions to execute on government housing policy. That setup caused the housing boom and threw prudence in lending out the window. It appeared, to the financial sector that housing in the United States was guaranteed by the government. This caused wild speculation in financial instruments by Wall Street. Now the politicians refuse to take the blame. So they are publicly accusing Wall Street for the financial collapse. The fact that the government bailed Wall Street out is an admission of guilt. This is what can happen when private enterprise and government is mixed together. There is reason to believe that the financial crisis would not have happened to this extent if hadn't been for government influence. Also, when the crisis happened, the market was taken out of play by the necessity of government intervention. What should have happened is that the financial institutions, who couldn't survive the crisis, should have been allowed to go bankrupt. This well meaning policy of house ownership for everybody created an unnatural and dysfunctional financial market. What we may have is a government financing arm for first time home buyers independent of the financial institutions.

When they start to regulate something it creates a false sense of security. When you do a little regulation over here, it creates the need to create more regulation over there—so it creates inflation in regulation.

According to Keynesian economics, during a recession, the government is not supposed to go in and "save" financial institutions but rather pump money and demand for goods and services into the private economy.

It's not that bad for the economy to go through cycles, because the down cycle causes innovation. When something gets too expensive to produce in one country and that production is moved to a low cost country, it benefits both countries involved in the transaction. Because what's being moved to the low cost country, is a better fit to that country than it is in the more advanced country. So if everything works the right way, the slack being created in the more advanced country spawns innovativeness and frees up capital to create for tomorrow.

So the private enterprise system, not only works well in one country, but it also works extremely well internationally—to make evolution take place.

The Sierra Club must take a big responsibility for the current crisis in CA with regard to energy, water, housing, and can even be made responsible for millions of people in CA living in ghettos and poverty. They can also be partially blamed for the fact that development in CA is happening on the most fertile agricultural land by having an emotional attachment to protecting hills and wildernesses. In a sense, they can also be made partially responsible for the overall economic crisis in CA in 2010 by being a proponent of zero development and their partially successful attempt to freeze CA in a status quo for the last 20 years.

When Obama says, "We need to make America more perfect," That is not what we need. The United States has been made too perfect already. And through this "perfection" the US is wearing out its own people. The pressure and stress by taxation and legislation demands is wearing everybody out! The biggest mistake that happened over the last 20 years was during the Clinton administration when they put 100,000 cops on the street. This caused an explosion in criminality.

My suggestion is take 100,000 cops off the streets because 90 percent of what they are doing is harassing the citizens.

The small businessman as the "new slave" is worn out! He doesn't want to carry the modern society on his back any longer. The small business owner is working 80-hour weeks to pay taxes and, at the same time, being legislated against. We have thousands of people in government jobs harassing the small business owners while living off "the fat of the land!" The private sector has become the slaves for the public sector.

There should be no tax on businesses with less than 10 employees and less than $1 million in sales per year. Then the corporate taxes should be progressive for larger and larger corporations. The billions of dollars in tax credits and guarantees in support of large corporations need to be stopped. Example—billions of dollars are being given to oil companies.

Companies with government contracts should be restricted with regard to dividend pay outs and be suspended from the stock exchanges. What we have today represents a massive transfer of wealth from the US taxpayers (citizens and businesses) into the pockets of stockholders in those companies. Small businesses and employees in the private sector are sick and tired of the massive wealth transfer into the pockets of large corporations, politicians, and bureaucrats. The small business owners and employees in the private sector have become the new economic slaves and it has to stop, otherwise, we will "shut you down"!

In the future, the individual tax payer should decide what the taxes should be used for. This would be a direct "democratization" of government. A web site should be set up where the tax payer can go and decide how his taxes should be allocated. The tax payer will be able to do simulations asking "what if" questions as to the consequences for his decisions and, based on these simulations a final decision can be made. This system will engage the citizens to a much higher degree and a much more efficient allocation of resources will be the result.

The government is supposed to work for us. We are paying for it. They are mostly parasites engaged in gross mismanagement. The mismanagement of the United States, especially since the Second World War, is jaw-dropping. Taxation, rules and regulations are so stifling that nobody can get anything done. All these rules have made it possible for a few individuals to amass huge amounts of wealth. In a truly fluid and free society it is impossible for mega wealthy people to exist in the long run because of competition.

Economics books state that you have a continuous increase in productivity coming from the learning curve itself in all aspects of the economy and also from the utilization of higher technology and more automation. This is a fundamental concept in economics. This has not happened during the last 50 years. The living standard for most people has gone down! The average working man in America in 1984 was making $40,000 a year and today (adjusted for inflation) he is making 35,000. That's a drop of more than 12 percent in purchasing power. However, 12 percent may not sound like all that much but it's actually coming off the top as discretionary money. This is a catastrophic drop in the living standard. There is nothing in economics that explains this. The only explanation left is gross government mismanagement. If we continue on this path staked out by our politicians and government there is reason to believe that in another 25 years most of the American population will live in poverty. That is not the people's fault. This is the fault of rulers.

I don't think this country needs any more "perfection!" What it needs is a lot more "imperfection" meaning that we need more freedom. We need less prosecution, less regulation, and less harassment. The environmental protection idea—and imagined terrorist threats—has become the biggest excuse for government to interfere, grabbing more power and slowing down progress even more.

Free economic progress utilizing new technology and competition automatically maximizes value and minimizes input of underlying resources. Assuming a somewhat rational consumer, the private enterprise system will automatically, go down the path consistent with environmental protection.

Rules and regulations by government will create a fair playing field and you could argue consumer protection. However, consumer protection is already inherent in the free enterprise system, especially today with access to information. Conceivably, in the future we will have a much more effective consumer protection by private companies that engage in consumer protection. This will be much more efficient than any government agency could ever dream. In fact, many government agencies set up to "protect" the people actually become rubberstamping and legitimize many products that are extremely harmful. Companies that manufacture them get an advantage over competition because of its resources and connections to government agencies.

Private companies that are engaged in evaluating companies, technologies and products will be more diligent and passionate because the consumer will pay for it out of their own pockets. Otherwise the consumer loses confidence in their services and stops buying their services.

There should be minimum taxes on manufacturing, distribution, entertainment, art, agriculture, healthcare, construction, transportation, education and energy. Everything else should be taxed higher to compensate for less tax revenues from those sectors. These segments of the economy should be taxed at a lower rate because they are the foundation for our living standard. Everything else is fundamentally parasitic!

Most fraud in business evolves through the interaction with or through government protection. The decision to invest has to be by the investors. Hence, the risk of investing has to be by the investors. Government regulation and protection only creates a false sense of security on behalf of the investors and a loss of responsibility for investment decisions. This ultimately leads to a more inefficient and stupid capital market with more waste of resources. Implied liability and responsibility is transferred by the investors to the government. This interference by the government in the capital market may ultimately destroy the private enterprise system. It has to be the ultimate stupor by the current system to create more control of the markets when in this crisis the capital markets have proven itself to work. Let them go bankrupt!

This leads to investors who rely on government to monitor things for them. The investor always feels that if things go wrong, he can sue the government or the corporation, or get bailed out!

The Multiplicator Effect of Taxes

Taking raw materials from the ground (40 percent labor tax)
+
Refinement (40 percent labor tax)
+
Components, parts, etc. (40 percent labor tax)
+
Finished goods (40 percent labor tax)
+
Distributors (40 percent labor tax)
+
Retail (40 percent labor tax) + 8 percent sales tax

If we do not have labor tax, we would be four times richer! The end products are four times more expensive from the cost of labor taxation as it is applied until it becomes a finished good.

All costs are labor costs! Any other cost does not exist! What's material cost on one level is the labor cost of the previous level. If you're going all the way back to matter transformation into products, we find that all costs are labor costs!

Hence, any government stimulus always turns into stimulation of labor in its entirety either domestically and/or internationally dependent of the content of import!

Noting has real value before it is turned into a finished product!

The living standard is created primarily from transforming matter into useful products and to distribute them to the end user. This includes manufacturing, construction, housing, agriculture, the distribution of food, transportation and other services that are offered and purchased by a free market to enhance well being.

Increasing living standards is not a matter of the money but a function of the products and services that are produced in a society at any point in time divided by its citizens.

If we decide to increase our salaries by 20 percent for the next year and the size of the "cake" to be divided only grows by 5 percent. We get 15 percent inflation.

Society's goal must be to maximize the growth rate of the "cake" over time and cause a fair distribution of that cake. The fairest system set up for that distribution is the private enterprise system.

Thought experiment: I have estimated that the sector of the economy that truly contributes to your living standard today is less than 50 percent. You could argue that it is as little as 25 percent. This means that more than 50 percent of the US population can be retired with the same salary as they had when they were working and nobody would experience a change in living standard. The question becomes, "How much of the over 50 percent do we want to convert again into contributors to our living standard? How much do we want to spend on "government" and its parasitic organizations and enterprises?"

When it comes to social security, military, justice, prisons and other government and regulatory agencies, the issue is not whether we can afford social security or health care. The issue is how we want to divide the money among different government sectors.

Social security and health care are a matter of priority.

The private enterprise system is capable of creating a super-efficient society that emphasizes maximizing the living standard. There is no inherent conflict between environmentalism and maximizing the individual's living standard. Through technology advancement in the private sector, less and less resources are needed to create a high living standard.

If we agree to this equation:
Cost or price = resources used = energy = finished products and services

The living standard can experience extreme growth. It also reduces resources used to produce that living standard. The goal of private enterprise is to maximize buyer value and minimize the cost = resources that it takes to deliver that consumer benefit. Faster growing companies will be the ones that maximize user benefits and minimize costs. The corporation or individual that grows the fastest in a free enterprise system also proves that they deserve to have power and manage a large part of the economy. They are justified in that they should manage a larger part of the economy since they are the most efficient producer with an emphasis on improving human living standards.

If we minimize that economy sector that is not participating in the creation of a high living standard we would also maximize the living standard and experience a great reduction of waste in the society at the same time.

Rather than living in a society that is a push (supply) economy. Services and products offered are pushed upon the individual either by legislation or supplied by tax revenues with little or no consumer choice. We must create a society that is a pull (demand) oriented economy where the consumer determines to a much larger degree than today what is produced and offered by directly paying for it out of their own pockets. If a person is not willing to pay for something, the big question is: Is what is offered needed?

To ensure that we have a super-efficient society and a healthy living standard, we need to maximize disposable income on behalf of the citizen.

Another important part of this equation is avoiding a de facto economic slavery. Every human being should have the freedom to decide to not work. Society must give all people the opportunity to not work to preserve freedom. This means we have to give people security so they are not subject to extreme poverty and misery. To effectuate this society we need to provide free services for all. We need reasonable government, health care and education.

Resources saved in a true, demand-oriented economy will be enormous. Products and services are weeded out by eliminating those not needed by the unwillingness of citizens who do not want to pay for them out of their own pockets. With the money saved, we can take a part of the excess tax revenues and distribute a minimum salary to everybody living in the US. This salary should be high enough to avoid poverty and misery. The other positive effect from this new economic freedom is the opportunity of the citizen to choose a life of self realization through art, science and entrepreneurship or whatever else you may chose to do. This way we have created a compassionate, free, fast-growing society.

The idea that the society has become more complex is a complete fallacy.

What do we really need?
- Food
- Shelter
- Transportation
- Entertainment
- Health care
- Education

We must create a consumer-driven government by creating a 25 percent flat tax for everybody. We must dismantle government as we know it. We take money saved and redistribute it among the people. Everybody gets, as an example, $10,000 a year just by living in the country. The benefits create a super-efficient society where nothing is offered or produced unless there is a market for it where each individual maximizes benefits from money spent. This will secure maximum benefits with a minimum use of resources:
- Get minimum environmental impact.
- The most environmentally friendly society.
- Economic democracy.
- Maximize people's freedom.
- No slaves under economic tyranny.
- Minimizing crime.

The redistribution of money: It will minimize crime because there is no or very little incentive for crime. We must allow people to choose what to pursue in life. This freedom should lead to maximum self realization based on interests and natural ability without fear.

Redistributing wealth will have absolutely no impact on the overall affluence of the society. In the short term the economics of a society is a zero sum gain. In the short term it causes a shifting in the kind of products and services offered. The total will be the same. In the long run there is reason to believe that the GNP will grow much faster.

How can the average person be worse off today than 30 years ago? This is absolute proof that government-managed GNP is destroying the affluence in the society by reducing and crowding out the production in the private sector and causing an incredible waste of human and natural resources.

The goal of the government needs to create a system through rules, regulation and control to maximize the size of the "pie" that is the goods and services offered in any year. We must make sure that people have maximum free choice between goods and services. The people need to "control" the largest possible part of the GNP.

If we want to make more money than the minimum salary, we must engage in useful activities for the society. This creates a super efficient-demand economy. It weeds out services and products from institutions that cannot stand on their own merit (Value contribution to the citizens). This forces a lot of government agencies to privatize. They will have to depend on the pocketbook and the value perception of the citizens for their existence. In other words, it would be "live or die" whether they (the citizens) want to buy their services or not after they have been privatized.

Because of government policies of injustice in other countries and the violation of the freedom principles, the government is giving aid to other countries as a bribery for "wars and threats" coming from one country against another. The surplus in the capitalist economies is spent on hopelessly inefficient international welfare to other countries, rather than leaving the surplus in the private sector for effective capital investment around the world where it creates affluence and development.

Hydro-electrical power benefits society the most. By creating multiple dams with possible (lakes) benefits the environment. This enriches floral and fauna, recreation, drinking water, water for irrigation, flood control and is non-polluting. Over time we have accumulation of silt and organic material on the bottom of the lakes. With appropriate intervals, this highly nourishing material can be harvested by evacuating the dam and used as fertilizer. Silt and organic material flushed into the ocean by free-flowing rivers have a negative impact on the ocean when the material is released. Lakes can also be used for freshwater fisheries and hence, direct food production.

Many government officials, bureaucrats and politicians who failed to create careers for themselves in private enterprise will have great difficulty believing that private enterprise can do what they cannot do after years of isolation from reality as a politician or bureaucrat. Projects of great complexity need very special and unique people to put them into reality.

"What you don't understand and can't do, you are afraid of or even in denial of."

This is some of the psychology inside government and among politicians. That is one of the reasons why government can never become creative but becomes a "no" destructive force. Creation has infinite complexity and there are an infinite number of ways to create something.

Stopping or restricting something only has one solution. "No" and destruction are the simplest ways to control an outcome and to make it not happen.

Politicians talk about tax cuts while it really doesn't matter in the long run for the economy. What really counts is productivity and people engaged in manufacturing, construction, and distribution. In fact, the tax-cut is inflationary unless it is supported by productivity growth.

Reducing regulations and restrictions are much more important to increase the living standard.

Even if 99.9999 percent of the population believes in something, that doesn't make it right.

All this mislead environmentalism thrives in times of plenty. But when fundamental growth resources such as energy gets in short supply, reality and the desire for development and creation kicks in, and the development of new resources takes place. Such as the energy crisis in 2001!

Because federal, state, county and city lands are most often hilly, mountainous areas, house and urban development is forced to take place on agricultural land. That is where most development takes place. Environmental protection is used as the argument to shun laying out hilly, barren, mountainous areas for development. Does this makes a lot of sense! Get rid of the most fertile land and protect and preserve the least fertile land?

How can we devastate the economy by doing something about pollution and global warming when we spend trillions on the military? In California, we spend billons on incarceration and "justice" while shutting down parks and cutting education?

Economic development decisions should not be made by politicians and the democratic vote. Automatically it spurs no development since the majority of people resist change out of fear for the unknown. "They" are happy with the way things are. Politicians choose no development as well, because that is the least energy and easiest to understand position. Interference by politicians and democratic vote on development issues violates the capitalistic system and stops evolution. What politicians, and ultimately the voters must do, is to create the right ramifications and regulations to maximize the power of the private enterprise system so it is fair and minimizes the negatives.

The Asian crisis with increased imports by the United States is what should happen because this stimulates the Asian economies. In the long run it benefits the US by increasing Asian export. This is the dialectic process in trade where two plus two equals five through mutual stimulation and benefit. The underlying advantage is the division of labor, specialization, and other natural advantages between nations. Ultimately, everybody wins. Commerce benefits immediately. In the long run, everybody wins.

How much something costs to produce including what is spent on government, military and any sector are a direct measure of how many resources are expended to create and maintain it.

The capitalistic system and freedom are the most efficient systems to maximize benefit to man with the minimum of resource expenditures. Consequently, this is the best for the environment.

Lending money is the mechanism to redistribute consumption.

"Given a certain size of the pie, the reason why the lower and middle class have to borrow money all the time is the unbalanced and wrong distribution of wealth. This is especially true with regard to the advantages that are given to government employees and the unfair taxation government has granted itself". Another very important factor is the manipulation of the economy by the banks circulating the money to their unfair advantage making everybody a debtor.

Fundamentals of the society: Priority from top to bottom
- Food
- Shelter/housing
- Health care
- Education
- Employment
- Careers
- Business formation
- Freedom

The economy is supposed to flourish! However, this is not true when society's organization and the economy's unfolding are severely controlled and restricted. Then, even fundamental individual needs cannot be adequately met, for food, housing and medical services.

The question becomes, "Where are the money and the resources going?"

Economic theory states that as technology develops and is adapted to the production and delivery of goods and services the living standard should continuously increase. In other words, the divided cake should experience a rapid increase during the 20th Century. The dynamics of technological development and productivity growth predicted that the living standard should increase exponentially. However, this has not happened. The living standard for large groups of people during the latter half of the 20th Century has been decreasing, manifesting itself in overcrowding and sparse housing. This leaves less money for discretionary spending.

In fact, growth and affluence created from the 1890s through the 1920s was incredibly more rapid than it was for the last 75 years. There is only one explanation for this reversal of living standard among the great majority of the population. It is attributable to increasing legislation and control by government agencies and spending on military and wars. For example, houses built in San Francisco from the turn of the century to the 1930s were much bigger and owned by "average" people. It was an incredible time of innovation, technological advance and science discoveries during 1890-1930. This period of time was characterized with an extremely low level of government rules and regulations of the Western Societies!

An example of development destruction is the car that was invented pretty much around the turn of the century. Fundamentally, it has not changed during the last 100 years. This lack of breakthroughs and innovation is directly attributable to government industry regulation. The same happened at the end of the 1990s—lawsuits filed by the government against Microsoft and Intel that destroyed another area of incredible innovation and growth. The government was directly responsible for the dot-com bust!

Government lawsuits and imposed regulations on economy growth sectors create an environment of uncertainly and end ups punishing the best and the brightest within that economic sector. The desire on the behalf of the government and the public with the mass media as a willing and participating player is trying to perfect something. While trying to weed out negatives and imperfections of that growing economic sector, they destroy the entire sector and its ability to continue to grow and prosper. This dynamic is one of the reasons why we are still living in a society where the average person can hardly survive. Because any surplus created in an economic sector that grows extremely fast in creating affluence is confiscated by the government for its own projects.

Justification to confiscate the surplus in a fast-growing sector of the economy is always done for moral reasons. Politicians and the government are subject to forces that they themselves don't even understand. They are doing damage in the name of "protecting the people."

What they don't realize is that the dynamics of government organizations and the desire on behalf of the individual for self realization will by necessity manifest itself as the attack and confiscation on the growth sectors of the private economy.

They are all well meaning, but their actions are destructive. According to ADM Corporation, one of the world's largest food processing companies advertises; "we have starvation around the world because of politics and government." They are right!

It is in the government's interest to destroy any truly independent business, enterprise or organization. Their interest is to make them dependent on the government for government's own well being and existence.

Too much government is not only a menace to the individual, but it destroys business. How can a judge's ruling in the Microsoft case reduce the value of Microsoft by over $100 billion, while sending NASDQ into a tail spin, reducing high-tech stock valued at more than 14 percent. This equals an incredible loss of value. This is complete idiocy!

The media aggravates the situation by inaccurately reporting the case. The reason we get an inflation threat and the economy has to cool down through interest rate increases is the prevention by government of the natural unfolding of the economy.

Example: Government restrictions on house building, infrastructure, new business formations and the free capital movement around the world. It manifests itself in inflation as a valve caused by heating up of the economy. The last thing we should do is to slow down the creative process by artificially increasing interest rates. Now it seems to be moving with regard to increasing the inflation.

- They increased rates.
- Making it too easy for people to borrow money.
- Changing demographics.
- Energy sucking from the economy to fuel wars.

You can argue that this approach stimulates the economy by the government spending more money by buying weapons from the military industrial complex. Money is spent in a semiprivate sector of the economy.

Economics 285

The problem with this scenario is that if the same money were spent in developing infrastructure, R&D, cutting of taxes on corporations and individuals, money would be directly spent to increase the growth rate of the economy. This directly benefits people rather than unproductive, non-living standard activities, destructive products and services.

The absolute obscene and criminal behavior of the US government and its policy of isolation and exclusion of Central and South America has stunted the growth of the rest of the Americas. A freeway should be built immediately that ties the US with Central and South America to facilitate communication and development. Freeways should be built from Canada to the south tip of South America. How can poverty exist in Central and South America after centuries of being next to the US if it were not for idiot policies by the US? Ask yourself!

The economy of the US was originally founded on a drug, "tobacco". Today other parts of the world such as South America, Afghanistan and Pakistan are prevented from getting their economies going by the rich part of the world, caused by their artificial and unnatural legislation against drugs.

If the drugs are so bad, how come the Americans, Columbians, Afghanis, and Pakistanis can survive? Especially when tobacco is a more addictive and damaging and killing more people than any of the other drugs from these countries.

We can choose between making every little wrinkle illegal and to create laws against it or, to minimize legislation and allow things to be imperfect. When does legislation and enforcement become counterproductive and represent general punishment of what is "normal"? When somebody is prosecuted for a "crime", rather than having one victim, the system creates at least two victims: 1) the subject of the crime 2) the perpetrator of the crime. This does not include dependents of the "victim" or the perpetrator, which would make the impact much larger. The justice system will reach a critical mass and experience explosive growth and turn everybody in society into a victim (it's happened already in the US). This is a "cancerous" growth that is in need of extensive tumor removal, in order to restore freedom and personal growth again.

Service, servant, survive

The company or person who serves and offers the best service survives. This is the essence of success as a business and personally that leads to happiness. This means that we need to let the ego go since it creates fear and doubts. To gain strength and confidence to create and serve, you need to tell yourself, "That I can only do my best." This means letting the "ego go". When you try to protect the ego it manifests as lack of confidence. The fear of possible hurt to the ego creates the fear.

Hence, when you let the ego disappear, fear and lack of confidence vanish. This translates into giving. The company or person, who gives the most, is the most successful. Entrepreneurs who are the brightest and most talented will always be the greatest creators and givers. When they achieve great monetary success by becoming a great servant, they continue to give even more as philanthropists.

Ultimately, each of us can become great creators of the future by giving and servicing humanity. Losers are the egocentric takers that end up victims. The ultimate takers are homeless people on the street. A successful person or business is a "fair giver," while a philanthropist is just a giver.

Pointers

- When it becomes more important to create, perform and impact society, the desire for ownership dies. The importance of ownership is empowerment for previously stated goals. Ownership only becomes important if it enables the individual to create.
- What is wrong with inefficient government agencies is that they are supply-driven organizations rather than demand-driven. If they were demand driven, nothing would be produced unless people are willing to pay for it out of their own pockets.
- The evolution of politics today is moving toward the decentralization of decision-making power to the states, cities and counties. The final evolutionary stage will empower and

decentralize to the individual = base income for all, combined with flat tax to create a super-efficient, demand-oriented economy.
- After women entered the workforce, their affluence has been cut in half.
- Ownership as we know it becomes meaningless when man takes the step into the universe.
- The increasing pace of company mergers to create monopolies is dismantling free enterprise. This is not surprising since freedom is being destroyed at the same rate. Eventually, we will end up with three privileged classes: politicians, employers and stockholders in monopolies. The price to pay is freedom, the slowing of evolution and declining living standards for all of us, including the privileged.

27
What is The Living Standard?

The social security debate is a fraud committed by the US government or they are ignorant about economics!

Less than 50 percent of the labor force actually creates the living standard by manufacturing beneficial products and is engaged in agriculture, distribution, construction, education and health care.

If we transfer money from all other "non-living standard" activities into social security, only 5 people are needed to work for every 5 people to receive social security. This means 5 people out of 10 people or half the US adult population can receive social security with no change in the living standard!

If a small tax cut is good for individuals and businesses—so the government says—larger tax cuts should be even better to create economic and job growth.

Tax codes and regulations promote the idea that it is bad to have a job. This must change to restore opportunities for wealth generation, pride and a sense of fulfillment for those who work.

There are vast employment opportunities in the environmental, business, entertainment, science and the arts. This explosion in meaningful jobs can only be created at the expense of the size of the government sector!

Quote: "The government that governs least governs best"! It's better to have it this way than to micromanage people. This is what the government is doing today!

Labor and management of private industry today understands that they have common goals to maximize the corporation's profitability and success so the company they work for can pay high wages to workers. Modern industry is dependent upon an affluent population with money to buy products. The only way workers and corporations in the private sector and for the society overall to increase the living standard for everyone, depends on how the resources/money are divided in society and how the money is spent. To increase the living standard for everyone, we need to maximize investments and production of products, housing construction and services that the population is voting on through their purchases (dollars spent).

The biggest drag on the living standard today is the money used for military, regulation, and other unproductive sectors of the economy. For example the waste of money—billions and trillions—to fund wars that directly affects the living standard of labor in a negative way. But that is just a tiny example of the incredible government waste. Today, the dividing line is no longer between labor and management/capital, but between people and government.

Business formation and investment need great degrees of freedom with great messiness to create "mulch" that from time to time will grow a rose with great value to the society. Business formation and capital flow need to be messy to make it happen and for a few great companies to sprout. If we destroy the mulch with overregulation, we are throwing the baby out with the bathwater.

"Cost of health care"

The government cannot owe money to itself. So the discussion about health care should not be about cost, but how much resources and manpower are allocated to health care. This should be determined as a percentage of GNP.

Living standard is created through efficient organization, level of technology and infrastructure to maximize the overall pie, its content and how it is divided among citizens. The free market best accomplishes this, excluding military, healthcare, welfare, education, and infrastructure.

The number one creator of high living standard is cheap energy. Cheap, non-polluting, and renewable energy must be the number one priority for humanity over the foreseeable future to meet the fundamental needs of man!

28
Organization of Society

The people who <u>know</u> how to solve a problem or to create something would also be the right people to solve the problem. If you appoint someone, as the government does, to do something, you will not get the optimal result. You may even get something that's useless after a lot of resources have been spent. This is another reason we need to have freedom and the private enterprise system.

The future will be based on a universal card with little ownership. You will only have things made available to you when you need it. This will maximize the living standard and minimize resources to achieve this standard. For example, you change cars as needed, different kinds and models. You only will have a camera when and where you need it. This way we can maximize living standard with the smallest amount of resources. We can create a super efficient society. It's just a matter of development and ease of acquisition and use.

Politicians and government employees need to face the consequences of their actions as private businesses are faced with through competition and the free choice of their customers that automatically "cultivates" the private sector.

Politicians and government employee's income should be tied to the performance of the stock market, deficit or surplus in the public sector and the performance of the GNP.

A strategy for defense should be a comparative technology assessment of superiority above any enemy capability. We should use a principle that basically states that with 20 percent of the cost we can achieve 80 percent of what is technologically possible. That way we can reduce investment and cost in weapon outlays four-fold with only a 20 percent reduction in weapons capability over what is technologically possible. And that will be completely adequate to completely overwhelm any enemy. The total US defense budget for 2010 is estimated to be $1.03 trillion ($1,030,000,000,000). That is approximately $9000 per US household for 2010. This is an enormous amount of money/resources that could be used to create rather than to destroy.

Pointers

- On the federal level legislation should only be associated with the regulation of business, preserve competition, defense and national security. The states should be able to decide whether they want their citizens to be free or to legislate morality. The people need to have the freedom of choice as to which system they want to live in within the United States. Decentralization is very important. In the US we can decide to give states much more autonomy than what they have today.
- We need to come together again to enrich ourselves and each other.
- Access to health care should be a right not a privilege. This should be written into the Constitution.
- Policies of the future should be less about money and more about how much freedom the individual should have to maximize self realization.
- The fight about welfare and taxes is going to subside!
- The building age driven by greed is coming to an end (ownership). The new age of resource management, exploration and science is starting.
- Getting rid of most unnecessary law-suits and laws for criminal prosecution, society will save a lot of money without destroying any of its wealth. When we create a purely demand-oriented economy, the standard of living does not drop since affluence is only created by transforming matter into food, consumable products, housing and transportation. There also needs to be a huge movement of resources into research and development, science and explorations. Other activities are a drag on the wealth creation. However, some of the other functions are necessary evils and need to be minimized.

If one dollar spent = one dollar in resources spent, we must maximize the following fraction:

$$\text{Living standard equals the maximizing of} \ldots \frac{\text{Wealth Creation}}{\text{dollars spent}} = \frac{\text{Transformation of Matter}}{\text{dollars spent}}$$

Figure 22
Wealth Creation

- We can only secure a super-efficient economy by creating a truly demand-oriented economy by maximizing the benefit to everybody with minimum resource input. This will also be the most efficient way to preserve the environment.
- These savings will support the minimum wage for everybody!
- The same principle should be applied to government spending, especially in the medical field!
- All government proposals should be subject to zero based budgeting reviews and these previously mentioned guidelines and principles should be followed.
- Reduction in technological advancements and services offered might be minuscule since the correlation between money spent, considering that to a large extent what drives technological innovations and performance is as much or more the brilliance and performance intensity of human endeavor, execution and innovativeness. We can get a lot more for the money than what we are getting today.

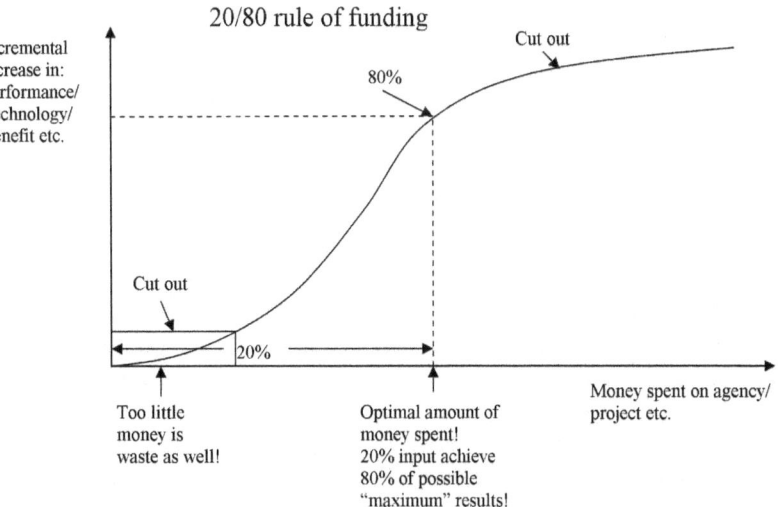

Figure 23
20/80 rule

- We need to focus on art, science and exploration of the universe to advance knowledge and consciousness. Space and cosmology will be the ultimate intellectual thrill for mankind.
- Affluence of a country or a community in the world is not so much about money as organization, stability, innovation, education, technology and access to raw materials.

29
The New Slavery

Student loans and government loans

They give you the loans when you are young to enslave the best and the brightest under the disguise that they are giving every person the same opportunity. These are the only loans that you are stuck with for the rest of your life because they can not be disposed of in bankruptcy. In a perverted and enslaved way you feel obligated for the rest of your life. Everyone who qualifies for a student loan today should no longer get loans but grants and scholarships with no obligation to pay them back.

We must educate a person who has talent as the best investment society can make without any strings attached!

Government policy now forces people to work in economic slavery rather than graduating students. When they graduate they work to succeed. They cannot do this as long as home prices and living costs have gone through the roof. The cause of increased living costs are payments to a huge government bureaucracy, through incarcerating millions, "protecting and securing" the country and individuals, and conducting wars and producing weapons of mass destruction.

To put people in jail and make their children grow up without parents perpetuates drop-outs and criminality that creates more criminality.
Bad policies include:
- Economic slavery by changing the bankruptcy law so we cannot dispose of debt.
- Reducing social security so we no longer have the choice to not work.
- Investigating and subpoenaing businesses and individuals.
- The probation system.
- IRS tax investigations and debt.
- Being paid by the government.

US aid to developing countries is used to make these countries slaves of the US government as they are saddled by enormous debt to the US.

Rampant corruption in governments and the United Nations (very sad) proves that government and its organizations should be minimized and heavily regulated. The private enterprise system is self-regulating and mostly immune from corruption.

Take away welfare and we no longer have the freedom to not work. Slavery is reinstated. The agenda to take away the welfare system is really to institute slavery. You no longer will have the freedom to not work. If welfare is taken away—and the rationale is that everybody should work—then nobody should be able to not work. This must include everybody including wealthy people or we have instituted slave labor once again. In fact, this solution will make everybody into slaves.

Laws passed that place modern people into slavery. For example,
- Child support Laws. If you don't pay, you go to jail.
- Student loans that cannot be discharged.
- Welfare Reduction.
- Draconian bankruptcy laws.

These are all forms of economic slavery!

30
Goals for Humanity

- Eliminate wars
- Eliminate poverty
- Provide shelter and food for all
- Education for all
- Health care for all
- Freedom for all
- Maximize the health and longevity of the earths biosphere
- Preserve life
- Explore and "conquer" the universe
- Acquire the power to recreate everything that ever existed and to create everything possible

Five percent of the earth's Gross Product should be dedicated to space exploration and travel, associated sciences and fundamental scientific research.

We have the power to create any future we want. I propose that we choose a future with freedom, triumph, meaning and purpose.

We must choose some worthwhile goals to achieve long and short term. I suggest that we explore the universe, attempt to preserve life forever, maximize technological development, our understanding of reality through science and ultimately acquire the power to recreate everything that have ever existed and to create everything possible.

I also suggest that we eliminate the idea that we have the right to impose our values on everybody else.

We must chose a life filled with fun and excitement without paranoid security and safety concerns.

We must allow things to be imperfect because "perfection" destroys everything including our ability to evolve.

I suggest that we choose to respect people around the world, regardless of values, religion or culture.

We must choose free trade and exchange of ideas rather than occupation, covert operations, exploitation and righteousness.

We must convert humanity from believing that a third party traditional "God" decides our future into knowing that we have freewill and the power to create our own brilliant destiny.

In other words, we need to convert humanity from unconsciousness to consciousness and enlightenment!

When you impose your values and beliefs on others you are committing a crime against humanity. You destroy other people's freedom to choose their own values and beliefs. As you destroy other people's freedom you do it to yourself and to your descendants and, ultimately, to all of humanity!

Through freewill we are not the object of creation, but the subject of creation, the Creator!

"Find the Truth"

Axioms ...

- *The pursuance of "perfection" destroys freedom and evolution.*
- *One person's values are no better and more valid than any other person's values.*
- *A person can live by their own values as long as they are not directly affecting anybody else's ability to live by their own values.*
- *A person or a group of people have no right to impose their values and beliefs on others through force or legislation.*
- *Pluralism is the impetus for the evolution of the society and excitement in living.*
- *Personal growth can only be achieved through personal responsibility under freedom to choose between "good" and "bad".*
- *Children belong to their parents until they are 18 years of age.*
- *The ultimate goal of man is to acquire the power to create and recreate everything that has been and that is imagined.*

"Now"

There it is in all its magnificent historical and futuristic glory
Yet it is the beginning of the end to this tumultuous story.
You see there is no future and there is no past
There is only "now" and is happening slowly and fast
It's happening right "now", right "now", and right "now" again
If you look real close "nows" are all we have my friends
Once you become enlightened and will it to be
You will notice that the observer is separate from the ego, and the me
Fear and anger and insecurity are yours to resist
The ego allows all of these things to exist
If you starve the ego and don't allow it to eat
You will never experience the feeling of defeat
Can you see that free will allows us to be free
It gives life purpose and meaning to you and to me
Now you can see that "now" is all we have in time
It's occupying my words, it even occupies this rhyme
The observer sees your thoughts as you give them a friendly read
The observer occupies your giving and the ego, your greed
I would like to remind you to be at service to yourself and others
In the final analysis we are all pretty much sisters and brothers
That's all for now, stand up and give humanity a hand and take a bow
Please remember to smile at yourself; never forget the magic of "now"
What happens is what it is
"Nothing" is the source of what is!

Poem inspired by and based on the teachings of Jim Knut Larsson.

Thank you!

Thank you for reading the book, study it! Go to our website; www.jimknutlarsson.com, view the videos, post your questions, read the commentaries, discuss it with coworkers, friends and family and you will find and experience the "final" revelation.

You are encouraged to join our organization to convert the world from" unconsciousness" to "consciousness"! Participate on our blogs, fundraisings, actions and events—it will give you peace and enlightenment!

All the best!

Jim Knut Larsson

Enlightenment

To turn humanity from "unconsciousness" into "consciousness" is to ...
- Know that we have freewill and can create the future.
- Experience the observer and creator inside to be different from the ego, thoughts and the body.
- Become the Creator.

The Goals:
- The first goal for humanity is to preserve life.
- The second goal is to "conquer" the universe.
- The third goal is to recreate everything that ever existed and to create everything that is possible.

"Find the Truth"

Jim Knut Larsson

info@jimknutlarsson.com

www.jimknutlarsson.com

Addendum: The Emperor's New Clothes
by Hans Christian Andersen

MANY, many years ago lived an emperor, who thought so much of new clothes that he spent all his money in order to obtain them; his only ambition was to be always well dressed. He did not care for his soldiers, and the theatre did not amuse him; the only thing, in fact, he thought anything of was to drive out and show a new suit of clothes. He had a coat for every hour of the day; and as one would say of a king "He is in his cabinet," so one could say of him, "The emperor is in his dressing-room."

The great city where he resided was very gay; every day many strangers from all parts of the globe arrived. One day two swindlers came to this city; they made people believe that they were weavers, and declared they could manufacture the finest cloth to be imagined. Their colors and patterns, they said, were not only exceptionally beautiful, but the clothes made of their material possessed the wonderful quality of being invisible to any man who was unfit for his office or unpardonably stupid.

"That must be wonderful cloth," thought the emperor. "If I were to be dressed in a suit made of this cloth I should be able to find out which men in my empire were unfit for their places, and I could distinguish the clever from the stupid. I must have this cloth woven for me without delay." And he gave a large sum of money to the swindlers, in advance, that they should set to work without any loss of time. They set up two looms, and pretended to be very hard at work, but they did nothing whatever on the looms. They asked for the finest silk and the most precious gold-cloth; all they got they did away with, and worked at the empty looms till late at night.

"I should very much like to know how they are getting on with the cloth," thought the emperor. But he felt rather uneasy when he remembered that he who was not fit for his office could not see it. Personally, he was of opinion that he had nothing to fear, yet he thought it advisable to send somebody else first to see how matters stood. Everybody in the town knew what a remarkable quality the stuff possessed, and all were anxious to see how bad or stupid their neighbors were.

"I shall send my honest old minister to the weavers," thought the emperor. "He can judge best how the stuff looks, for he is intelligent, and nobody understands his office better than he."

The good old minister went into the room where the swindlers sat before the empty looms. "Heaven preserve us!" he thought, and opened his eyes wide, "I cannot see anything at all," but he did not say so. Both swindlers requested him to come near, and asked him if he did not admire the exquisite pattern and the beautiful colors, pointing to the empty looms. The poor old minister tried his very best, but he could see nothing, for there was nothing to be seen. "Oh dear," he thought, "can I be so stupid? I should never have thought so, and nobody must know it! Is it possible that I am not fit for my office? No, no, I cannot say that I was unable to see the cloth."

"Now, have you got nothing to say?" said one of the swindlers, while he pretended to be busily weaving.

"Oh, it is very pretty, exceedingly beautiful," replied the old minister looking through his glasses. "What a beautiful pattern, what brilliant colors! I shall tell the emperor that I like the cloth very much."

"We are pleased to hear that," said the two weavers, and described to him the colors and explained the curious pattern. The old minister listened attentively, that he might relate to the emperor what they said; and so he did.

Now the swindlers asked for more money, silk and gold-cloth, which they required for weaving. They kept everything for themselves, and not a thread came near the loom, but they continued, as hitherto, to work at the empty looms.

Soon afterwards the emperor sent another honest courtier to the weavers to see how they were getting on, and if the cloth was nearly finished. Like the old minister, he looked and looked but could see nothing, as there was nothing to be seen.

"Is it not a beautiful piece of cloth?" asked the two swindlers, showing and explaining the magnificent pattern, which, however, did not exist.

"I am not stupid," said the man. "It is therefore my good appointment for which I am not fit. It is very strange, but I must not let any one know it;" and he praised the cloth, which he did not see, and expressed his joy at the beautiful colors and the fine pattern. "It is very excellent," he said to the emperor.

Everybody in the whole town talked about the precious cloth. At last the emperor wished to see it himself, while it was still on the loom. With a number of courtiers, including the two who had already been

THE HUMAN PATHWAY 303

there, he went to the two clever swindlers, who now worked as hard as they could, but without using any thread.

"Is it not magnificent?" said the two old statesmen who had been there before. "Your Majesty must admire the colors and the pattern." And then they pointed to the empty looms, for they imagined the others could see the cloth.

"What is this?" thought the emperor, "I do not see anything at all. That is terrible! Am I stupid? Am I unfit to be emperor? That would indeed be the most dreadful thing that could happen to me."

"Really," he said, turning to the weavers, "your cloth has our most gracious approval;" and nodding contentedly he looked at the empty loom, for he did not like to say that he saw nothing. All his attendants, who were with him, looked and looked, and although they could not see anything more than the others, they said, like the emperor, "It is very beautiful." And all advised him to wear the new magnificent clothes at a great procession which was soon to take place. "It is magnificent, beautiful, excellent," one heard them say; everybody seemed to be delighted, and the emperor appointed the two swindlers "Imperial Court weavers."

The whole night previous to the day on which the procession was to take place, the swindlers pretended to work, and burned more than sixteen candles. People should see that they were busy to finish the emperor's new suit. They pretended to take the cloth from the loom, and worked about in the air with big scissors, and sewed with needles without thread, and said at last: "The emperor's new suit is ready now."

The emperor and all his barons then came to the hall; the swindlers held their arms up as if they held something in their hands and said: "These are the trousers!" "This is the coat!" and "Here is the cloak!" and so on. "They are all as light as a cobweb, and one must feel as if one had nothing at all upon the body; but that is just the beauty of them."

"Indeed!" said all the courtiers; but they could not see anything, for there was nothing to be seen.

"Does it please your Majesty now to graciously undress," said the swindlers, "that we may assist your Majesty in putting on the new suit before the large looking-glass?"

The emperor undressed, and the swindlers pretended to put the new suit upon him, one piece after another; and the emperor looked at himself in the glass from every side.

"How well they look! How well they fit!" said all. "What a beautiful pattern! What fine colors! That is a magnificent suit of clothes!"

The master of the ceremonies announced that the bearers of the canopy, which was to be carried in the procession, were ready.

"I am ready," said the emperor. "Does not my suit fit me marvelously?" Then he turned once more to the looking-glass, that people should think he admired his garments.

The chamberlains, who were to carry the train, stretched their hands to the ground as if they lifted up a train, and pretended to hold something in their hands; they did not like people to know that they could not see anything.

The emperor marched in the procession under the beautiful canopy, and all who saw him in the street and out of the windows exclaimed: "Indeed, the emperor's new suit is incomparable! What a long train he has! How well it fits him!" Nobody wished to let others know he saw nothing, for then he would have been unfit for his office or too stupid. Never emperor's clothes were more admired.

"But he has nothing on at all," said a little child at last. "Good heavens! listen to the voice of an innocent child," said the father, and one whispered to the other what the child had said. "But he has nothing on at all," cried at last the whole people. That made a deep impression upon the emperor, for it seemed to him that they were right; but he thought to himself, "Now I must bear up to the end." And the chamberlains walked with still greater dignity, as if they carried the train which did not exist.

Addendum: War Commentary

We, the people of the world are sick and tired of the self-serving circus created by governments and media called terrorism. We demand that the leaders of the nations of the world solve the terrorist problem—by taking away the underlying reasons for it. The terrorist threat is a self serving "problem" to governments around the world and especially for those government organizations "feeding" upon the frenzy. These government organizations only incentives are to fight terrorists, not to solve the terrorist problem. We, the people want a solution to this problem. Here is the solution which has to be creative, not destructive:

- Solve the Israeli/Palestinian problem by setting up Palestine as a separate state.
- The US occupation of Iraq, Saudi Arabia, and Afghanistan must end.
- Allow the Middle East to take responsibility for their own destiny.
- Start massive employment programs in the Middle-East.
- Do a massive investment in education in the Middle-East.
- Have respect for the Muslim faith.

That's it!!!

Do it now!!!

If you do not believe in this solution, ask any leader and intelligent person in the Middle-East who does not have a vested interest in the continuation of the madness!

Instead of spending hundreds of millions of dollars on the war, that money should be spent on employment and infrastructure investments in the Middle East—that will immediately turn the US into a benefactor. It would immediately silence the terrorist threat. What we are doing through the killings is to create more and more terrorists. We are killing fathers, sons, daughters, grandmothers, uncles—that is not working.

If the governments around the world can not solve the problems around the world without killings, then the governments around the world are no better than the people they are killing. The principle needs to be—Do Not Kill! When you have to kill to solve a problem, then you are too stupid to solve the problem in a constructive way.

The world does not need that kind of stupor, any more!!!

Mankind, today, is acting as if it is still suffering from the ignorance of the middle ages. We, the people of the world, have advanced beyond this ignorance—obviously the governments around the world have not. In the eyes of most educated people, most governments of the world act and look like idiots with a complete lack of ability to look clearly at a problem and find a peaceful, logical solution.

The final question: Do they think they are going to solve the terrorist problem by continuing to kill people in the Middle East?

Government thinking: "We need to have troops in Afghanistan and Iraq in order to isolate Iran." That argument has no foundation in reality at all. It's created as an excuse to keep all the interest groups busy and provide them with a purpose and employment. It's like the US government is suffering from complete fear of success—because if it is successful, then most of the interested parties involved would no longer have anything to do. The mantra among all these constituents would be, if we are successful, in solving the terrorist problem it would be "I saw my livelihood and my meaning and purpose in life, disappear." The deepest fear, at the top level, is to be confronted with something truly complex and that is to manage the United States and the world for prosperity. The terrorist problem is the eternal excuse for everything and a "cover-up" for gross mismanagement of the country and the world!

What is it with the western world that it feels that it must force its beliefs and values upon the rest of the world? Historically, it has been Christianity that has been forced upon others. Now, that has changed into being our culture, government and laws. There is no real difference between the two! Let us make a thought experiment: An old tribal leader in the Middle East is looking at the western world seeing that most marriages are ending in divorce, women dressing and behaving like whores, premarital sex, young girls "going wild" and an explosion in homosexuality and lesbianism (there is nothing wrong with that, people are free to choose, but to have a desire to have well-behaved children and grand children that lives a "normal" lives have that become wrong too?). He would naturally think that he does not want his granddaughters to be and behave like that and would fight any attempt of the western world trying to impose its values, government and laws upon his family and his country. On this background; would it be right for us to force our culture and values upon this other country? Most people both in the western world and in other countries want to be left alone rather than being micromanaged by people who think they are superior to them!

When a government starts killing people, it cannot stop because if they do, they are admitting that the killings were wrong in the first place. It will be an admittance of murder! That is why it is extremely difficult to stop a war and the killings! All killings of people are murder except for crimes of passion. Just like George Bush when he was governor of Texas could not stop executing inmates. He even denied DNA testing to find out if the prisoners on death row were innocent. This testing could not be allowed on the remaining inmates as the statistics of innocence or guilty would indicate how many innocent inmates were already killed. Hence, it was more important for George Bush and the justice system to avoid embarrassment than killing innocent people!

Addendum: Personal Stories of Injustice

Police follow a common operating procedure when they falsely charge a person with felony assault and battery charges—often it's the police who have caused the bodily harm and injury. Officers regularly file charges against innocent people who are falsely arrested.

The latest publicized example is the November 2009 arrest of a white man by Bay Area Rapid Transit (BART) police at the West Oakland Station. The video clearly shows no resistance from the victim. The video plainly reveals an assault by an officer who is blatantly inuring an innocent victim.

A similar incident also happened to me as I was leaving a night club in San Mateo, California, in 1985. A jealous bouncer asked me to leave the club as I was dancing with his girlfriend (a relationship of which I was not aware of at the time). Walking out to the parking lot, I flicked a cigarette butt in the direction of the two bouncers, who were following me. The butt landed at least 20 feet from the two "bar enforcers." Meanwhile, a friend had arrived to pick me up, was waiting with the car running.

As I got ready to open the car door, the two bouncers attacked me and threw me violently to the ground. My head slammed into the concrete. The two men then ripped my suit and restrained me on the ground until police officers arrived. I was arrested and taken to jail. Around 5 a.m. I was taken out of my cell for interrogation. Being a Norwegian immigrant—and not knowing my rights—I told the officer exactly what had happened. It turned out that the bouncers were San Mateo Police Academy students. When I finally saw the police report, I discovered that it was a complete lie. Much of the profanity alleged by the officers was not even in my vocabulary. I could not understand some of the phrases they accused me of making. The police report went on to state that I had attacked the bouncers. I was charged with assault. It was absolutely not true. In order to protect their own hides, the police charged me the crime that they actually had committed. My case eventually was reduced to a misdemeanor trespassing charge. My attorney advised me against pressing charges against the police for lying, brutality and assault, warning that I might lose my case in front of the jury and wind up serving a jail sentence. Never in my life have I felt a greater sense of injustice than, during this encounter with the American Criminal Justice System.

I believe it is important to realize that every piece of legislation passed also reduces the freedom of legislators and their families. In the end they also will fall victim to the legislation they've passed. It is painfully clear that the rest of us are victimized by this irreprehensible legislation. The lawmakers' punishment for violating their own legislation should be much more severe than which is applied toward the average citizen—for equal crimes. Ask yourself: If we cannot trust our own legislators and enforcers, who can we trust?

Another example is my good friend Aldo, who I met through my girlfriend living in San Mateo. Aldo is an immigrant—just like me—from Malta, a tiny island country in the Mediterranean Sea. He is doing very well for himself with his sole proprietorship, as an electrical contractor in San Mateo.

Aldo loves to ride motorcycles. He was working out in a gym as a bodybuilder at the time of his heinous arrest. We both started crying when he told me his story. For me this is significant, because the only other times I've cried is when I lost my dad at 17 and again upon losing my mother three years later.

Aldo was driving home on his motorcycle from a restaurant when the police stopped him for running a stop sign. Aldo, who has a temper, resisted arrest. The police took him down and isolated him in a cell. A few hours later, he was taken out of his cell, stripped naked, and asked to get down on his knees with his butt up in the air and his head against the wall. The officers told him they "were going to give him a tune-up." Then they used their batons in the most vicious way, beating his buttocks until my friend was screaming in pain. What the San Mateo Police Department did to my friend is unconscionable. Obviously the arresting officers were homosexual sadists. There is nothing wrong with giving or receiving a spanking if it is between two consenting adults. It can be a satisfying sexual experience by both participants, whether sadist or masochist. However, when this is done against an unwilling party, this is a violation of that person's being. Aldo was neither a masochist nor a consensual party to the assault—he was the victim of a most humiliating act with no possibility to defend himself. It is not surprising that similar incidents occurred in Iraq by US prison guards who sexually humiliated prisoners. These disgusting occurrences are common operating procedure in US prisons. Prison guards in Iraq were trained and supervised by US police enforcement officials.

How sad it is that we have the audacity to pass legislation against minor infractions against people—even elevating punching and slapping into felony assaults. Then the justice system, under the cover law, commits the most seditious, sadistic and heinous crimes against its citizens in US prisons. Crimes committed by the justice system far exceed 90 percent of the crimes committed by regular citizens.

All of us—for better or worse—are fundamentally no different that anybody else. We, as human beings, must acknowledge the duality—the *yin* and *yang*—of our own personalities. The only way humanity can go forward is to minimize serious crimes against humanity, to ensure freedom and to control institutionalized power.

Ann Story One

When the son of my friend, Ann, was about five years old, his shoulder had a tendency to come out of the socket. She took him for treatment at a hospital in Marin, California, where they live. Two months later he again dislocated his shoulder, and again six months after this, which required additional medical treatment.

A few days later, two people from the state Child Protective Services (CPS) knock on her door and ask to come in to talk to her. She learns that they believe that her son is being physically abused by his mother and father. One CPS worker decides to take her son into a separate room for interrogation. After about an hour they leave.

The sad aftermath of this event is that Ann's son is petrified that he will be taken away from his mother. Now he refuses to sleep alone in his own room. Instead, he insists on sleeping with his mother every night in her bedroom. The critical observation is that this one incident with CPS caused more trauma and fear in her son than any other incidences in his entire upbringing. This is a typical example of well-meaning legislation that causes more traumas to a child than almost anything the parents could have done.

Ann Story Two

Ann's license plate on her corvette is "MISSWORLD" as she won several beauty and fitness competitions. Her competition led to her crowing as Miss World Beauty and Fitness in London. Ann lives in Marin County, north of San Francisco, an affluent area. Since Ann is partially Polynesian, Brazilian and French, her fantastically beautiful skin tone is considered dark. Ann is repeatedly stopped by the police for no infractions when she drives in her hometown. In one incident she was wearing a short skirt. When asked for her documents in her glove box, she leans over causing her skirt to rise. She immediately notices the officer stooping down to look up her skirt. She confronts him as she feels deeply violated. The police officer tells her that if she tries to do anything about the encounter that "no one will believe you." Ann, who has been through a lot in her life, said she never felt more violated and helpless than from this incident.

I want you to email me your own personal stories about injustice, indicate if the story can be publicized. You must speak the truth on your honor! Aldo and Ann in the stories above are fictitious names to protect their privacy!

Submit to: testimonials@jimknutlarsson.com

Addendum: What to do in Case of Arrest?

One in every 100 Americans resides behind bars, and over 40% of the male population has some kind of criminal record. Each year, close to six times more people are arrested than die of the top ten leading causes of death, combined. As a nation, we spend vast amounts of money trying to prevent and cure disease. As individuals, many of us exercise, try to eat well, and generally do our best to become more informed as to the specifics of these diseases and how to avoid them.

So why is it that we devote precious little time and effort to the preparation for the possibility of being arrested? Relying on the belief that simply because you are a law abiding citizen, you'll never be crushed beneath the wheels of our steam roller criminal justice system, is a bit of dangerously flawed logic that could throw your life into a tailspin unlike most people are ever forced to experience.

Since the reinstitution of the death penalty, over 130 formally convicted felons have been exonerated from any wrong doing whatsoever—this after spending close to an average of ten years behind bars for crimes they never committed. As further evidence that the system has and is continuing to punish innocent people, let's call attention to the fact that during capital cases, the system grants the accused far more leeway and allowances than would be afforded to people accused of lesser crimes. In California it is estimated that we spend close to $250 million per execution of inmates on death row. In other words, during those 130 trials, in which our system yielded such disastrous results, the courts were operating at a level of maximum accuracy, and still they failed. So for lesser crimes, in which the accused is offered far fewer avenues for which to prove their innocence, it only stands to reason that the rate of false convictions is much higher.

This writing is not intended so much to explain what can be done to improve the system, but rather to examine the way it is now and how you can attempt to extract some measure of justice from what has become a very flawed and unbalanced system. Once you've been arrested, it will do you no good to focus on the injustice of it all—the only prudent thing to do at that point is to deal with things as they are, not as they should be.

As we'll see later, one of the biggest downfalls of the system, lies within the plea bargain process. If you think that you're safe because you'd never take responsibility for a crime you didn't commit, let's examine for a moment, the way in which the plea bargain system works. There is a body of evidence which suggests that the greater the likelihood that the accused will be able to prove his/her innocence at trial, the wider the gap will be between the punishment that would be administered upon conviction and that offered in exchange for an admission of guilt. In other words, in order to avoid the embarrassment of accusing an innocent person, the prosecutors are hedging their bets. Now suppose for example, that upon conviction you stand to face the next six years in prison. And supposing further, that the DA is offering you a plea bargain that allows for no more jail time or just a tiny fraction of the time you'd face as a result of a conviction—in exchange, of course, for a plea of guilty. If the system were 100% accurate 100% of the time, then I'd say that the plea bargain system is treating innocent detainees fairly. Because, armed with the knowledge that every case that goes to trial, will result in an accurate verdict, innocent people could confidently ignore the disastrous consequences that would be the result of a loss. But since this is not the case, you now find yourself in the position of being forced to decide on the likelihood of an accurate outcome at trial, and then weigh that against the consequences of a loss.

Given all of this, it's often to the advantage of the accused—guilt or innocence notwithstanding—to take the drastically reduced punishment associated with accepting the plea agreement. Because of the way the system is functioning today, it's no wonder that 95% of all felony convictions are achieved through this process and that so many innocents feel compelled to perjure themselves in court by admitting to something they didn't do. Those who say they're guilty aren't always criminals! And those who get convicted aren't always guilty.

In the end it's a win-win situation all around, except for the most crucial link in the chain of players within our criminal justice system—the accused. Upon conviction, the DA has just received another feather for his or her cap, the police have made an arrest which has now been validated by the conviction, the judge has just cleared another proceeding from the docket and depending on which way you've decided to go, the public defender has just resolved another case, or your attorney has received another substantial boost to his or her bottom line. With all these forces arrayed against you, it's vitally important that you realize that the odds are not stacked in your favor, and that sometimes, the best thing that you can do is simply to mitigate the damage.

Although there are many changes which could help to improve the accuracy of our system, precious little is actually being done. So it behooves each of us to do what we can to try to understand the system as it stands today, and prepare for the possibility of falling victim to the blundering of a system which all too often, simply doesn't work. This piece was written in an effort to help convince you not only that you need to prepare, but also to help you do that.

Sometimes, prior to the dreaded moment when officers of the law take you into custody, you may have an inkling that an arrest is imminent. If you're in this situation, then it's important to move quickly. The first thing you need to do is to make a full and accurate assessment of the totality of your financial resources. Then make an estimate of what your bail will be—if you have some idea of what your charges might be, bail guidelines can easily be found on the internet. If, through your own financial strength, you feel as if you'll have enough to bail yourself out, then you can move on to the next step, otherwise you need to have a heart to heart with friends, family—anyone you can, and make arrangements with them to cover the balance of your bail amount. And finally with regard to finances, you'll need to find a trusted individual who will agree to manage your money, organize the assets of your friends who've agreed to help, and then post your bail.

The next step in your preparations for the possibility of being arrested is to make a list of all the accusations that may be raised against you. Be broad in your thinking in order to facilitate a wide range of possibilities. Now go out and gather as much evidence to refute the items on your list as possible. Good sources are surveillance cameras located in public places, like public transit vehicles, shopping centers and banks. The reason it's so important to do this immediately is because most of these loop and record over old records on a three to 14 day cycle, and some are even daily. If the holders of this video evidence are unwilling to give you copies without a court order, then simply ask them to set the evidence aside because you have a court order pending. If eventually you are arrested and accused of doing something illegal at a certain place and time, think how valuable it would be to have a video surveillance tape of yourself in a completely different location.

Another great source of evidence is signed and dated credit card receipts from whatever businesses you happen to frequent. Do you suspect that someone may try to frame you for something you didn't do such as an angry lover, or jealous ex-girlfriend/boyfriend? Or maybe you have a husband or wife who's trying to set you up as a child abuser for the sole purpose of gaining full custody of your kids. How valuable would it be to have audio recordings of that person threatening to commit such a fraud? But use this tactic with caution—unless you feel yourself to be in danger, it's against the law to make audio or video recordings of a person without their knowledge. However, should you later use such recordings to prove your innocence as a defense against false accusations and an arrest, the DA will be hard pressed to come back and charge you for recording things with the intention of proving that you are innocent. However, this turns out, the negative consequences of making those recordings are likely to be far less severe than those attached to whatever else with which you may be charged.

If you are at home when the doorbell rings and you are unfortunate enough to have a couple of cops standing on your doorstep, DO NOT OPEN THE DOOR! The police may try to intimidate you, or coerce you in some other way. But whatever you do, do not let them into your house. If you let them into your house, the police are free to arrest you on the spot. However, if you don't let them in of your own volition, they cannot arrest you without a special kind of document from a judge or magistrate called a Ramey warrant. If you ask them for this, through the closed door, and they don't have one of these in their possession, then they will obliged to do nothing more than simply go away and not come back until they've obtained the proper paperwork. This will now give you some time to prepare yourself, as outlined above.

Even if you are arrested, the simple fact that you've posed the question about the warrant will put you in good stead. It's not the police that you're communicating with, it's the DA. By establishing your knowledge of the law up front, you'll be letting he or she know that you can't be pushed around and that any conviction achieved won't come without a fight.

If, however, they do have a Ramey warrant, then invite them into your home and politely ask if you may grab your shoes, cash, and glasses or whatever else you may need before they put on the cuffs. Many people are drawn to the profession of law enforcement because the idea of having power over others appeals to them, and given the opportunity, they won't hesitate to exercise their positions of authority and use you as the target for their frustrations. This is not to say that all officers are this way, but on the chance that you have encountered one of these bad apples it's important that you exercise the proper caution. It is extremely important, at this point, to seem as reasonable and polite as possible. If your blood is boiling then fake it. Any aggressive actions you take—like pulling your hands away from the cuffs, backing away for the police, or uttering foul language will only hurt you, not them.

Physically speaking, you need to be as docile with the police as a new born kitten. It's on the intellectual level, that you can and should apply all of your aggression. This does not mean, you should be mouthing off to them. You need to carefully consider the potential consequences of anything you say before uttering even a single word. If the time comes that they've decided to arrest you, simply ask them why—again you need to be as non-confrontational and cooperative as possible.

If you're innocent then tell them. Explain as clearly as you can the circumstances of the incident in question. If you suspect that there are witnesses that may be lying, explain to them what you believe to be their motivations. The police don't want to make a bad arrest any more than you want to be arrested, so if you look at it as a group project—it may be helpful. Phrasing your questions with this in mind, will likely help to elicit some empathy and cooperation from the police. This is your greatest and best chance of mitigating the damages of whatever may have happened.

Being cordial and cooperative—making the officer's job as easy as possible can only help you. The more personal interaction you can have (without annoying the officers) the better off you'll be. It's a personal connection you are looking for; just be careful not to give away any information that could later hurt your case. Given the fact that your natural instinct will be fight or flight, this will be difficult to pull off, but giving in to these urges can only make matters worse for you. It is under these circumstances where levelheaded calmness will win the day. To the extent that the police reports reflect your attitude during the arrest, the DA will perhaps be more lenient with the initial charges.

Remember that the arresting officers will have an impact on how you are later charged by the DA and in the event of a trial, will be likely to testify against. Their opinion of you, be it positive or negative, will have subtle, yet powerful affects, especially with regard to their body language, tone of voice, and other nonverbal forms of communication.

If you are innocent of the charges, then it is important to remember innocent people are convicted every day. So if you can use clear concise language to convince them that they are making a mistake, not only do you stand a chance of getting the cuffs removed, but should they arrest you any way, you may be able to have an effect on the severity of the charges that you'll later be forced to deal with.

Should you exercise your right to remain silent? If you are guilty and the charges aren't overblown, then absolutely remain silent. If, however, you're innocent or the charges overstate the crime that you committed, start talking. Remember to remain docile and respectable with regard to your body language, demeanor, and tone of voice, while still asserting the truth about what happened. Keep your sentences short and concise, and tell your truth as plainly as you can. The police don't want a false arrest on their record any more than you want to be arrested. So if, in the first few sentences of what you say, you can cast some doubt on the possibility of your guilt, you will get their attention. In the best case scenario, of course, they'll release you on the spot. But even if they don't, you may succeed in inducing them to reduce the charges.

Once a person within any organization takes an action, it is their natural tendency to want to justify that action—after the fact. This is basic human psychology. So after an arrest has been made, it is only natural that the police will place more emphasis on evidence which supports what they have done and less on anything which supports the idea that they have made a false arrest. Unfortunately there is no law that states that there must be a team of police dedicated to finding evidence that proves your innocence to balance out the ones who are trying to prove that you are guilty. Although, in theory the burden of proof falls on the prosecution, after your arrest, the de facto burden of proving your innocence rests squarely on your shoulders and that of your attorney.

Immediately after the booking process and as soon as you have access to a phone, call the trusted friend, that you've made arrangements with before, and have them bail you out as soon as possible. Even if you find that jail is somehow tolerable, don't try to cut corners and save this money. There are many reasons for this, but the most important is that; more than likely, the DA is still deciding on how to charge your case. By bailing yourself out you'll be communicating to the DA that you have some financial backing and that you may have the possibility of paying for an attorney. The biggest fear for any DA is that a defendant takes a case to trial and wins—thereby proving that they've charged an innocent person with a crime. People, who can't afford to bail themselves out of jail, have a far lesser chance of being able to afford an attorney, so the likelihood that they'll be able to win at trial is greatly reduced. This in turn emboldens the DA to overcharge the accused, thereby setting themselves up for success during the next stage of the process—the plea bargain.

The DA will almost always attempt to level as many charges at the accused as possible, because this will strengthen their position during the bargaining process. The greater the charges faced by the accused, the more the leverage the DA will have to put pressure on the defendant to accept responsibility for a crime which they may or may not have committed.

Should you hire a paid attorney? If you have the money, have some compelling evidence as to your innocence, and feel that it's possible to prove the truth, then the answer is yes. However, at this point, it's important to proceed with caution. Your attorney is not your friend. He or she is simply someone who has procured a license to practice law and knows the "ins and outs" of our justice system. They are nothing more than business people operating in a free enterprise system. And as such, their primary motivation is to achieve maximum profit for the least amount of effort. The more money that you can throw at the situation the better the attorney that you'll be able to afford and the stronger your defense will be—in other words, justice in this country is something that needs to be bought. In theory, everyone has the right to even handed justice, but in practice this right is all too often overlooked within a system that favors the well to do. If public defenders were just as good as private attorneys, then why would anyone bother to spend their money on the latter?

Since 95% of all felony convictions are achieved through the plea bargain process, it's important that you come to grips with this early on and gear your efforts and conversations with your attorney toward this end. "But I'm innocent, you might say, and a good attorney should be able to prove that at trial." Well maybe, but here's the deal. Taking a case to trial requires vast amounts more time and energy for your attorney than simply running through the relatively quick and far easier process of setting up a plea agreement. Remember two things: Your attorney is not your friend. And he or she is a business person whose primary goal is to maximize the profits. Although taking a case to trial will earn them more money, which of course you'll have to pay, it's often far more profitable for them to make their money through volume, by churning through far more plea bargain cases than they could if they took most of their cases to trial. So don't be deluded into believing that simply because you're innocent that that will be proven in a court of law. Remember the 130 people who've been wrongfully convicted of murder, within courts that were operating at the peak of our system's accuracy? So unless you have buckets of money to throw at the problem, when you're interviewing for an attorney, don't ask how many cases have they won, but rather what kind of plea bargains have they achieved?

To draw this all together, just remember that throughout the process it's important to keep in mind the incentive structure of every individual with whom you'll be dealing. The police want to do their jobs and make arrests without getting the blemish of a bad arrest on their record. The prosecutors want to achieve that all important conviction, and the defense attorneys, both public and private want to churn through as many cases as possible in order to achieve the greatest profits or, in the case of public defenders, the highest possible marks on their efficiency rating for churning through as many cases as they can.

For an account of the randomness and how an innocent person can be accused and get trapped in the justice system, please read *"Blundering Justice"* by Kellog Stover!

www.blunderingjustice.com

Addendum: Recommended Readings

A Brief History of Time by Stephen W. Hawking
A Briefer History of Time by Stephen Hawking
A New Earth by Eckhart Tolle
A short History of Nearly Everything by Bill Bryson
The Ages of Gaia by James Lovelock
Adolf Hitler by John Tolin
The Ancestor's Tale by Richard Dawkins
Beyond Einstein by Michio Kaku and Jennifer Trainer
Beyond the Quantum by Michael Talbot
The Big Bang by Joseph Silk
Big Bang by Simon Singh
The Black Hole War by Leonard Susskind
Black Holes & Time Warps by Kip S. Thorne
Black Holes and Baby universes by Stephen Hawking
The Blank Slate by Steven Pinker
Blasphemy by Douglas Preston
The Blind Watchmaker by Richard Dawkins
Blundering Justice by Kellog Stover
The Book of Secrets by Deepak Chopra
Breaking the Spell by Daniel C. Dennett
Buddha by Deepak Chopra
Chaos by James Gleick
The Complete Conversations with God by Neale Donald Walsch
The Constants by John D. Barrow
The Cosmic Blueprint by Paul Davies
The Cosmic Code by Heinz R. Pagels
Cosmic Coincidences by John Gribbin
Cosmic Jackpot by Paul Davies
Dark Cosmos by Dan Hooper
Death by Black Hole by Neil DeGrasse Tyson
Deep Time by David Darling
The Demon-Haunted World by Carl Sagan
The Dreams of Reason by Heinz R. Pagels
The Edge of Infinity by Paul Davies
The Elegant universe by Brian Green
The End of Faith by Sam Harris
The End of Time by Julian Barbour

Endless Universe by Paul J. Steinhardt and Neil Turok
Engines of Creation by K. Eric Drexler
Entanglement by Amir D. Aczel
Exploring Chaos by Nina Hall
The Fabric of the Cosmos by Brian Greene
Faster than the Speed of Light by Joao Magueijo
Faster than the Speed of Light by Nick Herbert, Ph.D.
The First Three Minutes by Steven Weinberg
The Fourth Dimension by Rudy Rucker
From Eternity to Here by Sean Carroll
Frozen Star by George Greenstein
Gnostic Secrets of the Nassenes by Mark H. Gaffney
The God Delusion by Richard Dawkins
The God Effect by Brian Clegg
God is not Dead by Amit Goswami, Ph.D.
God is not Great by Christopher Hitchens
God the Failed Hypothesis by Victor J. Stenger
The God Theory by Bernard Haisch
The Golden Ratio by Mario Livio
The Goldilocks Enigma by Paul Davies
The Grand Design by Stephen Hawing
The Greatest Show on Earth by Richard Dawkins
The Holographic Paradigm by Ken Wilber
How Order Emerges from Chaos in Sync by Steven Strogatz
In Search of Schrodinger's Cat by John Gribbin
In Search of The Big Bang by John Gribbin
The Infinite Book by John D. Barrow
Infinite in All Directions by Freeman Dyson
Infinity and the Mind by Rudy Rucker
Intelligent Life in the Universe by Carl Sagan and I.S. Shklovski
The Intelligent Universe by James Gardner
Interactions by Sheldon L. Glashow
The Invisible Universe by George B. Field and Eric Chaisson
Irreligion by John Allen Paulos
Jesus by Deepak Chopra
Justice by Michael J. Sandel
The Language of God by Francis S. Collins
The Large, the Small and the Human Mind by Roger Penrose
The Left Hand of Creation by John D. Barrow and Joseph Silk
The Lightness of Being by Frank Wilczek

The Living Energy Universe by Gary E. R. Schwartz and Linda Russel
The Living Universe by Duane Elgin
Margins of Reality by Robert G. Jahn and Brenda Dunne
The Matter Myth by Paul Davies and John Gribbin
The Mind-Boggling Universe by Neil McAleer
The Mind's Sky by Timothy Ferris
The Nature of Reality by Richard Morris
The Nothing that Is by Robert Kaplan
Nothingness by Henning Genz
The Omega Point by John Gribbin
Order out of Chaos by Ilya Prigogine and Isabelle Stengers
Origins of Existence by Fred Adams
Parallel Universes by Fred Alan Wolf
Perfect Symmetry by Heinz R. Pagels
The Philosopher's Stone by F. David Peat
The Physics of Consciousness by Evan Harris Walker
The Physics of Immortality by Frank J. Tipler
Physics of the Impossible by Michio Kaku
The Power of Now by Eckhart Tolle
Practicing the Power of Now by Eckhart Tolle
Programming the Universe by Seth Lloyd
Quantum by Manjit Kumar
Quantum Reality by Nick Herbert
The Recursive Universe by William Poundstone
The Restless Universe by Max Born
Science and Creation by John Polkinghorne
The Science of Good & Evil by Michael Shermer
Science Order, and Creativity by David Bohm and David Peat
The Self-Aware Universe by Amit Goswami, PhD
Space-Time and Beyond by Bob Toben and Fred Wolf
Space Warps by John Gribbin
The Spiritual Brain by Mario Beauregard and Denyse O'Leary
The Spiritual Universe by Fred Alan Wolf, PhD
Spontaneous Evolution by Bruce H. Lipton and Steve Bhaerman
Star Wave by Fred Alan Wolf
Stephen Hawking's Universe by Stephen Hawking
Stillness Speaks by Eckhart Tolle
Superforce by Paul Davies

Superstrings and the Search for the "theory of everything" by F. David Peat
The Symbiotic Universe by George Greenstein
Synchronicity by Allan Combs and Mark Holland
Synchronicity by F. David Peat
The Tao of Physics by Fritjof Capra
Theories of Everything by John D. Barrow
The Third Jesus by Deepak Chopra
This Will Change Everything by John Brockman
Time's Arrows by Richard Morris
Turbulent Mirror by John Briggs and David Peat
The Turning Point by Fritjof Capra
Uncommon Wisdom by Fritjof Capra
The Unexpected Universe by Loren Eiseley
The Unfinished Universe by Louise B. Young
Until the Sun Dies by Robert Jastrow
The View from the Center of the Universe by Joel R. Primack and Nancy Abrams
The Web of Life by Fritjof Capra
Wholeness and the Implicate Order by David Bohm
Wrinkles in Time by George Smoot

About the Author

Jim Knut Larsson was born in Stockholm, Sweden and grew up in Raufoss and Oslo, Norway. He was an excellent student with top grades. He especially excelled in math and physics. He also won the county championship in cross country skiing when he was 14. Started a pop band when he was 12, which won a talent competition when he was 14, by the time he was 15 he played in one of the most popular bands in Norway. He lost his father when he was 17 and his mother died three years later. After High School, he went in for one year of military service. He earned his bachelor's in business in Norway as a top student and was granted scholarships to earn an MBA at Arizona State in the US, which he finished in one year. He respectfully declined a scholarship for a PhD. as he was driven to go into private industry. After various assignments as a strategic planner for companies both in the US and Europe (Siemens, Teledyne Systems and Optical Coating Laboratories), he founded Gloria Munde International in 1983 as a 29 year old, a cosmetic and image design company. He pioneered color analysis and image design and grew the company into a million-dollar business in nine countries. He also had eight fashion stores and makeover centers. Gloria Munde International was sold in 1995. He founded another company, GAIA in 1997 as a private label manufacturer of holistic anti-aging skin care products, nutritional supplements and the GAIA brand (incorporated in September 2001 as Knutek, www.knutek.com & www.knutekpro.com). He has developed many skin care products and nutritional supplements and has taken a leadership position in using nano technology for transdermal delivery of nutrients. The successful development of a stable nano emulsion for delivery of oxygen to the skin cells is a major achievement in this field. He has now two patents pending in nano technology. The Knutek brand is currently sold through skin care salons, day spas and clinics both in the US and overseas. He is an innovator of breakthrough products in cosmeceuticals and nutraceuticals and a makeover artist. He is the creator of "Makeology™"/the science of making and becoming. He is also an award-winning educator in skin care, a makeover artist and has "starred" in TV and radio infomercials and commercials. His grandfather, Josef Larsson, was a representative at the League of Nations, the precursor to the United Nations. He led the largest union in Norway for 37 years before his retirement. He also endured four years in Nazi concentration camps and is considered a national hero. The author's father, Knut Larsson, fought the German occupants in WW2 for three years as an insurgent in Norway and was later trained in Scotland as a "Spitfire" pilot in 1945. He became the president of Luma Inc. by the time he was 44, but died three years later. He was also a colonel in the Norwegian air force reserves . . . Jim Knut Larsson has a daughter, a granddaughter, sister and brother all living in Norway. He resides in Berkeley, CA.

Enlightenment

To turn humanity from "unconsciousness" into "consciousness" is to ...
- Know that we have freewill and can create the future.
- Experience the observer and creator inside to be different from the ego, thoughts and the body.
- Become the Creator.

The Goals:
- The first goal for humanity is to preserve life.
- The second goal is to "conquer" the universe.
- The third goal is to recreate everything that ever existed and to create everything that is possible.

"Find the Truth"

Jim Knut Larsson

info@jimknutlarsson.com

www.jimknutlarsson.com

www.thehumanpathway.com

www.ingramcontent.com/pod-product-compliance
Lightning Source LLC
Chambersburg PA
CBHW050124170426
43197CB00011B/1706